Jihadism, Sectarianism and Politics in a Changing Middle East

ISBN 978-94-6301-344-4

Eburon Academic Publishers, Utrecht, The Netherlands
www.eburon.nl

Cover design: Textcetera, The Hague
Graphic design: Studio Iris, Leende

Jihadism, Sectarianism and Politics in a Changing Middle East

Adib Abdulmajid

Eburon
Utrecht 2021

Contents

1. Introduction 7

Part I Sectarianism 13

2. Sectarianism: Concept and Characteristics 15
3. Emergence and Development of Sectarianism in the Islamic History 19
4. Cultural Diversity at Stake 33

Part II Jihad and Jihadism 43

5. Jihad: Term and Concept 45
6. Jihad as a Classical Notion 48
7. Jihad and the Sect: Sunni and Shia Interpretations 60
8. Salafi-Jihadism 66
9. Jihad and Militancy 78

Part III Islamism and Salafism 83

10. Foundations and Core Objectives 85
11. The Struggle for an Islamic System 103

Part IV The Rise of Modern Middle East: Aspirations and Challenges 113

12. The Collapse of Ottoman Empire and the Emergence of Nationalism 115
13. Sykes-Picot and the Development of National Borders 122
14. Post-Independence: States in Turmoil 129

15. Arab Spring 138
16. Political Islam and the Islamization of Popular Uprisings 142

Part V Sectarian Extremism 151
17. Sectarianized Politics and Religionized Extremism 153
18. Politico-Sectarian Roots of Contemporary Islamist Extremism 165

Conclusion 189
Note on Transliteration 192
Glossary 194
Appendix 223
Notes 241
Bibliography 261
Index 271

1. Introduction

The Middle East has encountered multiple challenges over the recent years, including armed conflicts and political rivalries, that are believed to hold serious consequences for the region's future landscape on political, social and economic levels. *Sectarianism* seems to have played a main role in the mounting rivalries and confrontations between key players in the Middle East, coupled with the formation of variable alliances in response to the surrounding developments. Meanwhile, the rise of various Islamist organizations across crisis-afflicted parts of the region raised questions about *Jihadism*-related doctrinal tenets to which such organizations claim attachment. Above all, the potentially devastating consequences of such developments on the populations inhabiting the region increase the interest in gaining a better understanding of the origins of the multifaceted crisis storming the region.

The cultural diversity that once enriched the Middle East on various levels, and the historic coexistence among the region's different communities, have been threatened and jeopardized by a few sectarian extremist groups whose atrocities reached every single social component with distinct religious, doctrinal or ideological tenets. Ethnic and religious minorities have become a target to radical groups, and sedition has been ignited and reinforced by the extremist discourse of sectarian organizations in the region, amid considerable failures by political leaderships.

Sectarianism forms one of the major challenges facing the Middle East, frequently arising in debates about geopolitical rifts and tensions throughout the region. Given the fact that the sectarian narrative has become one of the main features of the crises that continue to beset the region, delving into the notion of sectarianism, its evolution throughout the history of the region, and the associated conceptions, interpretations and developments, appears inescapable if one tries to understand the background of the contemporary Middle Eastern landscape.

Furthermore, the rise of Islamic militancy over the past few decades and the alleged attachment of various extremist groups to *Islamic jihad* (*jihād Islāmī*) have paved the way for a widespread controversy about the actual relationship between *jihād*, as a concept, and *Jihadism*, as a movement characterized by a radical worldview. Hence, exploring the origins of *jihād* in the Islamic tradition, the various interpretations of this notion and its eventual employment by Islamist extremists as a doctrinal basis to justify their actions, seems crucial.

In order to rise and establish itself, extremism undoubtedly requires a fertile ground. As two of the major hotspots of the Middle East, Iraq and Syria emerged in the first two decades of the 21st century as main incubators to extremist Islamist groups in the region. In the aftermath of the 2003 war, Iraq suffered from a widespread chaos and security vacuum, coupled with intensifying sectarian rifts, which erupted at a governmental level and later reached the very core of the society. These were key factors that led to the rise of sectarian Shia militias such as al-Hashd al-Shaabi and the radical Sunni ISIS group. Meanwhile, as the Syrian uprising of 2011 descended into a civil war, extremist organizations like al-Qaeda and ISIS found a sufficient foothold and joined the conflict under the pretext of protecting fellow Muslims. The rise of religious extremism considerably deprived the people of the region of their legitimate aspirations in establishing a pluralistic form of government based on democratic principles and willing to demonstrate respect to basic human rights. Thus, this anti-tyranny revolutionary age has been largely infiltrated and hijacked by some radical movements that tirelessly sought to forcibly impose their extremist agenda on exhausted populations, particularly in war-ravaged areas.

The emergence and growth of sectarian Islamist militant organizations such as Sunni-based al-Qaeda and ISIS, and Shia-guided al-Hashd al-Shaabi, whose leaders have constantly emphasized their commitment to an extremist version of *jihād*, can be seen as a fruit of the emerging radical theorizations, interpretations and elucidations on the conception of *jihād*, which have continued to flow and unfold throughout the 20th century, and the evolution of the movement of *Islamism* in general. The tactics, targets and arenas of operation pursued by such groups in the recent years indicate the dramatic evolution of the movement of *Jihadism*. Such a development constitutes an unprecedented transformation of the basic idea of *jihād* into a radical concept upon which some of the most fanatic and atrocious organizations are based in terms of thought, ideology, discourse and course of action. Besides, globalization and the digital age surface at the heart of the propaganda and recruitment campaigns launched by such radical groups to attract as many members and sympathizers to their alleged cause as possible, and *jihād* has been hereby exploited as a brand to provide a religious legitimacy to their cause and emotionally manipulate the recipients of their increasingly ideological discourse.

In order to understand the emergence of the contemporary political landscape in the Middle East and the developments attached to it, beside the rise of *Jihadism* and *sectarianism* as major challenges, shedding light on the modern history of the region seems vital in terms of studying, understanding and analyzing the multifaceted topic at hand.

This book tackles questions of core significance for the comprehension of the current religio-political scenery in the Middle East, the doctrinal tenets associated with the emergence of influential Islamist organizations, the ultimate rise of sectarian-based extremist groups, and the challenges encountered by the culturally-diverse populations amid such developments. It provides the reader with a study of *sectarianism*, *Islamism*, *Salafism* and *Jihadism*. It also delves into the historical events that have shaped the Middle East as we know it today. It further explores the key factors behind the rise of the most influential extremist sectarian-guided, jihādi-based groups in the recent years.

The main objective of this book is to help the reader understand the complex religio-political scene in today's Middle East and the ideological tenets of key influential movements whose beliefs and actions ultimately jeopardize the cultural diversity in the region. This is accomplished through a comprehensive literature-based study and analysis of the various aspects associated with *sectarianism*, *Islamism*, *Salafism* and *jihadism*, the multifaceted context within which these concepts and currents evolved, and their eventual impact on the political landscape and the society at large. This book also strives to thoroughly identify and analyze the main factors behind the rise and expansion of sectarian-guided extremist Islamist organizations and the associated threat to the cultural diversity in crisis-stricken parts of the region, particularly Syria and Iraq.

This book comprises five parts. *Part I* primarily focuses on the concept of *sectarianism*, sheds light on the emergence and development of *sectarianism* in the Islamic history, and further delves into the cultural diversity in the Middle East and the threats encountering this melting-pot. *Part II* explores the multifaceted notion of *jihād*, the various interpretations of the concept, the rise of *Salafi-Jihadism* and the eventual employment of Islamic *jihād* by militants. *Part III* investigates the emergence and development of the movements of *Islamism* and *Salafism*. *Part IV* looks into the historical events that have contributed to the rise of the modern Middle East, including the emergence of national borders, the Western influence, the state of turmoil across post-independence states, the aspirations associated with recent revolutionary movements and the challenges accompanying the Islamization of popular uprisings. *Part V* thoroughly scrutinizes the politico-sectarian roots of contemporary Islamist extremism.

Part I

Sectarianism

Sectarianism constitutes one of the significant challenges encountering the Middle East. The concept emerges frequently in debates about the geopolitical tensions and rivalries among major powers and key players in the region. It arises at the core of the crises that hit various parts of the Middle East over the recent years. While the roots of the sectarian divide, as tackled in the context of this volume, originate in the early history of Islam, its manifestations have taken various forms and continue to re-emerge as one of the defining dimensions of the political rifts and armed conflicts that persist to afflict the region today. Given the fact that the sectarian narrative has become a defining feature of major crises striking the Middle East, it seems crucial to tackle the notion of sectarianism, its evolution throughout the history of the region, and the associated conceptions, interpretations and developments.

2. Sectarianism: Concept and Characteristics

In discussions about the Middle East and regional rifts and conflicts such as the case of Syria and Iraq, the term *sectarianism* (*al-Ṭā'ifiyya*) is frequently mentioned, often without a sufficient explanation or a sharp definition.[1] Although the concept of *sectarianism* remains largely undertheorized, several definitions of the term and explanations of its characteristics have been produced over the years.[2] *Sectarianism* is defined by Liechty and Clegg as a system of "attitudes, actions, beliefs and structures, which arises as a distorted expression of positive, human needs especially for belonging, identity and the free expression of difference and is expressed in destructive patters of relating."[3] It is believed to function at personal, communal and institutional levels, constantly involving a religious element as well as a negative mixture of politics and religion.[4] According to Brewer, *sectarianism* can be considered as "the determination of actions, attitudes and practices by practices about religious difference, which results in them invoked as the boundary marker to represent social stratification and conflict."[5] The term thus refers to a bunch of beliefs, ideas and myths about religious difference mainly used to turn religion into a social marker and make disdainful comments and statements about other groups. In tensions between Sunni Muslims and Shia Muslims, or between one religious group and another like between Muslims and Christians, each group tends to identify itself with the religious and political features displayed in the discourse of its leadership, separating it from other communities in the area they inhabit and leading to some discriminatory statements about the alleged 'other'. *Sectarianism* is further deemed to be a set of prejudiced attitudes, policies and types of treatment based on religious difference, occurring at the levels of ideas, individual action and social structure.[6] In its modern context, *sectarianism* implies reference to the deployment of religious heritage as a key marker of modern political identity. It is ultimately "an act of interpretation that shapes as well as is shaped by religious mobilizations and violence in the modern world."[7] *Sectarianism* is described by Makdisi in his *The Culture of Sectarianism* as "a disease that prevents modernization."[8]

The academic discussion around the notion of *sectarianism* in the recent years has been increasingly driven by the rise and development of intra-religious strife, whether within Islam, Christianity or Judaism, leading many scholars to study and explore the nature and origins of sectarian rifts and struggle. One of the key aspects of *sectarianism* is the growth of in-group sentiments and an extreme attachment to a certain set of values and beliefs that emerge in contrast with that of other groups within the same society. Despite the various disagreements within the scholarly discussion of *sectarianism*, there is a relevant degree of agreement on what defines belongingness to a particular sect, which implicates "being a member of a group that has a shared identity, belief or ideology that defines them from the rest of the society."[9] While the term is basically employed in the context of discussing differences among religious communities with negative connotations involved, the concept of *sectarianism* has further expanded to include political as well as ethnic minorities. In order to understand the fundamental dynamics of *sectarianism*, it is of great importance to consider Ibn Khaldun's idea of *ʿaṣabiyya* or group feeling, which entails a process of developing group relations and ties as a key factor for empowering a community and ensuring the survival of its identity and basic values against any outside danger.[10] Hence, attributing negative connotations to the perceived "others" and subsequently excluding other groups for not sharing similar values, beliefs and ideological tenets emerge at the core of the notion of *sectarianism*. Its discriminative nature often leads to social divide that may eventually manifest itself in the form of violent strife aimed at the survival and prevalence of one's own sectarian identity over others.

Although the term is basically used in reference to animosity, grudge and prejudice toward individuals or groups with different beliefs, *sectarianism* also holds a political dimension. Mabon and Royle strongly disagree with the narrative that suggests that *sectarianism* is inherently violent, arguing that violence only occurs when the sectarian differences or identities are politicized.[11] The notion of *sectarianism* is widely used in describing a country's social and political divisions with religious implications involved. The Middle East has witnessed numerous of such examples. Saudi Arabia, the major Sunni power in the region, has repeatedly witnessed suppression of predominantly-Shia movements in the Kingdom, where the authorities accused Iran, the major Shia power in the Middle East, of supporting such movements to destabilize the region. In Syria, rebel groups fighting the regime of Bashar al-Assad in the aftermath of the 2011 uprising were mainly characterized by their Sunni-based struggle, striving to overthrow the Alawites from power. In Iraq and Bahrain, tensions and struggle for power are mainly based on the deep Sunni-Shia cleavage. Another example of the political dimension of the concept of *sectarianism* is Lebanon, where the political system is formally based on the distribution of power between Maronite Christians, Shia and Sunni Muslims. In this context, competitive or hostile political relationships between communities defined by their religious characteristics and traits are expressed through a sectarian discourse. This basically applies to tensions and conflicts between groups adhering to a broad faith community such as Muslims, where widespread disputes and clashes between Sunni and Shia have been taking place, similar to tensions between Protestants and Catholics in Europe, and also between completely different faiths like between Muslims and Christians.[12] Hence, a religious identity is employed as a marker of difference among diverse communities, leading to rifts and tensions over power and political matters, where questions of marginalization, discrimination and exclusion on the basis of religious affiliation are raised. Illustrative cases are to be found in different parts of the Middle East, taking various forms and bearing multiple consequences. As a minority religious group in northern Iraq, the Yezidi Kurds were exposed to socioeconomic marginalization by Sunni Kurds in the Kurdistan Region. This led many Yezidis to deny the ethnic and cultural ties they share with the Kurds and claim to constitute a unique ethnoreligious community with own history, culture, religious customs and traditions. Under Saddam Hussein, the Shia suffered exclusion and suppression by the Sunni-led regime, and in post-2003 Iraq the situation reversed as the Shia took power and pursued oppressive and exclusionary policies against the Sunnis. In Syria, the Alawite regime of Assad excluded Sunnis from power circles for decades. The Lebanese suffered over fifteen years from a sectarian-based civil war that exhausted the country and devastated its people.

3. Emergence and Development of Sectarianism in the Islamic History

In the Islamic world, *sectarianism* has for long played a defining role with regard to key rifts and differences that have emerged and surfaced within the Muslim society over centuries in the aftermath of the major Sunni-Shia split. Issues of rightful religious authority and eligible political leadership arise at the heart of intra-Islamic *sectarianism*. In the early history of Islam, strong disagreements erupted between the Islamic elite regarding grave issues affecting the *'umma*. One of the most bitter and definitely the longest lasting issues was the rift that occurred over the political succession to the Prophet Muhammad. A Sunni-Shia split emerged as a consequence of the different claims to the leadership of political Islam. Other political disputes occurred between those who had been the earliest converts and companions of the Prophet (*Ṣaḥāba*) and those who had joined Islam much later on, mainly the elders of the Quraysh tribe. These disagreements threatened to tear apart the community.[13]

Subsequent to the death of the Prophet Muhammad in 632 A.D., a split within the Muslim community took place, mainly due to political disagreements. Two major branches of Islam emerged, the largest of which was the Sunni, the followers of *Sunna* or tradition and known as *'Ahl al-Sunna* or the People of the Tradition, and the second was the Shiʿa or Shiʿites, a name derived from the Arabic *Shiʿat ʿAli* or the party of ʿAli. Controversy and dispute arose at the *Saqīfa*[14] assembly following Muhammad's death over the required qualifications and the precise functions and duties of his successors to lead the Muslim community. Hence, the question of the succession of the Prophet Muhammad was a central issue that divided the Muslim community between those who favored allegiance to successors from the Prophet's household and those who considered the political leaders of the pre-Islamic era as the more eligible candidates.[15]

The Shiʿites stressed the spiritual function of the Prophet's *Caliph* or successor, referred to as *'Imām*, who reflects the Prophetic Light.[16] According to the Shia, Imāms are divinely safeguarded against error and sin and possess an impeccable and infallible knowledge and understanding of the Qur'ān. They considered members of the Prophet's family or *'Ahl al-Bayt*, basically descendants of his daughter Fatima and her husband ʿAli ibn Abi Talib (the prophet's cousin and son-in-law), as the only ones qualified to become Imāms. The Shia insisted that Muhammad had on several occasions referred to ʿAli and his male descendants as the righteous successors of the Prophet. One of these occasions, which has been mentioned in authentic and authoritative Shia and Sunni sources, has been interpreted by the Shia as a formal approval and authorization of ʿAli's right to succession by the Prophet. While on his way back from his last pilgrimage to Mecca, on the eighteenth day of the month *Dhul-ḥijja* of the eleventh year of his Hijra in 632 A.D., at a place called *Ghadīr of Khumm*, the Prophet Muhammad reportedly made a crucial declaration, stating: "He for whom I was the master, should hence have ʿAli as his master *(fa-hādha ʿAlīyun mawlāh man kuntu mawlāh)*."[17] For the Shia, the alleged circumstances that took place at the *Ghadīr of Khumm*, referred to as *Waṣiyyat ʿAli*, constituted the single significant piece of evidence on the basis of which they legitimized the succession of ʿAli and his descendants.[18]

Although the Sunni Muslims recognize the authenticity of the *Ghadīr of Khumm* story, they have interpreted the Prophet's use of the term 'master' differently. According to the Sunnis, the term 'master' (*mawlāh*) as used by the Prophet Muhammad on that occasion should be understood as 'patron' or 'friend' rather than leader. The event of *Ghadīr of Khumm* was included in the Ibn Ḥanbal's collection of *Ḥadīth* (narratives of the Prophet's words and actions). Nevertheless, most Sunnis who accepted the event as a historical fact largely denied the Shiʿite interpretation of it. The Sunnis believe that the Prophet had left the issue of succession open on purpose, in a bid to provide the Muslim community (*'umma*) with an opportunity to elect the most qualified person to lead them. In response to the succession crisis, the Sunnis developed a doctrine implicating that the Caliphs were all legitimate successors of the Prophet. They were elected through a political process and were considered as both temporal and religious leaders. However, the Caliphs were not given the same degree of religious authority as the Shiʿites attributed to the Imāms.[19]

Regardless of the true intention of the Prophet Muhammad in his proclamation, the Sunni perspective prevailed at the *Saqīfa* assembly at the time. Subsequently, Abu Bakr al-Siddiq, a distinguished and prominent member of the community and Muhammad's father-in-law, was chosen as the first Caliph (successor) of the Prophet. ʿUmar ibn Khattab, also a close companion of Muhammad and his father-in-law, succeeded al-Saddiq as the second Caliph after being nominated by the latter on his deathbed, followed by ʿUthman ibn ʿAffan, a member of the prominent Umayyad clan at Mecca and the Prophet's son-in-law, who was elected by a council (*majlis*). ʿAffan was murdered by a rebel group in 656, and ʿAli ibn Abi Talib received a huge popular support to assume leadership as the last of the four Rightly-Guided Caliphs (*'al-Khulafā' 'al-Rāshidūn*). Hence, the Rightly-Guided Caliphs or the *Rāshidūn* include the first four Caliphs who succeeded the Prophet, namely, Abu Bakr (632-4), ʿUmar (634-44), ʿUthman (644-56) and ʿAli (656-661). The expression *Rightly-Guided* signifies their actions as being accepted by all Muslims as the closest to the Prophet's example. After the Prophet Muhammad, the words and actions of the Rightly-Guided Caliphs were deemed to be the most authoritative source on Muslim behavior.[20]

However, by the time ʿAli took charge, the rapidly growing Muslim community had witnessed remarkable changes. The expansion of the Islamic territory brought about greater resources and wealth, where some families and clans assumed new power-contenders and had little sympathy with ʿAli's insistence on accountability and transparency in the management of the affairs of the Muslim community, and they refused to respond to his call to return to the firm and strict regime applied at the time of the Prophet. ʿAli ibn Abi Talib was murdered in 661 after a five-year Caliphate that was largely marred by civil war, famously known as *fitna*. Interestingly, during the Prophet's lifetime, intercommunal conflicts were remarkably contained. The first civil war within the Muslim community erupted during ʿAli's reign as the fourth Caliph, namely the Battle of the Camel that broke out on the background of the killing of ʿUthman, the third Caliph. The battle took place in Basra, Iraq, in November 656. ʿAisha bint Abu Bakir, Muhammad's widow, heard about ʿUthman's death while she was on a pilgrimage to Mecca. During her journey, she decided to head to Kufa in order to discuss the incident with ʿAli, but the situation then developed into an armed battle, as ʿAli asked for time to punish ʿUthman's murderers. The Battle of the Camel was led by ʿAisha against ʿAli, but she was eventually defeated. The battle became known as the *First Fitna* or Muslim civil war. ʿAli was later involved in a second, larger, civil war that put him in confrontation with the Umayyads. The tension developed into a major battle known as the Battle of the Ṣiffīn, where ʿAli's supporters fought against the supporters of Moʿawiya ibn Abi Sufian, the founder of the Umayyad dynasty. ʿAli was eventually assassinated by a Khārijite, known as Abdur Rahman ibn Muljam, in January 661 in Kufa. The *Khawārij* (deviants) were a rebellious sect that emerged during the *First Fitna*, operating in accordance with the belief that any authority they considered as illegitimate and not abiding by God's dominion had to be overthrown for "judgement belongs to God alone."[21]

Following ʿAli's death, Moʿawiya ibn Abu Sufyan, a close relative of ʿUthman and governor of Syria during ʿUthman's rule who had been involved in tensions with ʿAli over the Caliphate, announced himself as Caliph in Damascus and established the Umayyad dynasty. However, the Shiʿites refused to recognize Moʿawiya's declaration and showed support to ʿAli's sons Hasan and Hussein, considering them the only rightful Caliphs of the community and the sole legitimate successors of the Prophet.[22] Hasan, the eldest son of ʿAli, was then forced to sign a peace settlement with Moʿawiya, but despite his weaker position he managed to include an article in the agreement that guarantees the return of the Caliphate to him after the death of Moʿawiya.[23] However, Hasan died mysteriously circa 669,[24] and his younger brother Hussein, who opposed the appointment of Moʿawiya's son Yazid as the next Caliph, was killed by Umayyad forces in Iraq's Karbala in the year 680. Afterwards, the Shiʿites were excluded from power, and their Imāms, descendants of Hussein ibn ʿAli, were banned from practicing political activities, kept under strict surveillance, arrested or killed by the Caliphs of the two powerful dynasties of Umayyad and Abbasid. The Umayyad Caliphate (661-750) emerged after the collapse of the Rāshidūn Caliphate. It took Damascus as its capital and it was characterized by heredity elections and territorial expansion. It became one of the largest unitary states in history. After overthrowing the Umayyad dynasty, the Abbasid Caliphate (750-1258) became the third Islamic Caliphate to succeed the Prophet, took Baghdad as its capital and ruled over a large empire for nearly three centuries. Furthermore, in 909, the Fatimid dynasty broke away from the Abbasids and formed a separate line of Caliphs until its decline and eventual collapse in 1171.

In the sixteenth century, with the establishment of the Safavid Dynasty in Iran, the Shiʿites were able for the first time to live under the rule of fellow Shia leaders. Nevertheless, according to the principle of *'Imāmah* (Imamate) or the leadership of the infallible Shia Imāms, the rulers won't enjoy an absolute political legitimacy in the course of waiting for the return of the Twelfth Imām al-Mahdi who, according to the Shiʿite's belief, has disappeared in the ninth century and will return at the end of time to bring justice to the world. The *Awaited Imām* al-Mahdi (*al-Mahdi al-Muntaẓar*) is deemed a kind of Messiah, called *al-qā'im* or the one who will be raised up by God. His name is Muhammad ibn al-Hasan al-ʿAskari, and he was born in the city of Samarra' in Iraq. Al-Mahdi, according to the Shia, had disappeared at the age of four or eight and he is allegedly still alive. He has several nicknames, including *al-Ḥujja* (the proof), *al-qā'im al-Muntaẓar* (the alive and the awaited), and *ṣaḥib al-zamān* (the owner of the time).[25] Thus, until the return of al-Mahdi, the *Mujtahids* (religious guides) and *Fuqahā'* (jurists) of the Shia community would be responsible for the interpretation of all legal issues and doctrines. This strict commitment has continued until the mid-twentieth century, when Iranian religious leader Ayatollah Ruhallah Khomeini initiated a radical interpretation of this doctrine, allowing what became known as the Absolute Guardianship of the *Faqīh* (the jurist), considering him a deputy of the Prophet and the Imāms in not only interpreting the Islamic laws, but also running the state's affairs on behalf of the *Awaited Imām*.[26] Today, the principle of the *Faqīh*'s Absolute Guardianship constitutes a crucial part of the current constitution of the Islamic Republic of Iran. The victory of the Iranian Revolution in 1979 and the setting up of the Islamic government by Imām Khomeini paved the ground for Shia *fuqahā'* to exercise comprehensive authority, and the Imām Khomeini was given power as the *faqīh* at the highest post in the government to practice his authority in everything that falls within the jurisdiction of the *walī al-faqīh*. The concept of the Absolute Guardianship of the Jurist implies that by occupying the highest post of government the *faqīh* enjoys all the prerogatives and rights required for governing and there is no difference between him and the infallible Imāms in this case. Furthermore, the Iranian Constitution clearly specifies three powers within the state; the legislative power, the executive power, and the judicial power. Nevertheless, Article 57 of the constitution states that these three powers are set to function under the supervision of the religious absolute guardianship.[27]

The Caliphate, as a political and religious institution, declined after the thirteenth century, despite the fact that the title *Caliph* continued to be used by some leaders of the Muslim community through the late stages of the Ottoman Empire, until its formal abolition in 1924 by Mustafa Kamal Ataturk, the first President of the Turkish Republic. After its elimination, the Caliphate turned into a significant religious and political symbol for some Islamist activists, particularly the Sunnis, throughout the nineteenth and twentieth centuries, who argued that by undermining the Caliphate, leaders in the Islamic world had abandoned the *true path* of Islam. This argument has remarkably inspired contemporary orthodox Sunnis to seek a restoration of the Caliphate institution as a way to return to the basic Islamic principles and values. However, the cultural diversity across the Muslim world, which is home to various groups with ethnic, religious, linguistic, socio-economic and political affiliations, constitutes a considerably serious challenge to the re-emergence of any pan-sectarian and centralized Islamic religious leadership.[28]

The Sunnis, who constitute the vast majority within the Muslim community today, endorse and approve the first four Caliphs, including ʿAli, as *'al-Khulafā' 'al-Rāshidūn* or the Rightly-Guided successors of the Prophet. This while the Shiʿites insist on the idea that ʿAli and his descendants were the sole rightful successors instead. Taking such a position with respect to the succession of the Prophet has resulted in branding them as *rāfiḍa* or rejectionists, which has become a pejorative word for Shia.[29] Despite the subtle differences in conducting obligatory prayers, both Sunnis and Shiʿites share a considerably analogous understanding of essential Islamic tenets. In terms of Islamic law, Sunni Islam includes four schools of jurisprudence (*madhāhib*) that present alternative interpretations with regard to legislative and judicial resolutions that affect Muslims' lives. Founded by Abu Hanifa in 767 A.D. in Iraq, the *Ḥanafī* (*al-Madhhab al-Ḥanafī*) is deemed the oldest school of Islamic law, and it is mainly prevalent in Iraq, Syria, Lebanon, Turkey and Jordan. It was followed by the establishment of the *Mālikī* school (*al-Madhhab al-Mālikī*), founded by Mālik ibn Anas in 795 in the Arabian Peninsula, and it is widespread in Bahrain, Kuwait and North Africa. The third Sunni school of Islamic law is the *Shāfʿī* (*al-Madhhab al-Shāfʿī*), founded by Muhammad ibn Idris al-Shāfʿi in 819, and it is common among the Sunnis of Egypt, Sudan and parts of Yemen. The fourth Islamic legal school is the Ḥanbalī (*al-Madhhab al-*

Ḥanbalī), founded by Imām Ahmed ibn Ḥanbal in 855, and it is prevalent in the United Arab Emirates, Qatar, Saudi Arabia and parts of Oman, among others.[30] These four legal schools place reliance on analogy in formulating verdicts and judgements, incorporating narrations and teachings of the Prophet Muhammad and his companions, known as the *Ḥadīth*, into their jurisprudential interpretations and verdicts differently. This illustrates that while the earliest split within Islam was political, the disagreements later on developed to eventually acquire theological and jurisprudential dimensions. Each of these schools has strived to develop practical and effective applications of *Sunna* as an ultimate objective of their efforts.

Shia Islam mainly spread and gained great following in Iraq, Iran and Yemen, and it is practiced among approximately 10 to 15 per cent of the world's Muslim population today, according to some estimates.[31] The Shiʿites consider ʿAli ibn Abi Talib as the first true leader of the Muslim people. He is referred to as *Imām*, a title that, according to the Shia, indicates leadership and signifies blood relation to the Prophet. ʿAli's descendants (*Imāms*) undertook the leadership of the Shia community. Serving as a political and spiritual leader, each Imām appointed a successor and passed down spiritual knowledge to the following leader, according to the Shia doctrine.[32] Amid the Shia decline after losing the political conflict with the Sunni leaders, the Imāms centered their efforts on the development of a spirituality that would constitute the essence of the Shia religious beliefs and practices. According to some of its foundational sources, Shiʿism defines itself as an essentially esoteric and initiatory doctrine that does not uncover itself easily. In a tradition traced back to several Shiʿi Imāms, it is stated, "Our teaching is secret, it is a secret about a secret. It includes an exoteric (*ẓāhir*), esoteric (*bāṭin*), and esoteric of the esoteric (*bāṭin al-bāṭin*) dimension."[33] The Shia spirituality is deemed to be complex, yet its practices and beliefs reveal some consistency and coherence in the essential role of knowledge and initiation, in the ambivalence of the *Imām*'s figure as the alpha and omega of Shiʿism. With the end of the line of Imāms descended from ʿAli, the *Mujtahids* or religious guides and leaders earned the right to explicate religious, mystical and statutory knowledge to the community, and those with the highest level of knowledge and understanding are known among the Shiʿites as *ayatollahs* (the signs of God). The most popular yearly ritual revived by the Shiʿites worldwide is the ʿAshurā', a ritualistic remembrance of the death of ʿAli's younger son Hussein, who was murdered during a battle with Sunni forces in Iraq's Karbala in 680. The Shiʿites believe that the tale of Hussein's martyrdom holds moral lessons for the community, and it considerably reinforced and strengthened Shia religious beliefs and practices.

Shia Islam is divided into three main branches. The *Twelver Shiʿism* (*Ithna ʿAsharis*) is the largest sect of Shiʿites, and its followers believe that the Prophet's spiritual authority and religious leadership were passed on to twelve of his descendants, beginning with ʿAli, Hasan and Hussein. The *Twelvers* believe that the 12th Imām, Muhammad al-Mahdi, known as the *Awaited Imām* or *Hidden Imām*, has disappeared from a cave below a mosque in 874 and will reappear at the end of time to bring absolute justice and peace to the world. The second largest Shia sect is the *Sevener Shiʿism*, also known as *Ismaili* (*'Ismāʿīli*), which emerged in the eighth century and its followers only recognize the first seven Imāms. The seventh Imām was named Ismail, thus the sect derived its name from his (*Ismailis*) and his position in the sequence of ʿAli's successors (Sevener). The *Ismailis* are historically known for pursuing territorial and military power and have founded strong states that took an active part in the Islamic history's development.[34] Shiʿism also includes the *Zaydis*, who form a minority sect of Shia Islam. The *Zaydis* only recognize the first five Imāms and differ about the identity of the fifth. The first five Imāms of the orthodox Shia include ʿAli ibn Abi Talib, his sons Hasan and Hussein, Hussein's son ʿAli Zayn al-Abidin and the latter's son Muhammad al-Baqir. However, the *Zaydis*, also known as *Zaydiyyah*, preferred the younger son of Zayn al-Abidin, Zayd, over his brother al-Baqir, as their Imām. This came after Zayd led a revolt against Caliph Hisham and was massacred, while his older brother al-Baqir didn't show any interest in politics.[35] The *Zaydis* reject the idea of the infallibility of Imāms and deny the concept of the *Awaited Imām*.[36] The *Alawite* sect is also derived from Shia Islam, and its followers consider the duties of Islam as symbolic rather than applied obligations. The deification of ʿAli is the basic doctrine of the *Alawite* faith. The *Alawites* interpret the *Pillars of Islam* (the five duties required of every Muslim) as symbols and therefore do not practice these Islamic duties, and many of their practices are secret. They consider themselves as moderate Shiʿites. As the roots of *Alawism* lie in the teachings of Muhammad ibn Nusayr an-Namiri, who was a Basran contemporary of the tenth Shiʿite Imām, the group is frequently referred to as *Nuṣayriyya* or *Namiriyya*. Another sect that originally falls under Shiʿism is the *Druze*. The *Druzes* are deemed an eleventh-century offshoot of *Ismaili* Shiʿism, but the community's essential beliefs are significantly different from those of mainstream Shia Islam.[37]

Furthermore, the political system developed by the Sunni Muslims holds different concepts than those developed by the Shiʿite *ʿulamā'*. The Sunnis embraced and promoted concepts deemed pragmatic in nature, such as *ijmāʿ* (consensus), *'ahl al-ḥall wal-ʿaqd* (elite scholars who loose and bind), *Khilāfah* (Caliphate), *Khalīfah* (Caliph), and *bayʿa* (swearing allegiance to the Caliph). The Sunnis, or *'Ahl al-Sunna wal-Jamāʿa*, believe that the Prophet did not designate anyone as his successor and that the Muslims would find a leader for themselves after his death. The pragmatic nature of the Sunni political practices stems from this belief. Therefore, a consensus among the Muslims and the role of *'ahl al-ḥall wal-ʿaqd* are deemed crucial is electing a Caliph to run the Caliphate after receiving *bayʿa*. The Shiʿites, on the other hand, distinguished themselves by promoting concepts like *'Imāmah* (imamate), *wilāya* (guardianship), and *ʿiṣma* (faultlessness and infallibility of the Imām), arguing that it was extremely unlikely that *Allah* (God) with his *luṭf* (benevolence) and *ʿadl* (justice) have left a crucial matter like the *imamate* (leadership) undecided. This is a basic argument by the Shia to legitimize ʿAli's succession. It was also emphasized through their interpretation of the event of *Ghadīr of Khumm*, in contrast to the Sunni interpretation of the same event, as illustrated earlier. Thus, this argument demonstrates a key point of difference between the Shia and the Sunnis. The Shiʿites emphasized the importance of Imāms in the *wilāya* (guardianship) of the community in the absence of God's messenger. From a doctrinal perspective, both Sunnis and Shiʿites share the basic religious principles of *Tawḥīd* (monotheism), *Nubuwwa* (Muhammad's Messengership), and *Maʿād* (Judgement Day). However, the Shiʿites included two additional principles to the ranks of doctrinal principles, namely, *'Imāmah* and *ʿadl* (divine justice). As a minority group among the Muslims, the Shiʿites historically sought a distinct identity as a strategy for survival.

The Sunnis are considered as a part of Islamic *orthodoxy* and they segregate the Shia as *heterodox* or even *heretical* sect. The orthodoxy of Sunni Muslims is mainly marked by an emphasis on the views and customs of the majority of the community (*'umma*), as distinguished from the views of peripheral groups. By developing an institution of consensus, the Sunnis were able to incorporate different customs and usages throughout history, although these had no roots in the Qur'ān. In Shiʿism, numerous Qur'ānic verses are explained in a hermeneutic way with reference to the primacy of ʿAli and the household of the Prophet, known as *'Ahl al-Bayt*. This exemplifies the reasons why the Sunnis consider the Shia to be *heterodoxical* or *heretical*.[38] Such interpretations reveal more about the ideological and intellectual climate within which these sects emerged than about the tension they claim to depict and symbolize.[39] The Sunni-Shia tension is thus viewed as a political quarrel about the course of history, with Sunnis advocating the status quo and the Shiʿites representing those who mainly contest such conformism. According to many contemporary world leaders, politicians, intellectuals and media commentators, the ongoing tensions and instability across the Middle East are attributed to ancient rancor and hostility between Sunnis and Shiʿites that emerged and developed since the dawn of Islam.[40]

Interestingly, this *sectarian narrative* has remarkably become a crucial explanatory feature of conflict in today's Middle East.[41] This narrative basically involves considering the seventh century Sunni-Shia split and struggle over the succession of the Prophet as responsible for the region's recent descent into unrest and, in certain cases, civil war. This millennium-and-a-half-old conflict has been reproduced over and over throughout the history of the Middle East, and is currently one of the key factors of instability in Iraq, Syria and other parts of the region, nourished and reinforced by the rise and expansion of extremist groups. The Iranian Islamic Revolution of 1979 led to the emergence of an extremist Shia agenda in the Middle East, challenged by conservative Sunni regimes. Over the past four decades, Iran has provided a remarkable support to Shia parties and militias in several countries, including Iraq, Syria, Lebanon, and Yemen. On the other hand, some Sunni-led states established relations with Sunni movements and developed an anti-Iranian discourse to confront Tehran's growing influence in the region. Today, multiple tensions in the region have a fierce sectarian overtone. Iranian troops and Iran-backed Lebanese Shia militia of Hezbollah have been involved in the Syrian war for years, defending the (Shia-affiliated) Alawite regime there against the Sunni-dominated opposition forces. Meanwhile, radical Sunni jihadist groups have repeatedly targeted Shia-controlled areas and their places of worship in Iraq and Syria.[42] Such conflicts have considerably contributed to the severity of sectarian divide between Middle Eastern communities, in some cases forcing the people to take sides as a condition for survival.

4. Cultural Diversity at Stake

This chapter is aimed at briefly introducing the reader with the cultural diversity in the Middle East as a relevant aspect within the framework of this volume, since sectarianism and the sectarian dimension of extremism constitute a serious challenge to this diversity and the peaceful coexistence among the various communities.

The term *Middle East* was coined in 1902, reflecting a European worldview, as imposed on the region through colonization. The Eurocentric regionalization of the Middle East is believed to have superseded indigenous geographical regimes.[43] The national borders in the Middle East, basically established following negotiations and in accordance with agreements between regional actors and European decision-makers, with the latter having the privilege of determining the final demarcations, considerably oversimplify or even erase many cultural identities.[44] The Middle East has historically embraced the rise of several prominent civilizations,[45] and is a place where various cultures intermingle and communities with diverse ethnic, religious and linguistic backgrounds meet to embody a cultural melting-pot and resemble a genuine social mosaic to be found in numerous cities across the region.[46]

Linguistic Diversity

Local languages are deemed essential for mapping and understanding the multiple identities of the Middle East. As the linguistic boundaries do not comply with the national borderlines in the region, it is of an extreme importance to grasp the linguistic map in order to obtain an image of the cultural diversity in the Middle East, given the key relation between language and identity. Identity is deeply bound up with the linguistic interaction among people. Group identities are deemed ways of conceiving the relationship of people to one another, and the same may be said of the individual identities that represent, in part at least, repertoires of these group belongings.[47] Languages provide more knowledge about histories than recently-drawn and colonially-imposed national borders.

The numerous languages that coexist in the Middle East mainly belong to three linguistic categories: *Semitic*, *Iranian* and *Ural-Altaic*. The *Semitic Languages* include Arabic, Hebrew, Aramaic/Syriac, among others. The *Iranian* (*Indo-European*) linguistic category includes Persian, Pashto, Kurdish, Baluchi and others. Under the *Ural-Altaic* category fall the Turkish and other Turkic languages like Azeri and Uzbek.

The Semitic languages derive their significance from being part of the identity of some ancient Semitic civilizations, including Sumeria, Aramaic-speaking communities,[48] Hebrew and Arab communities. Today, Arabic is the most common spoken language in the Middle East, with over 300 million speakers, yet with various Arabic dialects.[49] Being the Qur'ān's formal language has given Arabic a prestigious and elite position across the Muslim world. The Qur'ān describes itself as being *ʿarabiyyun* (Arabic) and *mubīnun* (clear). These two attributes, according to Versteegh, are intimately connected.[50] In Q43:2-3, we read, "*wa-l-kitābi l-mubīni: 'innā jaʿalnāhu qur'ānan ʿarabiyyan laʿallakum taʿqalūn*" (By the clear Book: We have made it an Arabic recitation in order that you may understand).

Persian or *Farsi* also occupies an important position among Middle Eastern languages, with an estimated 80 million speakers, mainly based in Iran. Turkish is another key language in the region, with more than 70 million speakers. However, the speakers of these three major languages in the Middle East are not all native-speakers. This includes, but not limited to, ethnic minorities such as the Armenians, Kurds, Amazigh, Assyrians, among others. The Kurds, who historically inhabit parts of Turkey, Syria, Iraq and Iran, have Kurdish as their native tongue beside speaking the prevalent or official languages within the borderlines of each of these countries. The Kurdish language unifies over 35 million Kurds and constitutes a key part of their cultural identity. Language constitutes a key instrument for the Kurds in their struggle for recognition as a people. Kreyenbroek and Sperl maintain that the Kurdish language "is both proof and symbol of the separate identity of the Kurds," and the significance of language in the struggle for maintaining identity was constantly emphasized by the advocates of the Kurdish rights in the Middle East.[51] Another prominent language of *Semitic* origins is the Hebrew. Hebrew is the main spoken language among Middle Eastern Jews, with approximately 5 million speakers, mainly in Israel. Other main languages spoken by Middle Eastern communities are Aramaic, Syriac, Baluch, Amazigh, Azeri and Armenian, beside numerous dialects and sub-dialects.[52]

This linguistic mosaic can be seen as a reflection of the diversity that characterizes the region and its populations, and is hoped to draw the reader's attention to the melting-pot of identities historically embraced by this region. The deep roots of the linguistic identities that enrich the Middle East have remained intact to a certain level, in spite of the challenges encountered by the populations of the region over the past and present centuries.

Religious Diversity

The world's three major religions –Judaism, Christianity, and Islam– have originated in the Middle East, a fact that reflects the significant role this region has played in the historical development of human civilization.[53] Today, the Muslims constitute a majority in the Middle East, the Christians live as minority groups across the region, and the Jews form a majority in Israel beside smaller Jewish communities residing in other countries. Interestingly, the term *minority* (*'aqalliyya*) was introduced to the Middle East by European powers during the second half of the nineteenth century with reference to the protection of Christians in the Ottoman Empire. According to some accounts, while the region was still under Ottoman rule, the concept of minorization was used as a pretext to justify European intervention into the Ottoman internal affairs.[54]

The Muslim community includes two major sects, namely, the Sunni, which forms the largest Islamic branch and is in power in most of Middle Eastern countries; and the Shia, the second powerful group of Muslims which in its turn is divided into subsects, including *Twelvers*, *Seveners*, *Zaydis*, *Alawites*, among others. Countries in the region with a great proportion of Sunni Muslims are Saudi Arabia, Egypt, Jordan, Syria, UAE, Qatar, Yemen and Palestine, and form a smaller community in Iraq, Iran and Lebanon. The Shia constitute a majority in Iran, Iraq, Lebanon and Bahrain, and live as a minority in countries like Syria, UAE, Yemen, among others.[55]

Christianity, on the other hand, is practiced by several communities in the Middle East, the largest of which is the Coptic community. The Coptic Orthodox Christian population consists of approximately 11 million people, most of whom reside in Egypt, and a part of the community exists in smaller numbers in Sudan, Libya, Israel and Jordan. The Maronites form another prominent Christian community in the region, with an estimated population of over 1 million, and are mainly based in Lebanon. The Middle East is also home for Syriac and Assyrian

Christians who constitute a part of the historical social mosaic in Syria, Iraq, southeastern Turkey and northwestern Iran. The Armenians also form a main part of the Middle Eastern Christian community, and are mainly concentrated in Lebanon, Syria, Jordan, Iran and Palestine. It is worth mentioning that the Christian communities in the Middle East were exposed to persecution, genocide and mass displacement. The Armenian Genocide is the most memorable example in this regard, when the Ottomans during the late phase of the empire (1915-1917) systematically exterminated approximately 1.5 million Armenians.[56] In conjunction with the Armenian Genocide, the Assyrian Christians were also exposed to mass killings by the Ottoman troops during WWI, and the death toll reached approximately 300,000 people. Such massacres were coupled with waves of mass displacement among the Christians in search of a safe haven in the region and abroad. Furthermore, the emergence of radical Islamist groups in the early 21st century led to terror attacks and military campaigns against Christian towns and villages in various countries in the region, the destruction of numerous churches, forced disappearance of many Christians and the emigration of a large proportion of the population toward the West. Today, the Christians are believed to have become a threatened minority in the Middle East.

Judaism constitutes the main religion in Israel, where Jews form over 73 per cent of the population. Although the Jews used to reside in most of today's Middle Eastern countries, most of the Jewish communities gradually emigrated their countries of origin in the mid-twentieth century amid a growing antisemitism movement and with the rise of the Arab-Israeli tension that followed the establishment of the state of Israel in 1948. However, some Jews still reside in Middle Eastern areas outside Israel, but in smaller numbers and as scattered communities.[57]

Nevertheless, the religious diversity of the Middle East goes beyond these three religions and finds its origins deep in the history of the region. Zoroastrianism, founded around 3400 years ago, is considered one of the oldest monotheistic religions, including two deities: *Ahura Mazda* (struggle for human goodness) and *Ahriman* (pushing toward evilness), and the *Avesta* is the Zoroastrians' sacred text. According to Zoroastrianism, as maintained in the *Avesta*, *Ahura Mazda* was the creator of life, light and all good things, and *Ahriman* was responsible for darkness, death and destruction.[58] Today's Middle Eastern Zoroastrian community includes approximately 20,000 members who are mainly concentrated in central Iran.

The Yezidis also represent one of the oldest Middle Eastern religious communities, with some Zoroastrian elements, worshipping a main divinity known as *Tāwsê Malak* or Peacock Angel. The *Tāwsê Malak*, also known as *Malak-Tāwūs*, is deemed to be the most important character of the Yezidi triad and is considered the essence of the Yezidi religion. In the Yezidi Statement of Faith, *Tāwsê Malak* is featured directly after God.[59] The Yezidis today number around 100,000 and are mainly found in Iraq, Iran, Syria and Turkey. Noteworthy, the Yezidis have been exposed to brutal acts of mass executions, forced displacement and sex slavery at the hands of extremist Islamists of ISIS during the group's expansion and invasion of Yezidi towns and villages in northern Iraq in 2014-2015. Religious minorities like the Yezidis are viewed by radical Islamists as heretical and Satanists, which has led the Yezidis to suffer heavy suppressive practices and encounter an existential threat represented by groups such as ISIS. Many Yezidi villages in northern Iraq remained deserted even after the collapse of ISIS, as mounting numbers of Yezidi survivors headed to the West in search of a safe haven.

Shabakism is another Middle Eastern religion and it shares some elements with the Yezidis. The Shabaks now number approximately 60,000 and are concentrated in northern Iraq. There are several other religious groups to be found in the region, including Mandaeans, Baha'is, Druze, Ishikis, Samaritans, among others, beside a limited and scattered number of nonbelievers.

Thus, the Middle East constitutes an incubator for various religious groups and identities, which have contributed to the rise and development of diverse civilizations and cultures. Despite the multiple challenges various religious communities, particularly the minorities, have encountered throughout the modern history of the region, the diverse values, principles, customs, and beliefs introduced by such communities remain undeniable elements and characteristics of the comprehensive identity of the contemporary Middle East.

Ethnic Diversity

The term *ethnicity* is used to refer to a group of people who identify with each other on the basis of similar characteristics, such as common culture, descent, society, language or nation, with a sense of belonging and affiliation involved.[60] Thus, an ethnic group is mainly defined by shared cultural heritage, history, language, homeland or customs among its members.

The Middle East is home to several ethnic groups and cultural communities, with only few groups forming the majority of the total population and numerous others living as minorities across the region. The Arabs constitute the largest ethnic group in most of Middle Eastern states, except Turkey, Iran, and Israel. The term *Arab* originally refers to the peoples of northern and central Arabian Peninsula, and subsequent to the historical expansion of Arab-Islamic empires the term became synonymous with Arabic speakers.[61] Today, the Arabs primarily inhabit 22 Middle Eastern countries –with a total population of over 300 million– that together form the Arab League.[62]

The Turkic people are the second largest ethnic group in the Middle East. They primarily inhabit Turkey, where they constitute approximately 80 per cent of the population that numbers some 70 million. The Turkic people share common historical background and language.[63] Another major ethnic group in the region is the Persian. Making up about 50 per cent of the population of Iran, the Persians share common cultural heritage, customs and traditions, and are native speakers of the Persian language. Beside the Persians, Iran is also home to several other ethnic communities such as the Kurds, Arabs, Lurs, Tats, Ballochs, Gilakis, Talshis, Azerbaijanis, Turkmen, Circassians, Armenians, among others. According to Lambton, the cultural diversity in Iran prevented the rise of nationalism, as the sense of being a Persian did not provide an adequate basis for nationalism in the modern sense, and the common feeling among the people as a whole was religious, not national. They shared a common religious background.[64]

The Kurds constitute the fourth largest ethnic group in the Middle East, with a population estimated at 35-40 million. The Kurdish people, deemed to be one of the largest stateless nations in the world, mostly inhabit contiguous areas stretching from southeastern Turkey (*Northern Kurdistan*) to northern Iraq (*Southern Kurdistan*), and from northern Syria (*Western Kurdistan*) to northwestern Iran (*Eastern Kurdistan*).[65] The common cultural, linguistic and historical heritage compose the basis for a shared identity among the Kurds.

Furthermore, there are dozens of other ethnic communities that inhabit the Middle East, some of which have played a key role in the development of the region throughout history and contributed to the establishment of its ancient civilizations. These include the Assyrians, Arameans, Armenians, among others. Today, many of these groups live as minorities across the region and have encountered and survived considerable hardships. The long list of ethnically-diverse communities of the Middle East stretches to include Lurs, Mandeans, Copts, Berbers, Ballochs, Samaritans, Mhallamis, Turkmen, Circassians, Tats, Talishis, and others.[66]

The cultural diversity that once enriched the Middle East on multiple levels, and the historical coexistence among the region's various communities, have been threatened and jeopardized by a few sectarian extremist groups whose atrocities reached every single social component with different religious, doctrinal or ideological tenets.[67] Ethnic and religious minorities have become a target to radical groups, and sedition was ignited and reinforced by the extremist discourse of sectarian organizations in the region. In addition, people from different social components were suppressed for their critical position toward radical groups –whose oppressive practices and atrocities undermined public liberties and deprived people of their basic civil rights.

Part II

Jihad and Jihadism

The rise of Islamist militancy over the past few decades and the alleged attachment of various extremist groups to *Islamic jihad* (*jihād Islāmī*) have paved the way for a widespread controversy about the actual relationship between *jihād*, as a concept, and *Jihadism*, as a movement characterized by a radical worldview. Hence, delving into the origins of *jihād* in the Islamic tradition, the various interpretations of this notion and its eventual employment by Islamist extremists as a doctrinal basis to justify their actions seems crucial. This part sheds light on the initial emergence of the concept of *jihād* in the Qur'ān and its multifaceted utilization within the ḥadīth, and provides an exploration of main interpretations of its aspects and the rise and development of Salafi-Jihadism.

5. Jihad: Term and Concept

Jihad (*jihād*) is deemed to be the most renowned and yet the least understood Islamic notion in contemporary public consciousness.[68] It is therefore of crucial importance to explore *jihād* as a term, concept and practice, and to outline its fundamental features and tackle the development of its basic tenets throughout history, for the sake of the general understanding of what it actually implicates. The word *jihād* basically means to "struggle" for a noble cause with determination or "striving" in the path of God (*jihād fī sabīl Allāh*). Knapp, in his *The Concept and Practice of Jihād in Islam*, emphasizes that, while different radical Islamist groups insist that their actions are determined by and fall within the framework of Islamic *jihād*, and with the Western media continuing to make an excessive use of the term to describe such actions, there remains a misconception and misinterpretation of what is basically meant by *jihād* in Islam.[69]

One of the prevalent misinterpretations of the notion is using the word *jihād* in a literal reference to *holy war*. However, war in Arabic is *ḥarb* and holy is *muqaddasa*, which combined make up *al-ḥarb al-muqaddasa*, a phrase that does not exist in any form in the Islamic tradition.[70] This emerges in contrast with the medieval Christian counterpart term of *crusade* or *the war for the cross*. Nevertheless, the continuous and ever-growing employment of the term *jihād* reflects a certain form of revival of the religious as well as military implications and connotations of the concept of *jihād* among the Muslims today. Therefore, *jihād*, known as the *sixth pillar of the Islamic faith*, remains largely in need of revisiting for the sake of illustrating what the term entails and what it essentially implies.

According to Egyptian Islamic scholar Yusuf al-Qaradawi, who provides an authoritative account on *jihād* and Islamic jurisprudential reasoning in his extensive work *Fiqh al-Jihād*,[71] the concept of *jihād* is quite multifaceted. With the term and its derivations mentioned in the Qur'ān thirty-four times, basically in reference to struggling, striving and bearing the burden of protecting the *'umma* and defending its core religious values and beliefs, the concept of *jihād*, however, goes deeper than the mere use of violence in such a struggle. Al-Qaradawi identifies several aspects and characteristics of what could be called "true jihād", including the prioritization of the community's interests over self-interest, the struggle against corruption and persecution, patience and endurance, combatting hypocrites, striving for invitation and clarification, and eventually fighting the enemies by force once peaceful options are exhausted.

Since the use of force emerges as a final form of *jihād* in its multilayered notion, framing *jihād* as a mere call for violence or use of weaponry in the face of enemies reflects a misconception and misinterpretation of what *jihād* essentially means. From a semantic perspective, the word *qitāl* (fight) is derived from *qatl* (murder), whereas *jihād* (struggle) is derived from *juhd* (effort). Furthermore, although the word *jihād* today is frequently associated with aggression and violence, where Islam itself is being perceived as a religion urging violence against other communities, the term *'unf* (violence) is never mentioned in the Qur'ān.

Nonetheless, al-Qaradawi's account on the definition of *jihād* remains prone to criticism for the ambiguity that certain concluding remarks hold. One such remark is his saying, "every fight is a jihād once it comprised a legitimate intention, but not every jihād is a fight."[72] While the second part of this statement appears well-founded, given the extensive analysis of religious texts he provides, the first part seems far from convincing since every self-proclaimed *mujāhid* could legitimize his intention in a way that may satisfy a particular group of fellow Muslims or a certain circle of Islamic scholars and seem "in the way of God" while bringing about harm and damage to innocents wrongfully designated as enemies.

Islamic scholars generally agree on the definition of *jihād* as the effort made by a Muslim to fight against evil inside himself/herself and in the surrounding community, and ultimately pursuing and combatting evil wherever it may exist. That is, fighting injustice, hypocrisy, oppression and forces hostile to the Muslim community. It is a multidimensional process that involves *ʿamalu l-qalb bil-niyya wal-ʿazm* (spiritual intention and determination); *ʿamalu l-isān bid-daʿwa wal-bayān* (communication for the sake of invitation and clarification); *ʿamalu l-ʿql bir-raʾī wal-tadbīr* (intellectual opinions and planning); and *ʿamalu l-badan bil-qitāl* (physical effort in combat).[73]

Within the framework of its classical interpretation, two basic types of *jihād* could be identified, namely, *Jihād al-Daf* (defensive struggle) and *Jihād al-Ṭalab* (proactive/offensive struggle). *Jihād al-Daf* mainly implicates involvement in a resistance movement against hostile forces which invade or occupy Islamic territories and attack Muslims and their properties. Whereas *Jihād al-Ṭalab* primarily entails carrying out premediated armed operations against enemy forces on their own soil (*fī ʿuqri dārih*), motivated by the preconceived urgency to expand the Islamic territory and to enable those living under the rule of enemy forces to receive the message of Islam. However, it is worth noting that the historical context and the surrounding circumstances are of key significance to understand the rise and development of such interpretations and jurisprudential reasoning about the notion of *jihād* among Muslims.

6. Jihad as a Classical Notion

In order to acquire a better understanding of the notion of *jihād* and comprehend its basic features and characteristics, delving into its initial rise in Islam and the associated religious tradition seems inevitable. Hence, revisiting the concept of *jihād* as introduced within the Qur'ān and tackled within the ḥadīth appears essential. References to *jihād* within these two fundamental sources have been frequently recited and reinterpreted for centuries by theologians and Islamic scholars. Thus, the classical notion of *jihād* is reviewed in this chapter by means of delving into its terminological and conceptual employment in the Qur'ān, the ḥadīth, and the manuscripts of some of the influential Islamic scholars.

In the framework of its appeal for struggle in the path of God, the Qur'ān established the basis for the notion of *jihād* as struggle for God's cause and godly order. This conception dismissed tribal goals and communal concerns within the holy struggle, even if the motivation was grounded in Islamic revelation.[74] Various accounts suggest that in the early seventh century, the first followers of the Prophet Muhammad did not take *jihād* as a struggle in the path of God wholeheartedly, as it implicated confrontation and fighting against their non-Muslim tribal kinsmen, given the high level of intertribal violence and heightened insecurity through the Arabian Peninsula immediately before the emergence of Islam.[75] Muhammad's message is believed to have played a key role in weaning tribal peoples away from their usual incentives for conflict, including material interests and tribal prestige.

The Qur'ānic declaration of *jihād* cannot be reduced to mere armed struggle, since virtually all instances of the root *j-h-d* speak primarily to the question of "true intention and devotion."[76] *Jihād* was viewed by Islamic jurists within the framework of struggle in a world perceived as divided between what came to be known as *Dār al-Islām*, or Islamic-controlled territory, and *Dār al-Ḥarb*, or territory of war that basically consisted of lands outside Islamic control and inhabited either by the "People of the Book", namely Jews and Christians, or polytheists.[77] Nevertheless, this division does not implicate a continuous warfare by Muslims to dominate what was known as *Dār al-Ḥarb*. Islamic jurists allowed a room for the negotiation of peace since "there is no compulsion in religion."[78]

Hence, exploring the real meaning of the term *jihād* and what it implies as a concept requires studying the context within which the term and its derivations were employed in the Qur'ān. The diverse forms of the term denote a divine test, like in the Surah Q47:31: "*And We shall try you until We test those among you who strive [al-mujāhidīn] their utmost and persevere in patience*". It emerges as a test to distinguish between tepid believers and those who aspire for God's satisfaction and sacrifice their body and soul in His path, as mentioned in various Surah's, or Qur'ānic chapters, such as: "*Those of the believers who sit still -other than the disabled- are not on an equality with those who strive in the way of Allah [al-Mujāhidūna fī sabīli-llāhi] with their wealth and lives. Allah hath conferred on those who strive [al-mujāhidīn] with their wealth and lives a rank above the sedentary. Unto each Allah hath promised good, but He bestowed on those who strive a great reward above the sedentary.*" (Q4:95); "*Those who were left behind rejoiced at sitting still behind the messenger of Allah, and were averse to striving [yujāhidū] with their wealth and their lives in Allah's way. And they said: Go not forth in the heat! Say: The fire of hell is more intense of heat, if they but understood.*" (Q9:81); "*And when a surah is revealed (which saith): Believe in Allah and strive [jāhidū] along with His messenger, the men of wealth among them still ask leave of thee and say: Suffer us to be with those who sit (at home).*" (Q9:86); "*O ye who believe! Choose not My enemy and your enemy for allies. Do ye give them friendship when they disbelieve in that truth which hath come unto you, driving out the messenger and you because ye believe in Allah, your Lord? If ye have come forth to strive [jihādan] in My way and seeking My good pleasure, (show them not friendship). Do ye show friendship unto them in secret, when I am Best Aware of what ye hide and what ye proclaim? And whosoever doeth it among you, he verily hath strayed from the right way.*" (Q60:1).

Jihād is primarily deemed to be a method of measurement to distinguish between authentic belief and disbelief or infidelity, and rating the degree of merit as well as the intention of the believers. This is tackled repeatedly in the Qur'ānic verses. To mention a few instances: "*So obey not the disbelievers, but strive against them [jāhidhum] with the utmost strenuousness [jihādan kabīran], with the Qur'ān.*" (Q25:52); "*Those who believed and left their homes and strove [jāhadū] with their wealth and lives for the cause of Allah, and those who took them in and helped them: these are protecting friends one of another. And those who believed but did not leave their homes, ye have no duty to protect them till they leave their homes; but if they seek help from you in the matter of religion then it is your duty to help (them) except against a folk between whom and you there is a treaty. Allah is Seer of what ye do.*" (Q8:72); "*And those who afterwards believed and left their homes and strove [jāhadū] along with you, they are of you; and those who are akin are nearer one to another in the ordinance of Allah. Lo! Allah is knower of all things.*" (Q8:75). Therefore, *jihād* emerges as the emblem and mark of the believers who demonstrate a high level of commitment, devotion and determination to fearlessly bear and bring forth the mission of God without a minimum degree of doubt or uncertainty (Q5:54 and Q49:15).

In its reference to the significance of *jihād*, the Qur'ān primarily stresses the level of dedication to God's cause vis-à-vis excessive attention to worldly matters (Q9:19; Q9:24; Q60:2). This emerges in contrast with how the concept of *jihād* is being generally perceived by many as a mere call for war and conflict. Various Qur'ānic verses signify *jihād* as meriting forgiveness and divine favor (Q4:95; Q4:96; Q9:20; Q29:6; Q29:7), indicating a basic element in one's relation with and orientation to God (Q22:78; Q29:69; Q61:11), which is, nonetheless, eventually known only to God.[79] The core idea of this orientation to God is clearly referred to in: "*O ye who believe! Be mindful of your duty to Allah, and seek the way of approach unto him, and strive in His way [jāhidū fī sabīlih] in order that ye may succeed.*" (Q5:35). The true devotion as a key characteristic of *jihād* rises in contrast with hypocrisy and disbelief (Q9:73). Thus, based on the Qur'ān, *jihād*, as a word and concept, entails devotion to God, commitment to His path, and dedication to the core values and teachings of His mission.

The Qur'ānic context further illustrates that *jihād*, with its various aspects and dimensions included, implies that one's conduct or action is carried out on the basis of righteous incentives and with a valid intention, and it therefore deserves divine reward for its conformity to divine command. One of the key Surahs addressing this in the Qur'ān is Chapter 9, *Sūrat l-Tawbah* (The Repentance), in which the 41st verse reads: "*Go forth, whether light or heavy, and strive with your wealth and your lives in the cause of Allah [wa-jāhidū by-amwālikum wa-anfūsykum fī sabīli-llāhi]. That is better for you, if you only knew.*" Other examples of Qur'ānic verses tackling this issue include: "*And those who strive for Us [jāhadū fīna] We will surely guide them to Our ways. And indeed, Allah is with the doers of good.*" (Q29:69); "*And Strive for Allah with the endeavor which is His right [Wa-jāhidū fyl-llahi ḥaqqa jihādihī]... So establish worship, pay the poor-due, and hold fast to Allah. He is your protecting friend. A blessed Patron and a blessed Helper!*" (Q22:78); "*Say: If your fathers, and your sons, and your brethren, and your wives, and your tribe, and the wealth ye have acquired, and commerce wherein ye fear decline, and dwellings ye desire are dearer to you than Allah and His messenger and striving in His way [wa-jihādin fī sabīlihī]: then wait till Allah bringeth His command to pass. Allah guideth not wrongdoing folk.*" (Q9:24). In this context, *jihād* basically means redeeming one's life before God, struggling in His path, and striving for His satisfaction.

The predominantly redemptive tenor that appears in the Qur'ānic context illustrates that *jihād* is first and foremost meant for one's own self, that is, for a person's ultimate purpose. This leads us to conclude that *jihād*, as manifested in the Qur'ān, refers to not warfare or armed activity per se, but a righteous cause and virtuous purpose before God. Nonetheless, different interpretations of what righteous and virtuous implicate with regard to *jihād* in the Qur'ānic context emerged and developed among the Muslims over the centuries that followed Islamic revelation, frequently influenced by historical events as well as surrounding socio-economic and political conditions.

In the *ḥadīth*, which is deemed to be the second most authoritative source of the Islamic law (*Sharīʿa*), *jihād* considerably implies a physical action or an armed activity in the cause of God. For instance, the *ḥadīth* 1297 reads: "*Death puts an end to all action, except in the case of one who patrols the frontier in the cause of Allah, for his activity continues to grow till the Day of Judgement and he is shielded against the trials of the grave (narrated by Abu Daud and Tirmidhi).*"[80] The *ḥadīth* 1300 maintains: "*Everyone who is injured in the cause of Allah will appear on the Day of Judgement with his wound bleeding, its colour the colour of blood and its smell like the fragrance of musk (narrated by Bukhari and Muslim).*"[81] Moreover, the *ḥadīth* 1302 concludes: "*Paradise becomes incumbent for those who fight in the cause of Allah even for the briefest space (narrated by Tirmidhi).*"[82] Also, the *ḥadīth* 1342 reads: "*He who shoots an arrow in the cause of Allah has merit equal to the freeing of a slave (narrated by Abu Daud and Tirmidhi).*"[83] The *ḥadīth* 1346 carries a comparable message, as it says: "*He who dies without having fought in the cause of Allah and without having thought of it in his mind dies with one characteristic of hypocrisy within him (narrated by Muslim).*"[84]

On martyrdom, as defined by the Prophet Muhammad with respect to *jihād*, the *ḥadīth* 1358 maintains: "*There are five who are martyrs: he who dies of the plague, he who dies of cholera, he who dies of drowning, he who is killed by the falling of a wall and he who becomes a martyr by fighting in the cause of Allah (narrated by Bokhari and Muslim).*"[85] Furthermore, the *ḥadīth* 1308 reads: "*The fire will not touch one whose feet are covered with dust in striving for the cause of Allah (narrated by Bukhari).*"[86] Also, the *ḥadīth* 1354 illustrates various aspects of *jihād* as maintained by the Prophet Muhammad: "*Strive [jāhidū] with your hands [fight], your tongues [Da'wah] and your wealth (narrated by Abu Daud).*"[87]

Thus, the *ḥadīth* generally tackles *jihād* from different angles, yet it remarkably sheds light on a physical embodiment of *jihād* as an activity of self-sacrifice, participation in armed struggle in the path of God and aspiration for *shahāda* (martyrdom) for God's cause. Although the *ḥadīth*'s approach to *jihād* was considerably bound to the events and developments that came to define the early stage of Islamic history, most Islamic jurists and theologians of the classical age (first few centuries) of Islamic history interpreted *jihād* in the context of armed struggle and tried to illustrate it in military terms.

Jihād was viewed by Islamic jurists within the framework of struggle in a world perceived as divided between what came to be known as *Dār al-Islām* and *Dār al-Ḥarb*.[88] Yet, this division does not implicate a constant warfare, given the room for the negotiation of peace allowed by jurists as inspired by verses such as: "There is no compulsion in religion" (Qur'ān 2:256). The concept of *Dār al-Islām* and *Dār al-Ḥarb* is believed to have been developed and reinforced during the rule of the first Islamic dynasty, the Umayyads (660-750 CE), who are said to have added an imperial dimension to the notion of *jihād*. With the rise of the Umayyads, *jihād* became a "convenient tool for dividing the world neatly into two camps: those under the control of Islamic state and those not."[89] Referring to the Islamic realm in political and territorial terms, rather than communal, was an imperial construct, as there is no Qur'ānic reference to indicate or explicate such a division. Moreover, during the rule of the Abbasid dynasty (750-1258 CE), *jihād* was viewed as both collective requirement and personal duty, increasingly in its offensive rather than defensive form, given the then remarkably expansionist mentality of the ruling authority. This emerged in contrast with the Crusades era, where defensive *jihād* as a communal duty was praised at a time when Islamic territory was under outside aggression.[90] Thus, the multifaceted interpretation of the notion of *jihād* by jurists, religious and political authorities illustrates the great impact of the surrounding circumstances on the way the concept was employed throughout history.

The core conception of *jihād* is believed to hold an objective beyond religious gains, that is striving for the establishment of a just and impartial political and social order. This is extensively tackled by al-Qaradawi, who maintains that true Muslims carry "a global message" implicating "prevalence of justice, goodness, incorruptibility, and the rise of the word of God on earth."[91] This message, the spread of which is deemed fundamental in the struggle in the path of God, entails struggling against weakness in the soul, aberration in the mind, deviation in behavior, corruption in societies, tyranny in governments, and grievance among peoples and nations.

The common understanding of the notion of *jihād* does not particularly implicate a requirement of every individual Muslim, known as *farḍ ʿayn*, but rather a general obligation of the Muslim community or a collective duty, known as *farḍ kifāya*.[92] Considering *jihād* as a collective requirement rather than an individual duty stems from the fact that the concept essentially entails a voluntary activity rather than a compulsory one.[93] An obvious indication of this argument is the fact that *jihād* doesn't literally emerge among the notorious pillars of Islam or the five duties incumbent on each Muslim, known as *'Arkān al-Islām*, which respectively comprise the Muslim profession of faith (*al-Shahāda*), prayer (*Ṣalāt*), the distribution of alms to the poor (*Zakāt*), the fasting of Ramadan (*Ṣawm*), and the pilgrimage to Mecca for those financially and physically capable (*Ḥajj*). Nonetheless, *jihād* arises in the *ḥadīth* as the sixth pillar of Islam, but in the form of a communal and collective requirement and not as an individual duty.[94] Once urged to perform *jihād*, mainly in the case of defending own territory against enemy assault or to combat injustice and corruption within society, it is sufficient for a group of Muslims to voluntarily carry the burden and perform the duty of *jihād* as representatives and defenders of the community as a whole.

However, this largely constrained, bounded, defensive and preventative conception of *jihād* did not persist as a sole version for long, as it was contested, reinterpreted and redefined by Muslim scholars and movements over the centuries. One of the most prominent Muslim thinkers who reshaped the core notion of *jihād* and contributed to radically shifting the debate about the then familiar version of *jihād* was Islamic legal philosopher Taqi al-Din Ahmad Ibn Taymiyya (1263-1328). According to Ibn Taymiyya, any form of authority or government is deemed illegitimate unless it enforced the *Sharīʿa* law in all aspects, including the fulfillment of *jihād*, considering power as a trust (*'amānah*) from God that needs to be exercised in accordance with the terms laid down in the *Islamic Sharīʿa.*[95] Therefore, any Muslim authority that fails to implement the *Sharīʿa* and the duty of *jihād* would be deemed insufficiently Islamic and hence loses its legitimacy to rule. One of Ibn Taymiyya's main arguments in this regard is that *fasād* (corruption) in religious and communal practice leads to *jahl* (ignorance), *ẓulm* (injustice), and argumentation based on *ẓann* (conjectural thought) and *hawā* (caprice) instead of commitment to the explicit rulings of the revealed law or *Sharīʿa.*[96] His spiritual texts on *jihād* have inspired many of modern day radical Islamic leaders, such as al-Qaeda leader Ayman al-Zawahiri who cited him in one of his speeches saying, "loving God necessarily requires *jihād*, because the lover loves what His beloved loves, and hates what He hates, and associates with whomever His beloved associates, and considers as enemies His beloved's enemies, he is pleased by what pleases Him, angered by what angers Him, commands what His beloved commands, forbids what He forbids."[97]

According to Ibn Taymiyya's philosophy of *jihād*, given that all creatures must live and die, "one ought to put one's life and death at the service of a goal that will guarantee true happiness, namely *jihād* which rewards one with either a divinely supported victory over unbelief or the prize of martyrdom."[98] His key concern was no longer the geopolitical integrity of Islam, but rather the Islamic religious identity, which was no longer protected following the fall of the Caliphate at the hands of the Mongols at the time. The rhetoric employed by Ibn Taymiyya is deemed considerably inspirational to today's extremist Islamists.

In his definition of *jihād*, Ibn Taymiyya quoted a *ḥadīth* recorded by Anas b. Mālik that reads: "Every religion has a kind of monasticism, and the monasticism of my religion is the *jihād*,"[99] which reflects an emphasis on the essentiality of committing oneself to *jihād* as a condition for being a *true* Muslim. His definition of the notion of *jihād* implicates fighting against *kufr*, *fitna* and *sharr*, that is disbelief, persecution, transgression and evil.[100] *Kufr*, in this context, may also apply to a Muslim in violation of the *Sharīʿa* law, that is, a professing Muslim who breaks with the faith is to be considered an apostate. In a bid to support his definition of *jihād*, Ibn Taymmiyya recites certain *ḥadīths*, such as: "He who deliberately abandons the duty of *jihād* will die as a *munāfiq* [hypocrite]."[101] Hereby he basically emphasizes the obligatory nature of *jihād* among the Muslims.

Ibn Taymmiyya differentiates between two types of *jihād*: "*jihād makkī*" and "*jihād madanī*". *Jihād makkī* refers to struggle with *ʿilm* (knowledge), as symbolized by the Prophet's *Daʿwa* or call to Islam in Mecca, which comes in the form of *jihād bil-ḥujja* (*jihād* with argument). Hence, *jihād makkī* implies the call for obeying the Islamic teachings and abiding by the *Sharīʿa* among the Muslims and the invitation to Islam among the non-Muslims. This type of *jihād* is referred to by several modern scholars as *inward jihād* and *jihād against the lower self*.[102] *Jihād madanī*, on the other hand, entails the employment of military force and combat alongside *Daʿwa*, which is stressed by Ibn Taymiyya as the best form of and true *jihād* for its potential efficiency. In order to support his claim, Ibn Taymiyya quotes the Qur'ānic verse:

"You are the best nation produced for mankind. You enjoin what is right and forbid what is wrong and believe in Allah. If only the People of the Book ('Ahl al-Kitāb) had believed, it would have been better for them. Among them are believers, but most of them are defiantly disobedient."[103] Some scholars suggest that since *jihād makkī* precedes *jihād madanī* in Ibn Taymiyya's categorization, *Daʿwa* or peaceful means of *jihād* are prioritized and recommended before taking action and engaging in military strife.[104] Nevertheless, promoting the second form of *jihād* as the excellent and true one reflects Ibn Taymiyya's tendency to recommend *jihād madanī* as the greater way to strive in the path of God. Given his emphasis on *jihād* as a significant part of duties assigned to Muslims by God, his well-founded argumentation on the necessity of applying the *Sharīʿa* by any Muslim ruler or authority as a condition to acquire and maintain legitimacy, his call for branding a professing Muslim who does not live by Islamic teachings as an apostate, and his promotion of a combination of *Daʿwa* and military force as the best and most appreciated form of *jihād*, Ibn Taymiyya is believed to have established an intellectual groundwork that has considerably inspired prominent contemporary radical Islamists.

Next to the classical view of *jihād* as a communal struggle for the protection and expansion of *Dār al-Islam* and Ibn Taymiyya's conception of active *jihād* as a key factor of legitimacy for any Muslim authority, another view of *jihād* has been introduced by the Sufi (*Ṣūfī*) movement, embodied by the doctrine of what they considered to be *greater jihād*. According to the Ṣūfīs, who constitute a mystical sect of Islam, *jihād* is basically deemed an *inner struggle* against the basic instincts of the body as well as the potential perversion of the soul.[105] Hence, the *greater jihād* is considered as a crucial component of the approach toward the acquisition of spiritual shrewdness and prudence. The Ṣūfī vision of *greater jihād* is viewed by many scholars as the "root" of the general concept of *jihād* and assigned to *'aṣḥāb al-bāṭin* (people of internal reality), which emerges in contrast with *jihād al-jazā'* (military *jihād*) that is primarily assigned to "kings and emirs" of Muslims and is deemed a mere "branch" of the *greater jihād*.[106] The Ṣūfī view of *jihād* emphasizes a fundamental contrast between the *greater jihād* (*al-jihād al-'akbar*), which entails an internal spiritual struggle in the path of God against worldly trials, and the *lesser jihād* (*al-jihād al-'aṣghar*), which refers to an external struggle for the sake of Islam, including fighting for God's cause on the battlefield or any form of physical action in defense of Islam.[107] Thus, given the various versions of and views on *jihād* that have emerged and developed over the centuries, it comes as no surprise that controversy over the meaning and significance of the conception of *jihād* still persists to this day.

7. Jihad and the Sect: Sunni and Shia Interpretations

Sunni and Shia Muslims principally agree on the application of *jihād* once certain circumstances coexist that basically justify striving in the path of God. Such circumstances include the defense of faith, territory, property and way of life.[108] *Jihād*, in its spiritual and physical forms, is thus deemed justified by both Sunnis and Shiʿites in the cases of repelling threats of invasion by hostile troops, protecting the Muslims and their properties, and guaranteeing the freedom of practicing and spreading Islam.

However, the issue of having an eligible and righteous authority to wage and direct *jihād* emerged as a divisive factor between Sunnis and Shiʿites. According to the Sunni interpretation of *right authority* that is deemed to be eligible to call for and direct *jihād*, all Muslim Caliphs, including the rightly-guided first four Caliphs and those who followed, possess the right to wage and guide *jihād* as long as they hold the political and religious authority and possess the support of Islamic scholars (*ʿulamā'*). Whereas the Shia believe that this right has been exclusively meant for the Imāms, but it was arbitrarily and wrongly stripped from them by the Sunni majority. This disagreement is deeply rooted in the Sunni-Shia original struggle over whether religio-political leadership was meant to be passed on by bloodline, known as the *Shia Imamate*, or through election, known as the *Sunni Caliphate*.[109] Hence, the jurisprudential variance between the Sunni and Shia conceptions of *jihād* is deemed to have been shaped by historical developments and the associated religio-political approach of the *ʿulamā'*.

Delving into the Shia perception of *jihād* illustrates that the historical suffering and grievances of the Shia are considered essential to the sect's understanding of the notion of *jihād* as intimately tied to these grievances.[110] One of the key incidents deemed crucial to the identity-building of the Shia was the martyrdom of Hussein, the Prophet's grandson and ʿAli's younger son, during a battle with Sunni Umayyad forces in Iraq's Karbala in 680 on ʿAshurā', the 10th day of the month Muḥarram according to the Islamic calendar. The Shiʿites believe that the tale of Hussein's martyrdom holds moral lessons for the community and has become a symbol for struggling against suppression and striving for justice. This interpretation, which constitutes a key element of the Shia doctrine, tends to draw a direct link between the martyrdom of Hussein and the fundamental notion of *jihād* as a struggle for God's cause and godly order. Another element of the Shia doctrine that considerably determines the perception of a majority of Shiʿites with regard to *jihād* is the *ghayba* or occultation of the Twelfth Imām.[111] The *Twelver Shiʿism* (*Ithna ʿAsharis*) is the largest denomination of Shiʿites, and its followers believe that the Prophet's spiritual authority and religious leadership were passed on to twelve of his descendants, beginning with ʿAli, Hasan and Hussein. The Twelvers believe that the 12th Imām, Muhammad al-Mahdi, known as the 'Awaited Imām' or 'Hidden Imām',[112] has disappeared from a cave below a mosque in 874 and will reappear at the end of time to bring absolute justice and peace to the world.[113] Thus, it is the *Hidden Imām* who, according to the majority of Shiʿites, possesses the true authority that would provide him with the right to direct *jihād*, and during the absence of the *Hidden Imām* the concerned *ʿulamā'* or *Mujtahids* –the most senior religious scholars– are performing this task until his return.

The main point of difference between the Sunni and Shia perceptions of *jihād* is thus the righteousness and legitimacy of an authority to initiate and guide *jihād*. According to the mainstream Shia scholars, while the *defensive jihād* that is aimed at protecting and defending the *'umma* against an outside attack is compulsory and may be authorized by the *Mujtahids*, the authorization of *offensive jihād* remains unlawful in the absence of the 'Hidden Imām'.[114] Having an identity marked by grievances and suffering, the Shiʿites perceive Sunnis as the main source of their miseries throughout history, and they therefore believe in the need to resist and fight against what they deem to be a long-standing injustice and oppression practiced against them. In terms of combatting fellow Muslims under the banner of *jihād*, a classical Shia interpretation of *jihād* is used as a main reference for authorization, which falls under *jihād of the sword*. It basically permits fighting even against fellow Muslims once those are found guilty of spreading discord, schism and injustice in the Islamic realm.[115] Such an interpretation has allowed for a greater divide to find its way into the Muslim society and contribute to the continuity and escalation of sectarian differences and confrontations between Sunnis and Shiʿites throughout history.

Both Sunni and Shia sects agree on the significance of having the proper *niyya* or right intention before declaring or calling for *jihād*. Engaging in armed *jihād* for the sake of "conquest, booty, or honor in the eyes of one's companions" would not be regarded as a true *jihād* and thus would go unrewarded, because the sole valid objective of *jihād* is to "draw near God" and hence struggle in His Path.[116] Once the right intention exists, other conditions would follow before the launch of *jihād* could gain its legitimacy. These conditions include offering the enemy the so-called triple alternative: accept Islam, pay the *jizya* (tax imposed on non-Muslim People of the Book, *'Ahl al-Kitāb*, residing in a Muslim-controlled area), or fight. The fundamental importance of *niyya*, agreed on by Sunni and Shia scholars, emerge in major literature on *jihād* for its key relevance to the Godly reward believed to follow *martyrdom* after joining an armed struggle for God's cause.

The jurisprudential literature of early Islamic history shows that for *jihād* to rise to the degree of truthfulness and righteousness, and in order for it to accomplish its intended divine purpose, two crucial conditions should exist inside each participant (*mujāhid*): the *niyya* (right intention) and *isteʿdād* (willingness).[117] Having the *niyya* to strive for God's cause would enable a Muslim to join *jihād* once called upon to do so, and those who appear unable to participate for certain justified reasons would still enjoy the privilege of having the *niyya* toward *jihād*. In this context, *isteʿdād* arises as a crucial and complementary building-block of *jihād*, for having the *niyya* without *isteʿdād* would impede the whole process. Hence, it is expected of each Muslim to have both *niyya* and *isteʿdād* with respect to *jihād* in order to contribute to the defense of Islamic territory once exposed to enemy attacks or when the safety of Muslims and their properties are threatened by hostile forces. Noteworthy, the discussion of the notions of *niyya* and *isteʿdād* with respect to *jihād* in major Islamic literature comes in the context of *Jihād al-Dafʿ* (defensive struggle), and under the assumption of considering *jihād* as a *farḍ kifāya* (collective communal duty). Nonetheless, the *righteousness* of the intention associated with *jihād* and its legitimate determiner remain controversial.

Furthermore, one of the fundamental differences between Sunni and Shia doctrines with regard to their approach to *jihād* is that the latter considers it a genuine pillar of Islam. While the Sunnis chiefly recognize the five duties incumbent on each Muslim –comprising al-Shahāda, Ṣalāt, Zakāt, Ṣawm, and Ḥajj– as the undisputable five pillars of Islam (*'Arkān al-Islām*), the Shiʿites consider *jihād* as another basic pillar (*rukn*) of the religion the commitment to which is deemed essential and at the core of the Islamic faith.[118] Yet, this approach underscores the key significance of legitimacy, right intention, and commitment to the basic ethics of Islam as fundamental elements that need to coexist in any form of *jihād* in order to be acknowledged as a true struggle in the path of God and eventually be rewarded. Once *jihād* was legitimate and justified (*mashrūʿan*), based on the right intention (*wa-ṣaḥḥat fīh al-niyya*), and was carried out in accordance with Islamic ethical principles (*akhlāqīyāt al-Islām*) and within the boundaries of God's teachings (*wal-tuzimat fīh ḥudūd Allāh*), it is to be considered the greatest way to worship God and get nearer to Him. The *Shia Imamate* notably refers to the kind of *jihād* that combines all these aspects to be acknowledged as the sixth pillar of Islam.

Hence, the Shia's belief that *jihād* is among other duties incumbent on each Muslim is to be viewed as the main point of difference with respect to *jihād* between them and the Sunnis, who insist on *al-'Arkān al-Khamsa* or the notorious five pillars. This goes beyond the question of determining the righteous authority to launch and direct *jihād*. Imām Ahmed ibn Ḥanbal (780-855), Islamic theologian, jurist and founder of the traditionalist Ḥanbalī school of law, considered *jihād* the greatest voluntary practice and the utmost form of sacrifice to demonstrate one's degree of commitment to Islam, a statement supported by numerous Qur'ānic verses and Ḥadīth quotes. According to al-Qaradawi, such teachings are deemed to be a source of inspiration for the Shia's insistence on embracing *jihād* as a genuine pillar of Islam.[119]

In a nutshell, while both Sunnis and Shiʿites agree on the basic principles of the conception of *jihād*, in its spiritual and physical forms, as a communal requirement to protect the faith and defend Islamic territory and the *'umma*'s property against any outside aggression, they still disagree on certain points in this regard. They also both agree on the necessity of having *niyya* and *iste*ʿ*dād* for any form of *jihād* in order to succeed and be rewarded. The question of legitimacy and righteousness of an authority to call for, initiate and direct *jihād* constitutes a fundamental point of disagreement between both sects. While the Sunnis consider any authority or leader that has gained consensus from the public to lead as eligible to launch and guide *jihād*, the Shiʿites, particularly the Twelvers, believe that this privilege solely belongs to the *Hidden Imām*, especially when it comes to *offensive jihād*, and that the *Mujtahids* are only allowed to lead the *defensive* form of *jihād* in his absence. The perceived long-standing grievances among the Shiʿites are deemed central to the sect's understanding of *jihād*, as crystallized in the classical Shia perception of *jihād of the sword* against fellow Muslims accused of spreading schism and injustice in the Islamic realm. Such interpretations were historically faced by Sunni reactions and contributed to the escalation of sectarian divide within the Muslim society and continued to surface into the modern era. Another aspect of difference between Sunni and Shia perceptions of *jihād* is whether to consider it a genuine pillar of Islam. The Sunni insistence to cling to the notorious *al-'Arkān al-Khamsa* as the only obligatory practices measuring one's commitment to the faith is faced by a predominantly-Shia perspective of embracing *jihād* as a considerably significant part of those pillars once justified, based on right intentions and carried out in accordance with the ethical principles of Islam and within the moral boundaries determined by the faith.

8. Salafi-Jihadism

Different radical Islamist groups claim attachment to Salafi-Jihadism or are branded as Salafi-Jihadi. This chapter strives to inform the reader on the different characteristics of the philosophy of Salafi-Jihadism and the rise and growth of the movement.

The term *Salafi* and what it designates remain ill-defined and repeatedly misunderstood and misinterpreted in the literature on this movement and in studies on Islamism in general.[120] Saudi Arabia's supreme clerical authority, the Permanent Committee for Scholarly Research and Fatwās, maintains that Salafism basically "refers to the righteous predecessors of the first three generations of Muslims", prominently known as the *al-salaf al-ṣāliḥ* or the pious predecessors.[121] These include the Prophet's contemporary companions (*al-Ṣaḥāba*), the last of whom died around the year 690; the generation that followed and known as *tābiʿīn*, lived until 750; and the third generation referred to as *tābiʿ tābiʿīn*, the last of whom died around 810. These three generations are viewed as the founders of and participants in a golden era of authenticated, attested and orthodox Islam. This arises in a *ḥadīth* of the Prophet in which he tackles the characteristics of the finest Muslims as "Of the generation to which I belong, then of the second generation, then of the third generation."[122] Hence, *Salafism* fundamentally entails the revival and maintenance of the version of Islam specifically as understood and practiced by the *al-salaf al-ṣāliḥ*.

In *Salafi-Jihadism: The History of an Idea*, which traces the evolution of the movement and its basic conceptions, Maher defines *Salafism* as "a philosophy that believes in progression through regression" where the "perfect life is realized only by reviving the Islam of its first three generations."[123] The legacy of *al-salaf al-ṣāliḥ* is deemed to be *authentic* and *pure* in this deeply revivalist doctrine. The core principles of *Salafism* implicate a consistent emphasis on *tawḥīd* (God's unity), and the preservation of *ʿaqīda* (doctrinal pureness). The Salafis consider themselves as the *al-ṭā'ifa al-manṣūra* or the sole triumphant group of Muslims, and *al-firqa al-nājiya* or the saved denomination.[124] The doctrine supports this claim by a *ḥadīth* in which the Prophet Muhammad is reported as saying, "A group of my followers will remain victorious till Allah's Order [the Hour] comes upon them while they are still victorious."[125] The *ḥadīth* refers to an anticipated divide within the Muslim community, marked by the rise of different currents, mostly deviant, except for one group of Muhammad's followers who will remain pure in their belief and practice Islam in accordance with God's Order and will thus eventually prevail.

Salafism is thus to be viewed as a doctrinal philosophy primarily focused on a supposedly exemplary form of Islam characterized by genuineness, purity and unconditional commitment to the teachings of *al-salaf al-ṣāliḥ*. In order to realize this vision, Salafi scholars refer to different methods (*manāhij*, s. *manhaj*). In a bid to explain the broadness and variance of methods to realize the Salafi version of Islam, Sheikh Salih ibn Fawzan provides a comparison between *manhaj* and *ʿaqīda*: "*Manhaj* is broader than *ʿaqīda*; *Manhaj* (method) occurs in *ʿaqīda* (creed), in *sulūk* (behavior), in *'akhlāq* (manners), and in *muʿāmalāt* (dealings), as a part of the life of every Muslim. As for the *ʿaqīda*, it constitutes the foundation of *'īmān* (faith)."[126] A similar contrast was outlined by Sheikh Naasir ud-Deen al-Albani, who maintains that *ʿaqīda* is "more specific" than *manhaj* in that it has a direct link with *tawḥīd* (monotheism), which forms "the chief and fundamental aspect of Islam." This while *manhaj* is deemed to be "broader than ʿaqīda and tawḥīd" in that it allows resorting to different methods for the sake of "conveying and actualizing Islam."[127]

Amid the rise of various *manāhij* (methods) meant to assist in the realization of the Salafi philosophy, one particular *manhaj* has gained the attention of the majority of Salafis since the 19th century, namely, *Wahhabism*. Introduced by Muhammad ibn Abd al-Wahhab (1703-1792), the followers of this *manhaj* are frequently referred to as Wahhabis, and the works and legacy of ibn Abd al-Wahhab are considered to be highly influential among and of great impact on contemporary Salafis worldwide. Ibn Abd al-Wahhab provided what some scholars consider to be a narrow definition of 'true faith', as it mainly focuses on the founder's teachings that have ultimately introduced the principles of *takfīr* (denouncing fellow Muslims as apostates) and *jihād* against the *kāfir* (infidel).[128] Hence, *Wahhabism* is deemed to be the most extreme manifestation of radical Sunni Islam.[129] *Wahhabism* mainly implicates a return to the basic values and teachings of Islam, and striving for the purification of the faith from any form of theological additions or philosophical speculations.[130] Ibn Abd al-Wahhab's extremely conservative thoughts stem from the fact that he was remarkably influenced by the teachings of the strictly orthodox and traditionalist Ḥanbalī school of law, and particularly by the works and thoughts of the Ḥanbalī-based legal philosopher Ibn Taymiyya. This has led scholars on *Islamism* to associate *Salafism* with the legacy of both Ibn Taymiyya and Muhammad ibn Abd al-Wahhab, who are seen as primary architects of today's *Salafism*.

Nonetheless, the notion and practice of *takfīr* emerged for the first time during the early Islamic history, particularly in the course of the first Muslim civil war, known as the *First Fitna*.[131] Amid a growing tension between ʿAli and the founder of the Umayyad dynasty

Moʿawiya ibn Abi Sufian, a rebellious group known as the *Khawārij* (deviants) emerged and embraced an extremist interpretation of obedience to God and His dominion. ʿAli was eventually assassinated by a Khārijite, known as Abdur Rahman ibn Muljam, in January 661 in Kufa, after being condemned for allegedly failing to abide by God's dominion. While the *Khawārij* initiated their gatherings and activities a few years earlier, this was the first time for them to take action on such a level. As a radical rebellious sect, the *Khawārij* operated in accordance with the belief that any authority they considered as illegitimate and not abiding by God's dominion had to be overthrown for "judgement belongs to God alone."[132] The Khārijite (*Khārijī*) way of thinking and acting is deemed an intolerant approach to defining good and evil, wherein a heavy stress is placed on obedience to God and governing by the Qur'ān. As verse Q5:44 declares, "*Whoever does not judge by what God has revealed is an unbeliever [kāfir].*" Coupled with a growing schism within the Muslim community and surrounding circumstances marked by conflict over religio-political power in the Islamic realm of the time, such Qur'ānic verses are believed to have partially inspired the rise of the *Khawārij*. According to the Khārijite perspective, there is no place for a conciliatory middle position: one is either a true Muslim abiding solely by God's dominion, condemning and avoiding any form of deviation from the Straight Path (*al-ṣirāt al-mustaqīm*); or a *kāfir* who deserves no mercy whatsoever and needs to be eradicated for the sake of preserving the pureness of the faith and the piety of the '*umma* intact.[133] This basically implicates either believing and acting in accordance with a narrowly defined orthodoxy in order to be recognized as a true Muslim, or being branded as a *kāfir* and hence eligible for punishment. Thus, within the Khārijite perspective, moderation is rejected and replaced by a rather extremist notion and practice of excommunication toward fellow Muslims, labelling them as *kuffār* and combatting them by all means possible. This perspective, and the implicated consequences for those involved, introduced the conception of *takfīr* and the doctrine of *takfīrism* for the first time in the Islamic history.

One of the defining categorizations within *Salafism* was introduced by Wiktorowicz, who points out that the movement can be divided into three categories: *purists, politicos,* and *jihadis.*[134] The *purists,* also known as *quietists,* are mainly characterized by their missionary *Daʿwa* activities while avoiding any involvement in politics. The *politicos,* also known as *ḥarakīs* or activists, are distinguished by their involvement in politics and political activities. Unlike the *quietists* and the *politicos,* the *jihadis* believe in the legitimacy of employing force as a form of *jihād* in order to accomplish the core objectives of *Salafism.* While being used as a reference by many scholars, Wiktorovicz's categorization remains prone to criticism. According to Hegghammer, *Salafism* is essentially a "theological, not a political category", which raises controversy about the basis upon which Wiktorovicz's categorization was fundamentally built.[135] Other attempts to contest this categorization were made by Hafez, who criticizes the terminology employed by Wiktorowicz while dividing *Salafism* into three separate groups, arguing that the term "purist" would have been better understood if replaced by "conservative", given that all Salafists are essentially purists.[136] Yet, the main problematic issue within Wiktorovicz's categorization is that its broadness makes it fail to depict how actors from these different groups within the movement interact with each other, the form of their approach to power and the manner in which they aspire to change it.

It remains unclear when the term *Salafi-Jihadism* first emerged, yet the Salafi-Jihadis employ the term today to describe their movement and what it essentially stands for. According to prominent Islamic scholar and theorist of *Salafi-Jihadism* Abu Muhammad al-Maqdisi, the term did not originate from inside the movement, yet it is commonly used in reference to it. "Jihadi-Salafism is a current that combines the call to monotheism in its totality with jihād for this end," al-Maqdisi maintains, "it is a current that strives to actualize monotheism by waging jihād against the false gods... Its jihād is not limited to a certain geographic spot; its [Salafi] jihadis are carrying out the jihād across the globe."[137] Other Salafi scholars tried to demonstrate the accuracy of the term in defining the movement and its doctrinal principles, such as Sadiq al-Karkhi, who illustrates the key characteristics of a member of *Salafi-Jihadism* as being "*Salafī-yul ʿaqīda* (Salafi in creed), *Jihādī-yul manhaj* (Jihadi in method)."[138]

In order to understand what *Salafi-Jihadism* basically entails, it is of key importance to tackle the characteristics that define the movement and what its philosophy primarily implicates. Several scholars have attempted to identify such characteristics. Hafez maintains that the movement has five key characteristics to be identified, which include *tawḥīd* (monotheism), *takfīr* (categorizing others as non-believers), *ḥākimiyya* (God's might and rule), *jihād* (struggle in the path of God), and a rejection of *bidʿa* (heretical innovations).[139] While agreeing with Hafez's reference to *tawḥīd*, *takfīr*, and *jihād* as basic characteristics of contemporary *Salafism*, Brachman rejects the inclusion of *ḥākimiyya* and *bidʿa* among those defining features, advocating the replacement of both notions with *ʿaqīda* (creed) and *al-walāʾ wa-l-barāʾ* (loyalty and disavowal) instead.[140] According to Alsulaiman, the main characteristics of the *Salafi-Jihadi* movement originally stem from

Wahhabism, which is defined by *tawḥīd*, *ṭāghūt*, *ḥākimiyya*, *al-walā' wa-l-barā'* and *jihād*.[141] Hence, the concept of *bidʿa* is hereby replaced with *ṭāghūt*, which refers to all kinds of notions and conceptions that seem to replace God, deviate a believer from His worship and eventually endanger the *tawḥīd* or monotheism—the cornerstone of the whole religion.

Delving into the conceptual building-blocks of *Salafi-Jihadism* requires tackling the broader set of Islamic jurisprudential notions. There are certain practical, theoretical and ritualistic jurisprudential concepts of significance in this regard. The practical dimension involves the concepts of *ridda/irtidād* (apostasy), *ḥisba* (accountability within the framework of Islamic call to command good and forbid evil), and *bidʿa* (heretical innovations), which are of concern not only to Salafi-Jihadis but also to other Muslim traditions and movements. The theoretical concepts fundamentally comprise *'īmān* (faith) and *ʿaqīda* (creed/doctrine), which are considered basic notions to be adopted by any Muslim in order to accept and embrace Islam. The ritualistic ideas include *shafāʿa* (intercession) and *dhikr* (frequent mention and remembrance of God), both of which are primarily practiced by Ṣūfī Muslims while considered by many Salafis as certain forms of heretical innovations or *bidʿa*.[142] Thus, although some of these concepts are shared by various Muslim traditions and movements, including *Salafi-Jihadism*, the interpretation and employment of certain aspects of these notions emerge in different forms within a current compared to others.

Despite the various perspectives and constantly emerging and developing theories on the defining features of *Salafi-Jihadism*, there remain five undeniably crucial characteristics of the movement and its philosophy which, regardless of terminological variance between sources, include: *tawḥīd*, *ḥākimiyya*, *al-walā' wa-l-barā'*, *takfīr* and *jihād*. Furthermore, an inescapable aspect of these defining features is that they mainly focus on two issues in particular: the protection of the faith and its promotion. The safeguarding and preservation of the faith is, in accordance with the Salafi-Jihadi doctrine, accomplished by means of *jihād*, *al-walā' wa-l-barā'*, and *takfīr*. Whereas the promotion of the faith is, first and foremost, attached to the concepts of *tawḥīd* and *ḥākimiyya*. "It is the first part of this equation that interests Salafi-Jihadis the most because it is battlefield-related," Maher emphasizes, "providing the *raison d'être* for their modus operandi."[143]

The Salafi-Jihadi thought and worldview could be traced and better understood through revisiting the group's selection of references and ideas, for these hold direct ties with the departure points of their philosophy and the objectives that the movement strives to realize. *Salafi-Jihadism* is thus concerned with the preservation of what it perceives as authenticity, legitimate and righteous authority, submission and revolution, with its doctrinal components set to serve these principles and to accomplish its objectives. It urges and enforces *tawḥīd* and *ḥākimiyya* in order to determine the legitimacy and righteousness of an authority and ensure the application of authentic teachings of Islam; it takes *al-walā' wa-l-barā'* as a basic doctrine to set up the rules and borderlines of loyalty and disavowal; it resorts to *takfīr* in a bid to protect Islam in its authentic form against perversion and violations from within the *'umma*; and praises *jihād* as a blessed *manhaj* that would guarantee the realization of the ultimate aspirations of the movement.

The rise and growth of *Salafi-Jihadism* come as a consequence of previous, highly relevant events and developments in the Islamic world. Tackling the evolution of the Salafi-Jihadi ideology necessitates revisiting certain historical occurrences of crucial significance to *Islamism*, as they have contributed to reshaping several predominantly-Muslim countries. Among those developments are the rise of *Wahhabism* and its incorporation into politics and state-leadership in Saudi Arabia based on an agreement between Muhammad ibn Abd al-Wahhab and the founder of the Saudi dynasty Ibn Saud in the 18th century; the rise of the Muslim Brotherhood and the suppression of its leading members by the Egyptian authorities throughout the 20th century; the American-sponsored Egyptian-Israeli Camp David Treaty of 1978 that was followed by the assassination of the then Egyptian President Anwar Sadat in 1981 by the *takfīri* Wahhabi-based al-Jamāʿa al-Islāmiyya (the Islamic Group), whose members are considered among the pioneers of *Salafi-Jihadism*; the Iranian Revolution of 1979 that brought Khomeini to power and transformed Iran into a Shia-based theocratic Islamic republic, led within the ideological framework of *Wilāyat al-Faqīh* (the guardianship of the theologian); the Afghan War between 1979-1989 and the associated developments, particularly the rise of armed Islamic militants (the *mujāhidīn*) and the eventual emergence of al-Qaeda; and the Algerian Civil War in the period between 1991-2002.[144] The employment of *Wahhabism* as an instrument for political objectives in Saudi Arabia is believed to have caused an internal split within the Wahhabi movement, especially in the 20th century, resulting in the emergence of two Wahhabi currents: one of them insisting on maintaining its purist-religious nature, and the other increasingly drawn into politics.

Given the impact of the surrounding developments and changes across the region, including the Egyptian-Israeli Camp David Treaty, the Iranian Revolution and the Afghan War, the Wahhabi movement faced increasing intra-confrontations during the 1980s, which led to a final split within the movement in the aftermath of the Gulf Crisis of 1990. Since then, two forms of *Wahhabism* came to the surface: one associated with and demarcated by its ties to the Saudi state establishment; while the other sought to reach Muslims across the globe, caught by a worldview implicating the *takfīr* of many fellow Muslims and considering contemporary Saudi, Arab, and international order as *ṭāghūt* that requires fundamental reformation. The latter doctrine and its philosophy came to be regarded as *Salafi-Jihadism* and its adherents are thus labeled as Salafi-Jihadis.[145]

There is a set of extreme Wahhabi tenets considered central to the Salafist tradition, and hence to Salafi-Jihadis, to be identified, including: the rejection of reverence for saints, 'holy' images or objects, places, shrines or graves, considering them as a form of heresy; the *taḥrīm* (forbidding) of shaving, smoking, swearing, alcohol, and musical instruments; and denying women leadership roles.[146] Such extreme teachings emerged at the heart of ISIS's regulations imposed on populations under the group's control in Syria and Iraq in the period between 2014 and 2017, providing an example of the most radical form of *Salafi-Jihadism*. The ideological and doctrinal philosophy of *Salafi-Jihadism* was adopted and brought forward by several groups over the past four decades, such as al-Jamāʿa al-Islāmiyya (the Islamic Group), Jamāʿat al-Tawḥīd wal-Jihād (Organization of Monotheism and Jihād), and Jamāʿat Anṣār al-Islām (Islam Supporters Group). With *Salafi-Jihadism* at the core of their doctrine and practice, these groups have inspired, equipped and contributed to the rise of remarkably violent and notoriously extremist Islamist groups, the most prominent of which were al-Qaeda and the Islamic State (ISIS).

Literature that is deemed to be of high significance to the ideology of *Salafi-Jihadism* and constitute the groundwork for its doctrinal philosophy was mostly developed in the 70s and 80s of the last century, such as *al-Farīḍah al-Ghā'ibah* (the neglected duty, 'jihād') by Muhammad 'Abd al-Salām Faraj; *Risalāt al-'īmān* (messages of the faith) by Sālih Sariyyah; *Kalimāt Ḥaqq* (the honest words) by Omar Abdulrahman; *Mithāq al-ʿAmal al-Islāmī* (the charter of Islamic activism) by al-Jamāʿa al-Islāmiyya; *Millat 'Ibrāhīm* (the community of Abraham) by Abu Muhammad al-Maqdisi; *'Ilḥaq bi'l-Qāfilah* (Do not miss the [jihād] convoy) by Abdullah 'Azzām; and *al-ʿUmdah fī 'Iʿdād al-ʿUddah* (the adequate preparation for the struggle) by Abdulqader Abdulaziz. All these pamphlets and monographs are primarily based on a strictly orthodox Wahhabi thought, taking the principal teachings of *Wahhabism* as a departure-point, extremely advocating and emphatically urging to preserve and revive the doctrines of *tawḥīd, ḥākimiyya, al-walā' wa-l-barā'*, *takfīr* and *jihād*. The Salafi-Jihadi literature basically tends to employ substantial Wahhabi teachings for the sake of feeding the ideological tenets of *Salafi-Jihadism* and adjust its recommendations in accordance with the movement's worldview. Yet the term *Salafi-Jihadism* was first referred to in a speech by the current leader of al-Qaeda Ayman al-Zawahiri in 1994, and its first appearance in academic research was in 1998 in two separate studies on the Algerian Civil War both by Gilles Kepel and Kamil al-Tawil.[147] Pargeter emphasizes that the term primarily reflects a "current of thought" to which individuals may subscribe, and it "should not be confused with a specific group as such."[148] Other scholars reiterate that the term *Salafi-Jihadism* is to be viewed as an ideological strain, or thought, that certain individuals may adhere to and follow, and it does not belong to any particular movement or organization.[149] It is deemed to be today's major Islam-based reactionary religio-political current. It holds sufficient features to be seen as a political religion in the sense of providing its adherents with a shared cause, belongingness, and a common purpose that creates a community unified under the same umbrella of ideological tenets within a framework of activism that turns politics into religion.

Thus, we may define *Salafi-Jihadism* as a strictly orthodox, religio-political Islamist current of thought, with ideological tenets mainly derived from *Wahhabism* and essentially inspired by the works of Ibn Taymiyya. It strives for the revival and maintenance of the version of Islam specifically as understood and practiced by the *al-salaf al-ṣāliḥ*. The Salafi-Jihadi doctrine implicates a struggle to protect what its adherents consider an original version of the faith through *jihād*, *al-walā' wa-l-barā'*, and *takfīr*, beside combatting *bid'a* and *ṭāghūt*. It also entails an aspiration to promote the faith by means of emphasizing the concepts of *tawḥīd* and *ḥākimiyya*. It embraces *jihād* as a blessed and efficient *manhaj* or method for the sake of realizing its objectives. *Salafi-Jihadism* is chiefly the product of a chain of historical developments, associated with the rise of a set of literary works aimed at further inspiring, ideologizing and feeding its adherents and guiding them toward the accomplishment of its goals. The Salafi-Jihadi philosophy, with its religio-political nature, has survived and evolved over decades to eventually inspire some of today's most radical Islamist groups such as al-Qaeda and ISIS, and the fact that it remains a current of thought to which various groups may adhere indicates its potential power to continue inspiring groups of individuals into extremism in the future.

9. Jihad and Militancy

Given the excessive employment of the notion of *jihād* by numerous Islamist organizations over the past few decades, studying the revival and transformation of certain aspects of *jihād* in accordance with the surrounding developments across the Middle East seems of key importance to the topic of this book. This chapter delves into the rise of jihad-based Islamist militancy and the associated impact of particular Islamic thinkers.

The 20th century has witnessed the rise of several Islamic theorists who have approached *jihād* from various standpoints and contributed to the revival as well as the transformation of certain aspects of *jihād* in accordance with the surrounding developments across the Middle East. One of the first Islamic thinkers to tackle the notion of *jihād* – considerably in its physical form– on a systematic basis in the 20th century was Sayyid Abu al-Ala Mawdudi (1903-1979), who considered warfare as a necessary means to not just expand Islam's political dominance but also to attain justice, including freedom of religion. Mawdudi views *jihād* as a *war of liberation* that is aimed at establishing politically independent Muslim states. His perspectives have played a key role in transforming the classical notion of *jihād* into a modern day-related concept, increasingly associated with contemporary questions and activities, such as national liberation currents and anti-colonialism movements.

This nationalist and activist conception of *jihād* was adopted by Egyptian Islamist thinkers Hasan al-Banna (1906-1949) and Sayyid Qutb (1906-1966), especially with regard to the establishment of what they considered as a true Islamic rule. Al-Banna and Qutb further integrated Mawdudi's conception of *jihād* with Ibn Taymiyya's teachings that recommend overthrowing any government that fails to enforce the *Islamic Sharīʿa.*[150] This revolutionary conception of *jihād* basically implicates that any ruler in the Islamic world who fails to show his absolute and unconditional commitment to the *Sharīʿa* as a sole legitimate source of government does not fit as a leader of *jihād*, and consequently needs to be toppled and replaced. Hence, Muslims are required to first direct their *jihād* toward the internal enemy before heading against the external enemy. Such strictly orthodox thoughts and teachings have paved the path for radical Islamists to refer to *jihād* as an obligatory duty on every individual Muslim and to reject its interpretation as a communal duty.

The influential theorization on the conception of *jihād* by prominent Islamic scholars in the early 20th century, and the associated projection on contemporary developments witnessed across the Middle East, eventually resulted in the emergence of a current known as *Jihadism*—later referred to as *Salafi-Jihadism*. Since its rise in the late 1970s, this movement of thought and action has evolved gradually and went through several phases. Wright *et al.* identify five phases defining the development of *Jihadism* over the past four decades, which comprise the inception, cross-pollination, causation, realization, and crossroads.[151] The first phase, known as the *inception*, was characterized by the impact of Islamic ideologues, such as Sayyid Qutb and his protégés in the Egyptian prison system, who advocated and promoted the rhetoric of *takfirism* or the excommunication of fellow Muslims. The second phase, viewed as a stage of *cross-pollination*, marks the process of intermarriage between the theological orthodoxy of *Salafism* and the Muslim Brotherhood's *Islamism*—which was defined by the group's religio-political activism after the expulsion of its members from Arab states and their resort to Saudi Arabia. This phase also implies the *Salafization of Jihadism* among various Islamic currents in the 1980s-90s, a process coupled with the employment of violent tactics and an increasing adoption of Salafi theology as a sole legitimate form of *jihād* among many jihadists. The third phase, identified as the *causation*, saw the light with the spread of Salafist activism that was driven and inspired by key events and developments across the region, including the Afghan War in 1979-89 and the first Gulf War of 1990-91, during which Saudi Arabia was perceived by Salafists as betraying Islam, causing the emergence of a movement referred to as the *Awakening*. The fourth phase, deemed to be a phase of *realization*, featured heavy operations, including the 9/11 attacks on the World Trade Center. This phase marked the rise of *Jihadism* as a major serious threat to the West, while for jihadist movements it was perceived as the start of a potentially greater era to grow and thrive. The fifth defining phase of the development of *Jihadism*, referred to as the phase of *crossroads*, began with the U.S. invasion of Iraq in 2003, where jihadist organizations witnessed shifts and adjustments in tactics, strategy, objective and identity. Such shifts have continued to take place into the years that followed, and the motives and inspirations among groups that fall under the umbrella of *Jihadism* remain diversified amid the development of capabilities on multiple levels that enable such organizations to mobilize greater numbers of recruits and maintain the sustainability of their ideological tenets.

Hence, the rise of various, mainly radical, interpretations of the concept of *jihād* by a new generation of Islamic scholars, who were increasingly driven by contemporary developments taking place across the Middle East and the world, has played a key role in inspiring and motivating numerous Islamist militant groups to emerge and grow. Extremist Islamists, whether Sunni or Shia, have found themselves equipped by a sufficient number of theological verdicts and decrees that allowed, and even urged them, to resort to force and violence under the umbrella of *jihād* allegedly for the sake of Islam and the *'umma*. Pamphlets and monographs developed by the pioneers of *Salafi-Jihadism* constitute a crucial source of inspiration for most of the Sunni-based militant groups that have emerged over the past few decades. Such sources feed the perspective on political violence as *jihād*, refer to the armed form of *jihād* as the heart of Islam and blame its neglect for the deterioration of Islam's position in the world. Combating pro-modernization Muslims, toppling secular or apostate regimes, establishing *Islamic Sharīʿa* rule in Muslim states, restoring the caliphate, and expanding Islamic territory are key objectives of *jihād* as promoted by the Salafi-Jihadi discourse and its literature.[152]

The sources to which Shia extremists resort in order to feed their ideological tenets and perspectives on *jihād* are no less significant than those of the Sunnis. Prominent Shia religious leader Ayatollah Ruhallah Khomeini (1902-1989) has tirelessly emphasized the necessity to expose and overthrow tyrannical rulers for not abiding by the Islamic laws of *Sharīʿa*, urging Islamic jurists to lead such a revolution and establish Islamic governments once the apostate rulers are removed. This was considered a call to all Muslims to struggle for the sake of establishing the *Sharīʿa* rule. Khomeini argued that once the genuine Islamic teachings have prevailed among Muslims, each member of the *'umma* can become a *mujāhid* or struggler for God's cause.[153] Other influential Shia theorists and ideologues, such as Murtaza Mutahhari (1920-1979) and Muhammad Hussein Fadlallah (1935-2010), advocated armed *jihād* and called for the use of force as a necessary means in the *jihād* against the enemies of Islam and Muslims. Speeches and pamphlets produced by such authoritative ideologues have inspired and triggered an undeniably remarkable wave of Shia militancy in the Middle East over the recent years, operating within the framework of a sectarian-based *jihād* comparable to that of Sunni extremists in violence and aggression.

The emergence and growth of Islamist militant organizations such as Sunni-based al-Qaeda and ISIS, and Shia-guided al-Hashd al-Shaabi, whose leaders have constantly emphasized their commitment to an extremist version of *jihād*, can be seen as a fruit of the emerging radical theorizations, interpretations and elucidations on the conception of *jihād*, which have continued to flow and unfold throughout the 20th century. The tactics, targets and arenas of operation pursued by such groups in the recent years indicate the dramatic evolution of the movement of *Jihadism.* Such a development constitutes an unprecedented transformation of the basic idea of *jihād* into a radical concept upon which some of the most fanatic and atrocious organizations are based in terms of thought, ideology, discourse and course of action. Furthermore, globalization and digitalization surface at the heart of the propaganda and recruitment campaigns launched by radical groups to attract as many members and sympathizers to their alleged cause as possible, and *jihād* has been hereby exploited as a brand to provide a religious legitimacy to their cause and emotionally manipulate the recipients of their increasingly ideological discourse.

Part III

Islamism and Salafism

This part investigates the rise and development of the movements of *Islamism* and *Salafism*. Understanding what *Islamism* and *Salafism* basically implicate and the key factors behind their emergence, growth and increasing popularity over the past few decades requires familiarization with the agenda of major Islamist movements and studying the foundational tenets and the ultimate objectives of these movements. It takes the reader on a journey into the early rise of both movements, to meet the architects and get acquainted with their works and significant role in establishing these movements and ensuring their continuity and impact. It also strives for providing an insight into the doctrinal principles that constitute the cornerstones of the contemporary worldview of *Islamism* and *Salafism* through the lens of key influential scholars of the past two centuries.

10. Foundations and Core Objectives

In order to understand what *Islamism* basically implicates and the reasons behind its rise and growth over the past few decades, a familiarization with the ultimate agenda of major Islamist movements is deemed essential. Within the framework of Islamism there is a dividing line between institutional Islamists, on the one hand, and jihadists, on the other. While these two categories differ in terms of the means to be utilized for the sake of reaching the objective of establishing a *Sharīʿa*-based form of government to rule the *'umma*, they both agree on the goal they claim to strive for. The political agenda attributed to the Islamists in general is shared by various Islamist movements, including the hardline jihādi-takfīris. Under the umbrella of Islamism, religion basically takes a political shape wherein different activities are directed toward the goal of establishing a political order coined as *Sharīʿa state*. Thus, Islamism can be defined as an ideology, with a religionized political agenda, that establishes a fundamental relationship between *dīn* (religion) and *dawla* (state) in a *Sharīʿa*-based political order. It ultimately implicates the imposition of a political system in the name of faith, known as *niẓām Islāmi*.[154]

Islamism, as a notion and phenomenon, refers to social and political expressions prevalent within Islamic societies, aimed at integrating and incorporating Islam into state affairs, politics, economics and legal systems. It is deemed a form of instrumentalization of Islam by certain individuals or organizations that seek political goals.[155]

Political Islam has its roots in the early stage of the Islamic history. Within a few months following the death of the Prophet Muhammad, different Islamic groups emerged and became involved in public affairs and political rivalry, amid rising scholastic and sectarian divide.[156] Ever since, Muslim political theorists have been engaged in debates about the nature of political authority within the Islamic tradition and the proper way to be a Muslim.[157] Muslim thinkers of the 19th and 20th century stressed that the characteristic institution of modern Europe –democratic government, patriotic loyalty and legal reform– were permitted by Islam, only if Islam was correctly understood.[158]

Reformist thinkers such as Jamal al-Din al-Afghani, Muhammad ʿAbduh and Rashid Rida called on Muslims to become part of the modern world that was based on reason and progressive activity, which they deemed essential in 'true Islam'. Adapting the Islamic law (*Sharīʿa*) to the needs of modern life became a point of emphasis for these thinkers. Reformist Islamic thinkers believed that Islam was a *rational* religion that could be applied directly to modern life. They believed traditional-bound Muslim leaders had led society astray and that religious thinking should instead be reformed and used as a vehicle for progress.[159]

Nevertheless, such reformist thoughts about Islam as a rational religion should be viewed within the framework of the long-standing tradition of *tajdīd* (renewal) and *'iṣlāḥ* (reform) in the Islamic history, reinforced by centuries-long debates about *'aql* (reasoning) and *naql* (transmission), as demonstrated through *ijtihād* (independent judgement) and a high-level philosophy. However, these debates haven't been as fruitful to develop methods of transition and the delegation of powers or tools to determine and preserve individual political and civil rights and freedoms. Throughout twelve centuries of Islam, the huge amount of debates hardly ever evolved into an independent Islamic political science, nor did they reach the extent of developing tools to define and protect personal political rights, public liberties, transition and devolution of power. As a matter of fact, the modern concept of reinstalling Islam into public life and considering politics an authentic part of religion was developed by the 19th and 20th century thinkers who were motivated by the provocation of direct contact with the West.[160]

One of the first pan-Islamic intellectuals to target the West and warn of the dangers of European imperialism to the Islamic identity and the Islamic realm was Jamal al-Din al-Afghani (1838-97). Shifting the focus from merely criticizing national regimes in the Muslim world, or the near enemy, to attacking the West, primarily Europe, or the far enemy, al-Afghani introduced an international vision of the Islamic movement. According to al-Afghani, the relationship between Europe and Islam is to be seen as antagonistic, stressing that the absence of strong morals among the *'umma* could eventually lead to the domination of European materialism throughout the Islamic world. Up until the rise of Sayyid Qutb (1906-1966) as a radical Islamic intellectual, al-Afghani was deemed the only Islamist to criticize the West and warn about its dangers to the region in terms of identity and culture. He anticipated a social breakdown in the east as a consequence of European imperialism, and therefore emphasized the urgent need for a new understanding of Islam as a strategy for the sake of salvation from this breakdown. Such a process will require a purification of Islam and a return to its basic traditional tenets.[161] By this, al-Afghani defined and introduced the *Salafism* movement (*salafiyya*), wherein he emphasized the need to return to the ways of the *salaf* as a condition for preserving and protecting what he considered as a *true* Islamic identity against the influences of modernism and Western imperialism. Together with his student Muhammad ʿAbduh (1849-1905), al-Afghani is considered the pioneer of *Salafism* as understood in the context of the modern age.

In order to crystallize their ideas about the required response from the Islamic world toward the threat of European imperialism and materialism, al-Afghani and ʿAbduh published the influential newspaper *al-ʿUrwa al-Wuthqa* (The Firmest Bond). Al-Afghani believed that a practical pan-Islamic response was needed in order to face the dangers waving from the West, and he then advocated a reformation of Islam in such a way that helps to shape a civilization sufficiently equipped to confront the Western threat. Nonetheless, transforming Islam to respond to challenges associated with modernism would not necessarily implicate secularizing it, according to al-Afghani, for Islam is already *rational* and does not need any form of secularization to thrive. Thus, Muslims could be modern *within* Islam, and there is no necessity to refuse or discard religious doctrines for that end.[162] Al-Afghani frequently emphasized the need for solidarity within the *'umma* in the face of Western encroachment. Such a solidarity should be based on a real unity among the Muslims, and one of the essential factors to accomplish such a *real* unity is to return and stay attached to a common religious conviction. Hence, the restoration of the Islamic strength and civilization primarily requires a fundamental return to *true* Islam. Al-Afghani's philosophy tends to combine *Islamism* and *Salafism* by means of emphasizing the need for political and cultural reforms, and shedding light on the necessity to return to the ways of the *salaf* as a true version of Islam that unites the *'umma*, for the sake of resisting Westernization, toppling tyranny, establishing an Islamic rule and inspiring Islamic unity.

The reformist ideas of ʿAbduh developed beyond those of his teacher al-Afghani, until he became recognized as the father of modern and secular Islam, beside his considerably essential contribution to *Salafism* and *Islamism* in general. ʿAbduh suggested that Muslims could be devout and modern at the same time. Following his appointment as the chief mufti of Egypt in 1899, ʿAbduh attempted to reform the al-Azhar into a nationalist university. His writings about *tawḥīd* and *ijtihād* (unity and interpretation), beside his attempts to advocate modernism within Islam through the revival of the Islamic tradition of the *salaf*, led some scholars to label ʿAbduh's approach as contradictory.[163] Eventually, he viewed pan-Islamism as the most efficient solution to the failures and challenges encountered by the *'umma*.

According to ʿAbduh, in order to face and overcome Europe's hegemony on the one hand, and the tyrannical regimes in the Muslim world on the other, a unified Islamic identity is needed, based on solidarity and striving for the establishment of governments that are willing and determined to embrace the Islamic *Sharīʿa* as a sole constitution for their rulings. Nevertheless, after distancing himself from al-Afghani, ʿAbduh's eagerness toward a radical political change in the Islamic world cooled, and he gradually turned into a moderate reformist and started to emphasize the need for educational and judicial reforms. Yet, in ʿAbduh's view, such reforms would require the revitalization of the *salafi* spirit of Islam, since the non-Islamic innovations made Islam weak and, thus, unable to face Western domination.[164] Hence, advocating the modernization of the *Sharīʿa* to meet contemporary needs and, at the same time, calling for the purification of Islam by means of returning to the ways of the *salaf* constituted one of the main contradictory theorizations pursued by ʿAbduh. His contradictory approach influenced and was further tackled by his student Muhammad Rashid Rida (1865-1935).

Rida took the radical views and ideas of al-Afghani and ʿAbduh through a more moderate and conservative tendency. He was initially inclined in the direction of the *Ḥanbalī* interpretation of Islam, which was characterized by its remarkably strict conservatism compared to the other three Islamic schools of law (*madhāhib*), namely the *Ḥanafī*, the *Mālikī* and the *Shāfʿī*. Rida was later drawn toward the Wahhabi branch of *Ḥanbalism*, wherein he advocated an orthodox interpretation of Islam and rejected what he labelled as false theological interpretations of the faith, such as Ṣūfism, for ignoring the *Sharīʿa*. According to Rida, the West has abandoned its religion for the sake of accomplishing its hegemony, which was supposed to be seen by Muslims as a warning to protect their faith by means of returning to the *Sharīʿa* and the ways of the *salaf*, and pursuing a strict orthopraxy, as the only path toward preserving their Islamic faith and maintaining the essential features of their distinct identity. He tried to share and spread his ideas and theories, supported by interpretations of core Islamic values and discussions of fundamental questions such as *tawḥīd* and *Salafism*, through his prominent Cairo-based journal *al-Manar* (The Beacon). Unlike his predecessors al-Afghani and ʿAbduh, who basically attempted to modernize Islam in a way that helps Muslims face Western hegemony, Rida's ideas reflected attempts to Islamize modernism. This became obvious in his frequent resort to the theological interpretations and jurisprudential views of Ibn Ḥanbal, Ibn Taymiyya and Ibn Abd al-Wahhab in a bid to tackle questions related to contemporary challenges faced by the *'umma*. He criticized secular nationalists for blindly imitating the West and the Islamic *ʿulamāʾ* (scholars) of al-Azhar for their mindless traditionalism, beside the hypocrisy and abuse of power attributed to these *ʿulamāʾ* for explicitly backing tyranny and implicitly promoting nationalism and corrupting the new generations of Muslims. His pan-Islamic position was crystallized by his emphasis on the need for a restricted *ijtihād*, because a flexible *ijtihād* would eventually open the path for Westernization to invade the Islamic world, according to Rida.[165]

Nevertheless, traces of the contradictory position taken by his teacher ʿAbduh surfaced through the gradual change of Rida's tone into a conciliatory one. Although he initially advocated the Ottoman Empire as an embodiment of Islamism, he later blamed the Ottomans for the weakness and disintegration of the Islamic world and called for collective religious and political reforms. He recalled al-Afghani's emphasis on the importance of solidarity and unity among the Muslims in order to face contemporary threats to their faith and identity, and he further sharpened his idea of unity by means of stressing the need to ignore distinctions between Islamic schools of law and to override sectarian differences between Sunnis and Shiʿites. One of the main methods proposed by Rida to accomplish a political reform in the Islamic world was a renovation of the *Sharīʿa*, either by merging the four Islamic schools of law (*Ḥanbalī*, *Ḥanafī*, *Mālikī*, and *Shāfʿī*) or through establishing a new legal system that meets contemporary needs and demands and ensures unity among the Muslims. Although the ideas of al-Afghani, ʿAbduh and Rida remained restricted to writings and have not inspired much action at the time, some of the literature they produced and the visions they proposed have been embraced by Islamists in decades to come.

The growing concerns about the future of the *'umma* and the Islamic identity and faith amid an increasing impact of nationalism and Western-inspired modernization have triggered a new generation of Islamic scholars in the region. Abu al-Ala Mawdudi (1903-79), one of the key influential Islamic thinkers of the 20th century, urged the Muslims to protect their faith and defend their culture against Western influences. Through his groundbreaking treatise *al-Jihād fi al-Islam* (Jihād in Islam), Mawdudi tried to inspire and incite a greater pan-Islamic movement against colonial powers and the associated diseases spreading within the *'umma*. Confronting nationalism and impeding the advance of secularism into the Islamic realm arose among the key objectives pursued by Mawdudi through his sermons, writings and political activities. According to Mawdudi, the main reasons for the decline of the *'umma* included foreign interventions, Western-inspired materialism, growing secular nationalism and corruption within governments. Such practices and 'diseases' have distorted the Muslim religion and deprived a large proportion of the *'umma* of its core values and principles.[166] Mawdudi tirelessly advocated a return to Islam's original beliefs and practices as the sole efficient solution to the decline of Islam and the deterioration of the conditions under which the Muslims found themselves.

Activism and involvement in politics appeared inevitable if one aspires to accomplish an actual change in government and society, and the Islamists were no exception with regard to this equation. Inspired by the thoughts and visions of al-Afghani, ʿAbduh, Rida and Mawdudi, Hasan al-Banna (1906-49) emerged as a major Islamic thinker, visionary and activist in the first half of the 20th century. He subscribed to the *salafiyya* doctrinal principles and *tawḥīd*, as a concept of social and political unity, introduced by his intellectual forebears. Yet, unlike his forebears, whose visions and ambitious agendas remained considerably restricted to writings, al-Banna sought to establish an organization capable of playing an active role in preserving the spirit of Islam and protecting the Islamic identity of the *'umma* amid the mounting Western impact on the region and the society. In 1928, al-Banna established the Muslim Brotherhood as a permanent organization for the sake of realizing the objectives aspired for by his forebears. The main goal of the Brotherhood, initially based in Egypt and later spread across the region, was to actualize the Islamic principles through concrete action.

The Muslim Brotherhood initiated its activities by founding charitable institutions, journals and newspapers, educational programs and the construction of mosques. The organization succeeded in attracting thousands to its ranks, and by 1948 its membership reached over one million members. Al-Banna's ambitious plans also led to the establishment of paramilitary battalions. While he initially advocated nonviolence and mainly focused on social justice, the outbreak of the Palestinian revolt in 1936 triggered him to call for bold anti-colonial activities and engagement in armed combat if necessary. The Brotherhood's position between nonviolent participation in politics and the advocacy of military force remained blurry. On the one hand, al-Banna announced twice his intention to run for parliamentary elections. On the other hand, the organization established the Secret Apparatus to launch war against the Zionists in Palestine. Several bombings and assassination attempts in Egypt were attributed to the Brotherhood, which led to a government ban on its activities on separate occasions and the imprisonment of many of its prominent members.[167] Yet, this did not hinder the continuity of the organization and the spread of its politico-Islamic agenda throughout the region. Al-Banna himself was assassinated in 1949, but his legacy -including the organization he established- continue to surface in today's Middle Eastern politics.

Amid the rise and growth of nationalism across the region in the mid-twentieth century, and the associated impact of secularism and modernism on the society, Muslim intellectuals struggled to rediscover the Islamic identity and culture in order to counter what they considered an existential threat coming from the West and invading the Islamic world. One of the most influential figures among those Muslim intellectuals was Sayyid Qutb (1906-1966). As a poet, author, literary critic and educator, Qutb initially embraced secular nationalism. Yet, he underwent a remarkable transformation from nationalism to Islamism amid instability in his home country Egypt, and eventually into radical Islamism under the impact of his personal experiences in prison. This transformation appeared through his writings both in theology and political Islam, the most prominent of which are *In the Shades of the Qur'ān* (*Fi Ẓilāl al-Qur'ān*), *Social Justice* (*al-ʿadāla al-Ijtimāʿiyya*) and *Signposts on the Road* (*Maʿālim fi al-Ṭarīq*). Qutb embraced the *salafiyya* movement developed by al-Afghani, ʿAbduh and Rida, according to which the ancestors' faith, beliefs and practices are to be embraced as exemplar for the entire Muslim society. Islamic activism, in his view, ought to be solely based on the *salaf*, the *Qur'ān* and the *Sharīʿa*. He increasingly emphasized that the Prophet and the *salaf* have provided a well-defined framework of proper behavior, faith and thought. Hence, Islam is not to be merely seen as a religion, but as an entire way of life; the Qur'ān as an instructional guide on how to transform society and maintain the welfare of its citizens; and history as not created by people, but determined by God.[168] The impact of the Ḥanbalī scholar Ibn Taymiyya (1263-1328) surfaced in Qutb's last major and most extremist book *Signposts on the Road*, wherein the *Khārijite* dogma seems dominant, implicating a strict intolerance toward diversity, hostility and grudge toward established governments, and a significant emphasis on God's dominion on earth. Qutb was enormously driven by a deep contempt toward Western materialism, sexual liberties and public emancipation, stressing the idea that the West has been suffering from moral degradation and ignorance (*jāhiliyya*). Thus, the Islamic *'umma* needs to spare itself from descending into such a path through maintaining its original identity, culture, values and principles.

It was anti-colonialism position and activities that have initially motivated several Islamic intellectuals and ideologues to delve into the practices and values of the *salaf*, rediscover defining features of the Islamic identity and civilization, and emphasize the *Qur'ān* and the *Sharīʿa* as the sole bases upon which the *'umma* needs to operate and act. Following the independence of various predominantly Muslim countries from Western powers, post-independence secularism, nationalism, materialism and modernity became the new enemies for such ideologues to struggle against, with the goal of purifying the *'umma* from such Western-inspired concepts and the associated activities that, according to them, tend to corrupt the very spirit of Islam and lead to deviation from its core values, morals and principles. Mawdudi's sharp criticism toward British imperialism and post-independence nationalism and modernism in India inspired Qutb's radical Islamism in Egypt. Based on Mawdudi's anti-Orientalist, anti-modernist perspectives, Qutb developed his theories about and interpretations of the concepts of *jāhiliyya* (ignorance), *ḥākimiyya* (the dominion of God and His laws), and *jihād* (the struggle by Muslims to move from the first to the second). These concepts were driven away from their classical definitions and reinterpreted in accordance with the surrounding circumstances in which scholars such as Mawdudi and Qutb found themselves, namely tyranny, corruption, and social immorality as main challenges allegedly brought about by Western modernity into the Islamic world.

The influence of Ibn Taymiyya's *Khārijite* and *takfīri* perspective emerged as obvious throughout the interpretations delivered by intellectuals such as Mawdudi and Qutb, particularly in terms of emphasizing the idea that true and pious Muslims should adopt and act within the framework of a narrowly defined orthopraxy and orthodoxy. Otherwise, they would be falling into *kufr* (unbelief), labelled as *kuffār* (infidels), and eventually be eligible for merciless punishment. Then, *jihād* becomes the most appropriate *manhaj* (method) and means for retribution, and the *shahāda* (martyrdom) becomes the ultimate objective of every true Muslim, or *mujāhid*, for it proves the idea that faith is more important than life itself.[169] It is this legacy that represents the most significant impact of these Islamic scholars, especially Qutb, among today's radical Islamists.

Islamists generally share the ambition of remaking the world. That's why the world order emerges as an essential question within the framework of Islamism. The neo-Arabic term *niẓām* (system) is deemed central to Islamist ideology, and the political order strived for by Islamists is also seen as a new world order. In contrast to secularism, Islamism envisions a world order that is sacral, based on the notion of *dawla Islamiyya*, wherein the state is primarily based on the *Sharīʿa* law and *ḥākimiyyat Allah* (God's dominion) –that is ought to replace popular sovereignty and ultimately develop into an international Islamic system.[170] The development of such a vision and agenda finds its roots in the historical events and experiences that have led to (re)shaping what was once known as *Dār al-Islām* into what we today call the Islamic world. In the course of its colonization by Western powers, the Islamic world made an effort for the sake of accommodating the new world order through joining the international system of nation-states. However, the Western model of modernization failed to completely transform the region into this international system. The Islamic world's historical memory of the old Empire was then subdivided into multiple nation-states, which created a state of confusion and frustration among a large proportion of the *'umma* that found itself struggling to preserve its religio-cultural identity and pride amid the attempt to move forward and embrace modernity. The failed development evolved into a crisis that has eventually led to the return of the sacred in a political form.[171] Promoting their agenda as a *ḥall* (solution) to such crises, Islamists tend to revive and construct multilateral memories about Islamic glory, claiming that by returning to history, Muslims could restore and enjoy that glory once again. Hence, according to the world order envisioned by Islamists, the restoration of the past constitutes the unique solution to the crises suffered by the *'umma*. The theocratic *niẓām* of *dawla Islamiyya*, based on the *Sharīʿa* and *ḥākimiyyat Allah*, is advocated by Islamists as a *ḥall* not only to the crises encountered by Muslims, but also to those suffered by people across the globe. The ultimate agenda is thus establishing an international Islamic system to replace the current world order, a vision that emerges at the core of the Islamists' ambition to remake the world.

The political agenda and global vision adopted under the umbrella of Islamism were developed and crystallized by the influential architects and philosophers of the movement. In his *Signposts on the Road*, Qutb predicted the collapse of the West and the downfall of democracy, envisioning the replacement of the West by an imagined Islamic power that will take over the world in a return of historical Muslim glory. "Humanity is at the brink... most clearly the West itself... after the bankruptcy of democracy... the rule of the Western man is about to break down," he wrote, "it is only Islam that possesses the needed values and method... It is now the turn of Islam and its 'umma community in the most tense time to take over."[172] This antipathy and rancor toward Western democracy, secularism and modernity is also shared by Mawdudi, who tends to define Islam and the Islamic system through consolidating a contrast between its principles and those of democracy. "Democracy stands in contrast to what you [Muslim brothers] embrace as religion and its dogma. The Islam that you believe in and according to which you identify yourself as Muslims differs in its substance from this hateful system [of democracy]," Mawdudi wrote in his *al-Islam wal-Madaniyya al-Ḥadītha*. "Where this system of democracy prevails Islam is in absence, and where Islam prevails there is no place [*lā makān*] for this system of democracy."[173] This hardcore position against the West and its democratic system continue to arise at the heart of the Islamists' efforts of promoting their international Islamic system as the most appropriate *ḥall* to the dilemmas encountered by humanity. According to Islamism, one can only overcome political, social and economic crises by embracing the Islamic solution.

As for Salafism, the only solution to the decline of the *'umma* is to follow the example of *al-salaf al-ṣāliḥ* and return to the pure roots of Islam. This utopian aspiration is, according to Salafism, the only way out of the contemporary setback encountered by Muslims. Unlike Islamism, which is mainly concerned with bringing about a *Sharīʿa*-based political order, Salafism delves into various aspects of life within its utopian Islamic state and claims to be able to cure all the grave illnesses of the society with idealistic prescriptions provided by *al-salaf al-ṣāliḥ*. Yet, the rise of various currents within the Salafi movement has led to different approaches toward realizing the goals of the movement. The *quietists* mainly focus their efforts on missionary *Daʿwa* activities while avoiding any involvement in politics; the *politicos* are distinguished by their considerable involvement in politics for the sake of bringing about the aspired change; and the *jihadis* believe in the legitimacy of employing force as a form of *jihād* in order to accomplish the idealistic world order set out by the movement's founders.

Understanding the Salafi worldview requires delving into the main features of the *ʿaqīda* to which the Salafists generally ascribe. The main cornerstone of this *ʿaqīda* is *tawḥīd* (the oneness of God). According to Salafism, the concept of *tawḥīd* comprises three main aspects: *tawḥīd al-rubūbiyya* (the oneness of the dominion [of God]), *tawḥīd al-'asmā' wa-l-ṣifāt* (the oneness of the names and characteristics [of God]), and *tawḥīd al-ulūhiyya* (the oneness of divinity). Some Salafists add a fourth aspect to *tawḥīd*, namely *tawḥīd al-ḥākimiyya* (the oneness of sovereignty); however, most Salafists agree that the *ḥākimiyya* constitutes a part and parcel of *tawḥīd al-ulūhiyya* and, therefore, does not form a separate component by itself. The *ʿaqīda* of Salafism further extends to include *'īmān* (faith in God), which consists of *al-iʿtiqād bi-l-qalb* (acknowledgement of faith in the heart), *al-qawl bi-l-lisān* (voicing faith with the tongue), and *al-aʿmāl bi-l-jawāriḥ* (demonstrating confidence in faith through activities with the limbs). According to ibn Ḥanbal, whose strict theological interpretations are embraced by the majority of Salafists, faith needs to not only be acknowledged in the heart and expressed by the tongue, but also be reinforced by a Muslim's activities and dealings.

In order to (dis)approve one's attachment to and compliance with these cornerstones of the *ʿaqīda*, Salafism extends in its creed to include *takfīr* or the excommunication of those who appear to be in violation with the basic principles of its doctrine. Salafi scholars generally distinguish between two types of *kufr*: *kufr aṣghar*, which occurs due to ignorance (*jahl*) or misinterpretation of texts, and it does not necessarily place the one involved outside the faith; and *kufr akbar*, which occurs while the one involved is fully aware of the fundamental principles of the faith and has correct and clear interpretations at his or her disposal, and it leads to labelling him or her as *kāfir* and consequently to *'iqāmat al-ḥadd* (carrying out punishment). The involvement in *kufr akbar* often concerns questions relating to *tawḥīd al-rubūbiyya*. It emerges as a result of *iʿtiqād* (belief) in the concerned behavior or action, an attempt to render that behavior permissible (*istiḥlāl*), or a conscious effort (*juhd*) to demonstrate one's rejection of Islam.[174] Nevertheless, the distinction between *kufr aṣghar* and *kufr akbar* remains somewhat blurry in practice, and many strict Salafists tend to apply *takfīr* even on those involved in the former.

While the beliefs, attitudes and actions of the *salaf* form a normative framework for Sunni Muslims in general, they are embraced by the Salafists as the sole code of conduct and source of inspiration in order to cure the calamities suffered by the *'umma* today. Nonetheless, the diversity found within the Salafi movement itself today reflects various degrees of disagreement that seem to go beyond the apparent attachment to this idealism. One of such disagreements between the different currents of Salafism concerns the concept of *takfīr* (excommunication of others as infidels). The *quietists* consider the *politicos* and *jihadis* as *neo-Khārijites* for legitimizing the use of force against other Muslims and for failing to differentiate between lesser sins (*kufr aṣghar*) and greater sins (*kufr akbar*), mistakenly labelling those involved in the former as *kuffār*, which is impermissible according to *quietists*. Therefore, the *quietists* brand the *politicos* and *jihadis* as *takfīris* (*'ahl al-takfīr*). On the other hand, the *politicos* and *jihadis* stigmatize the *quietists* as *neo-Murji'a* for refusing to apply *tafīr* on those involved in un-Islamic practices and grave sins, and for failing to excommunicate political authorities that do not strictly abide by the *Sharīʿa*, rule by man-made laws (*qawānīn waḍʿiyya*) and refuse to recognize God's dominion (*ḥākimiyyat Allah*).[175]

Another point of disagreement among the various currents of Salafism, which reflects an ideological intra-conflict, concerns the notion of *al-walā' wa-l-barā'* (loyalty and disavowal). While the three currents agree on the basic theoretical features of the notion, which essentially implicate "to love and hate for the sake of Allah," they still disagree on the way this doctrine is supposed to be applied in practice. Unlike the *quietists*, who appear to be solely attached to the puristic dimension of the concept, the *politicos* and *jihadis* suggest that there are other aspects of *al-walā' wa-l-barā'* that need to be embraced and acted upon as well. *Politico-* and *jihādi*-Salafists maintain that there is a political dimension involved as part of *al-walā'* (loyalty), which involves the question of *al-istiʿāna bi-l-kuffār* (asking the unbelievers for help or forming alliances with non-Muslims during conflicts). According to the *politicos* and *jihadis*, Muslims have an obligation to show solidarity with each other during conflicts and to refuse any help from non-Muslims, and definitely not to ask for such a help against other Muslims. This question arose during the Golf War of 1990, when Saudi Arabia resorted to the U.S. for military support against the regime of Saddam Hussein during the Iraqi invasion of Kuwait. The U.S. sent over half a million soldiers to protect the Saudi borders against Iraqi advance, and several Western powers were involved in thwarting the Iraqi invasion of Kuwait. In order to legitimize his call for U.S. support, King Fahd of Saudi Arabia had then demanded the *quietist* Islamic scholars of the Kingdom to issue a *fatwā* backing the decision of receiving protection from non-Muslims if necessary to deter threats from a Muslim state, in this case Iraq. With the Saudi *quietists* issuing such a *fatwā*, the *politicos* and *jihadis* launched an aggressive campaign of criticism that targeted the *quietists* for complying with and supporting the Saudi King in his call for protection from *kāfir* Americans against fellow Muslims. This in itself was, according to the the *politicos* and *jihadis*, an act of *kufr* on the part of the *quietists*. They considered such a *quietist fatwā* as a violation to the principle of *al-walā' wa-l-barā'*, since it undermined the concept of absolute loyalty to God, Islam and Muslims, and tried to redefine this principle in accordance with the wishes of the Saudi regime, which was eventually seen as a breach of the fundamental doctrine of *tawḥīd*. The *jihadis* have taken the political dimension of the notion of *al-walā' wa-l-barā'* even further by means of condemning not only *al-istiʿāna bi-l-kuffār* (asking infidels for help), but also *iʿānat al-kuffār* (providing support to the infidels). This modified definition of loyalty and disavowal arose amid the post-11 September cooperations between Muslim states and Western powers in the fight against terrorism, which targeted Salafi-Jihadists in particular. The *jihadis* view such cooperations as a Muslim support to the unbelievers against supposedly fellow Muslims, and they eventually labelled all those involved as *kuffār*. By this, the *jihadis* emerged in disagreement with their fellow Salafists from the *quietist* and *politico* currents with regard to the interpretation of the notion of *al-walā' wa-l-barā'*.[176] Thus, the diversity of views on the basic principles of Salafism among the different currents shows that the movement is internally divided over certain core ideological and doctrinal values and beliefs, which can be seen as an indication of the fragmentation that the Salafi movement seems to encounter within its own ranks.

11. The Struggle for an Islamic System

For the sake of understanding *Islamism* and *Salafism*, it is crucial to delve into what the project members of such movements strive to accomplish looks like, and what the defining features and characteristics of the system they are set to realize comprise. One of the very few Islamic thinkers who succeeded in providing a concrete Islamic project and advocate its theoretical implications and practical dimensions is Sayyid Qutb. This chapter examines Qutb's theories and ideas on the *Islamic system* (*niẓām Islāmi*) aspired for by many contemporary Islamists.

In an attempt to reintroduce, reestablish and redefine certain aspects of Islam and Islamic traditions to ensure their validity through the contemporary context, Qutb labelled his understanding of the faith and its teachings as *the Islamic concept*. This concept comprises rules and regulations that are supposed to govern and organize the relation and correlation between humanity, nature, the universe and God. It explores the meaning and purpose of life; the relationship between humanity and the Creator; and the functions of men and women in society. Qutb's *Islamic concept* is chiefly focused on assisting the Muslim *'umma* in the process of acquiring a comprehensive understanding of the notions of unity, struggle, obedience, worship and social justice. It seeks to help Muslims better understand the distinctive features and characteristics of their religion for the ultimate objective of generating a certain course of political action that may save the *'umma* and ensure its prosperity. Such a political action should be based on a practical understanding of the Qur'ān, which requires sincere efforts focused on reshaping the current system in order to reestablish a true Islamic life.

Our aim is not some frigid knowledge that deals only with men's minds and adds to the accumulation of "culture." Such an aim does not deserve pain and effort, for it is a cheap and foolish aim. We seek "movement" as a stage beyond "knowledge." We want knowledge to transform itself into a motivating power for realizing its meaning in the real world. We seek to enlist the conscience of man to achieve the purpose of his existence, as traced out by this divine concept. We seek to return humanity to its Lord, to the plan He had drawn up for it, and the noble and elevated life that conforms to the nobility that God prescribes for mankind.[177]

According to Qutb, there are three types of knowledge: an absolute divine knowledge, a privileged prophetic knowledge, and a limited human knowledge. There are nine key characteristics to be identified in the *Islamic concept*, which include *al-rabbaniyya* (divinity), *al-thabāt* (stability), *al-tawḥīd* (unity), *al-shumūl* (comprehensiveness), *al-'īmān wal-ʿamal* (belief and practice), *al-tawāzun* (balance/moderation), *al-'ījābiyya* (positive orientation), and *al-wāqiʿiyya* (realism). Qutb's *Islamic concept* allegedly provides a comprehensive ideal model for human belief and practice that introduces Islam as a movement that allows the society to move from *jāhiliyya* (ignorance) to *ḥākimiyya* (God's dominion) by means of *jihād* (struggle in the path of God). It seeks insights from the practices and values of the *salaf* in terms of politics, economics and civilization for the sake of freeing the Muslims from foreign pressures, accomplishing equality for all pious believers who acknowledge God's authority, and realizing and acting upon the truth of God's message conveyed by the Prophet Muhammad as "the final handbook for practical life."[178]

The struggle for an *Islamic system* that may correct that path on which the contemporary Islamic society finds itself and move the *'umma* from *jāhiliyya* to *ḥākimiyya* has led to the emergence of an updated conception of *jihād* as a necessary means for such a movement to take place and succeed. Qutb redefined *jihād* within the framework of his efforts to develope his *Islamic concept* into a comprehensive *Islamic system*. Such efforts resulted in the rise of four modified types of *jihād*: *jihād bil-qalb* (jihād of the heart), *jihād bil-lisān* (jihād of the tongue), *jihād bil-yad/bil-ḥaraka* (jihād of the hand/activism), and *jihād bil-sayf* (jihād of the sword). The first type of *jihād*, namely *jihād of the heart*, refers to an internal struggle to purify one's inner self of immorality, man-made laws and false beliefs. According to Qutb, every individual is, first and foremost, required to fight against his own desires, ambitions, personal interests and those of his family and nation, and against anything that is not derived from Islam and that may become an obstacle in the way of worshiping God and the implementation of His divine authority on earth. The second type, namely *jihād of the tongue*, concerns preaching, which is only realizable once people are free to listen and decide on their own. This type of *jihād* is originally inspired by the Prophet's 13 years in Mecca calling its inhabitants to Islam. Qutb advocated activities aimed at educating people and convincing them of the necessity to build up an Islamic society based on the fundamental beliefs and values of the religion. Hence, preaching essentially entails that faith cannot be forcefully imposed upon people; it rather needs to evolve from within, based on freedom of choice. This dynamic method of Islam, according to Qutb, demands the bearers of the Islamic message to comprehend and understand the interrelationship between the construction of belief and the practical organization that led to the rise of the *'umma* in the first place. As long as there are no obstacles to preaching, forceful methods are excluded. The third type of *jihād* introduced by Qutb in his discussion of moving from *jāhiliyya* to *ḥākimiyya* as a necessary condition for establishing an effective *Islamic system* is *jihād of the hand*, which implicates taking action. However, such an action does not necessarily imply militancy. It primarily entails engagement in political activities, organizing campaigns, planning and implementing community development programs and projects. Such activities should be concentrated on freeing human beings from servitude to anyone other than God. Given that this initiative is in the very nature of Islam, Qutb advocates the universality of the Islamic message that is aimed at liberating the whole mankind, regardless of geographic or racial limits, from evil, chaos, darkness and servitude to lords other than God, arguing that truth and falsehood cannot co-exist. Finally, *jihād of the sword*, which implicates the use of force as a necessary means to allow other types of *jihād* to accomplish their goals, is meant to clear the path of any obstacles impeding the process of moving from *jāhiliyya* to *ḥākimiyya* and establishing the aspired *Islamic system*.[179]

According to Qutb, Islam is a completely practicable social system in itself, as it includes beliefs, laws and a social and economic system that is open to growth through application and development. "It offers to mankind a perfectly comprehensive theory of the universe, life, and mankind," Qutb maintains, "[It offers] a theory that satisfies man's intellectual needs. It offers to men a clear, broad, and deep faith which satisfies the conscience. It offers to society legal and economic bases that have been proven both practical and systematic. Islam bases its social system on the foundation of a spiritual theory of life that rejects all materialistic interpretation; it bases its morals on the foundation of the spiritual and moral element, and it rejects the philosophy of immediate advantage. Thus, it is very strongly opposed to the materialistic theories that obtain ground in both the Eastern and the Western camp."[180] Hence, the *Islamic system* he advocates forms a comprehensive and integrated set of social ties and relationships, established on the basis of Islamic teachings, values and principles to cover all domains of a unified society, including political, economic, moral, cultural, and civilizational. The *Islamic system* aspired for is said to be both material and spiritual. Through such a combination, this system tends to establish a social unity based on the *tawḥīd* of God and his dominion on earth, which is believed to bring people together into a single cooperative and harmonious society. Qutb argues that the spiritual aspect of this system makes it unique when compared to other systems. The *Islamic system*, in his view, is flexible enough to develop into a system that praises diversity in terms of the nationalities, races and ethnicities of the people coexisting side by side under its shadow. It derives such an inclusiveness from its unique recognition of piety and devotion, regardless of the backgrounds of the members of the single harmonious society it tends to rule.

In order to defend the *Islamic system*, Qutb tirelessly drew contrasts between this system and other man-made ideological systems, such as secularism, modernity, nationalism, capitalism, socialism, communism and democracy. Secularism and modernity, in Qutb's view, represent a gross violation of *tawḥīd* (God's unity). In Islam, belief and practice go hand in hand to contribute to a divine unity; religion and wordly affairs are believed to be intertwined, unlike in the Western-based separation of religion and state. Qutb tried to promote Islam as a religion and a way of life that needs to be followed by all humanity. Besides, nationalism is deemed one of the principal adversaries to the *Islamic system*, as it promote ideas such as loyalty to a territorially-based ethnic group instead of loyalty to God. According to Qutb, nationalism divides people, which basically undermines the unity of God and His creations; it produces asymmetrical distinctions between people based on ethnic, cultural, racial and political affiliations, which emerges in contrast to the *tawḥīd*-based *Islamic system* that unites and brings people together on the basis of belief, practice and submission to God's dominion and authority. Furthermore, Qutb considers capitalism as a force that could accomplish a certain degree of progress, but at the expense of the community and its ordinary members. Such progress was basically accomplished by means of bank interests and crass consumerism, and such interests are among the main prohibitions in the *Sharīʿa*. Islam allows income and wealth from the ownership of property but in moderation, unlike in capitalism where the right to property is believed to be abused in such a way that violates community values and norms that Islam protects and supports. According to Qutb, capitalism (re)produces inequalities in societies through favoring the interests of the individual and placing them above those of the community, unlike in Islam where all members of the community are perceived as equals, operating based on communal interests, and are treated in accordance with the degree of piety and devotion to God and His dominion. Qutb also condemns socialism and communism as crassly secular and materialistic, and totally devoid of faith and spirituality. None of them acknowledges God's authority or submits to his laws; they marginalize religion and constitute a part of *jāhiliyya*. In socialism, helping the poor is meant to establish some political stability, especially for the ruling class; whereas in Islam, helping the poor by means of *zakāt* is a heart-felt component of a greater dynamism that is mainly aimed at enhancing unity, stability and harmony without igniting any conflicts between the components of the society. For Qutb, communism was yet another man-made secular and materialistic system which abolishes individual rights and enables the state to become the owner, arbiter and ruler of the society. While communism views classlessness as a product of revolution, which eventually produces a supreme state authority and control, the Islamic system sees classlessness as an instrument to accomplish unity and harmony within the society for the ultimate goal of worshiping and submitting to God. Qutb maintains that classlessness in Islam arises from the common faith and spiritualism shared by Muslims and the eventual marginalization of inessential identities. Given that social justice in communism is not based on faith, it remains prone to change and instability; whereas in Islam, social justice is permanent and stable. Qutb also draws a contrast between the *Islamic system* and democracy, arguing that democracy, as a man-made system, has its own rules, regulations, and ideas of freedom and justice, which can change in accordance to the surrounding circumstances. This while Islamism constitutes a permanent system created by God, wherein people cannot vote out or change the *Sharīʿa* and overtake authority from God to themselves. Qutb emphasizes that justice, equality, freedom and truth in Islam are derived from the Qur'ān, and they therefore cannot be reshaped based on human self-interest, desires and weakness. Any system that shifts principles and values is hence a *jāhilī* system that needs to be overthrown and replaced by the *Islamic system* that holds eternal and divine values intended for all humanity. Thus, all these doctrines and systems are, in Qutb's view, sterile and defeated. Islam is believed to be the only true and genuine system that reflects God's will and the human nature created by God. No other system acknowledges and combines both the spiritual and the material dimensions of social life. All other ideological systems are imported from abroad and imposed on the Islamic community to harm, weaken and incapacitate the *'umma.* These ideologies, branded by Qutb as *forces of jāhiliyya*, tend to distort

Islam and tear the *'umma* apart. The failure of these systems in the Islamic world asseverate the fact that they cannot find a fertile ground to thrive. Thus, Muslim societies would do better if they adopt the *Islamic system*, for it is more authentic and natural to their civilization, history and culture, according to Qutb. His extensive advocacy of the *Islamic system* was driven by the principle of proving that Islam, as a faith and a governing system, generates social integrity, unity, and harmony, and condemns division, schism and discord. Imported ideologies such as secularism, nationalism, capitalism and democracy are blamed for the state of chaos and disorder storming the Islamic world. While such a disorder may benefit and empower a small circle of the society, the majority of the population is destined to suffer unbearable conditions under such inappropriate systems. Qutb argues that governments are to blame for the flourishing of *jāhiliyya* and the deterioration of Islam and the *'umma*. In order to save and revitalize Islam and its spirit, passion, dynamism and struggle are required to overthrow the current regime and replace it with the *Islamic system*. Only then would the *'umma* regain its glory and greatness.[181] The *Islamic system* will eventually ensure the establishment of *ḥākimiyya* (God's dominion) on earth for the salvation of not only the Islamic community, but also the whole mankind from remaining steeped in *jāhiliyya* (ignorance) through the universal message of Islam.

Qutb's vision and ideas have inspired a multitude of extremist Islamist groups to struggle for actualizing the *Islamic system*. Leaderships of contemporary Islamist organizations continue to seek inspiration and guidance from Qutb through exploring the manifesto he provided to revitalize the spirit of Islam and to regain greatness and dignity to the *'umma*. Qutb's antagonism and hostility toward the West and all man-made laws and systems, which reemerge over and over again in his post-radicalization works, have stimulated an ever growing movement of radical Islamism. Although today's extremist Islamists seem far more equipped than what Qutb would have imagined while writing down his advocacy of the *Islamic system*, the struggle for actualizing this system remains far from fruitful. Nonetheless, on the path of striving to impose and enforce such a system, many non-adherents and opponents have been victimized, especially over the past two decades in crisis-afflicted parts of the Middle East, which basically illustrates the exclusionary nature of such an agenda, in contrast to what Qutb once claimed to be an inclusive system. The preferential and tendentious foundations upon which Qutb's system is principally built, especially when it comes to man-made laws, systems and currents of thought, can be viewed as an indication of the theocratic totalitarianism it tends to accomplish, and a reflection of how essentially unappreciative of diversity this system seems to be.

Part IV

The Rise of Modern Middle East: Aspirations and Challenges

In order to understand the emergence of the contemporary political landscape in the Middle East and the developments attached to it, beside the rise of *Jihadism* and *sectarianism* as major challenges, shedding light on the modern history of the region seems inescapable in terms of studying, understanding and analyzing the multifaceted topic at hand. Although our journey through the history of the Middle East will be brief and mainly focused on the past and current centuries, relevant developments in earlier phases of the history of the region will be recalled for the sake of clarity and to provide a sufficient insight into this historical background. This part delves into the historical events that have contributed to the rise of the modern Middle East, including the emergence of national borders, the Western influence, the state of turmoil across post-independence states, the aspirations associated with the Arab Spring and the challenges introduced by the Islamization of popular uprisings in the region.

12. The Collapse of Ottoman Empire and the Emergence of Nationalism

Throughout the Islamic history, there has always been a certain level of consciousness about the differences between Arabs, Turks and Persians. These three nations are considered the main bearers of the Islamic history, and the ethnic, cultural and linguistic differences between them had not hindered their efforts to maintain the Islamic heritage and had never been so deep as to break down the shared religious identity as Muslims despite the sectarian disputes, except in later stages that accompanied the rise of nationalism and the emergence of the modern Middle East. Historically speaking, the religious identity brought Muslims from different ethnic groups together to submit to their rulers within an Islamic state or empire, to serve it, fight in its name and strive for its prosperity. For instance, the expansion of the Ottoman Empire into Arab-majority territories brought the Ottomans into a direct contact with the most ancient Muslim urban civilization, namely, the great schools of Cairo, Damascus and Aleppo, with the main stream of Islamic theology and law, and with an urban class which would bring into the new universal Islamic state its own tradition of social leadership and of a balance between government and the forces of society. The Ottomans became rulers of the holly cities: of Jerusalem; of the Shiʿite holy cities in Iraq, Najaf, Karbala and Kazimayn; and of Mecca and Medina, and the main routes of pilgrimage to them. Every year pilgrims from Egypt and Africa gathered in Cairo, pilgrims from Turkey and the Caucasus, Syria, Iraq and Iran in Damascus; they had to be led and defended on the way to Mecca, the holy cities and their inhabitants had to be protected and nourished, and the orthodoxy of the religion in the name of which the pilgrimage was made had to be preserved.[182] Thus powerful was the shared religious identity to reconcile and suppress differences of other kind. However, the rise of nationalism in the Middle East in the early twentieth century brought with it unprecedented developments at various levels, including strong attachment to territorial and ethnic affiliations, beside the growth of nationalist movements amid the gradual collapse of the Ottoman Empire and the emergence of national identities that have ever since demarcated the relationship between the previously integrated communities.

The Ottoman Empire, which had developed into a universal empire during its historical expansion, had remarkably held together different regions, ethnic groups and social orders within a designated framework of administration and loyalty to a ruling family. Various regions fell to the Ottoman reign –which lasted for over 600 years– including Asia Minor, West Asia, the Balkans, North African Coast and Egypt. The Ottomans governed diverse ethnic groups, such as Arabs, Kurds, Turks, Greeks, Rumanians, Armenians, Bulgars and Serbs, among others. Moreover, different religious communities came under Ottoman rule, including Jews and Christians of different ethnoreligious minorities such as Copts, Maronites, Armenians and Assyrians, among others. The empire had also imposed its power over various social orders, governing urban as well as rural populations. This shows the power of the Ottoman Empire at the time in holding together and ruling a multitude of different communities.[183] Nevertheless, the predominance of Turks over the empire's inner power circle undermined other ethnic identities, like that of Arabs, Kurds, Armenians and others. In some cases, tensions emerged where the state pursued merciless policies to punish a certain community for opposing its rule and seeking equality. The Armenian Genocide is the most memorable example in this regard, when the Ottomans during the late phase of the empire (1915-1917) systematically exterminated approximately 1.5 million Armenians.[184]

Furthermore, the Sultan was deemed an embodiment of the greatness of Islam. It is noteworthy that the title of *Sultan* has remarkably replaced the title of *Caliph* within the Ottoman Empire until mid-nineteenth century, when the Sultan began to seriously claim to be the Caliph of all Muslims. This step came in a bid to gain more loyalty and support from Muslims even outside the empire and to confront the then growing European threat. Besides, the Ottoman Empire promoted itself as a Sunni commonwealth, and this conscious sectarian distinction was nurtured and sharpened by the disputes and tensions with the Shia Safavids. The Ottoman Empire and Safavid Persia, then the two major powers in the Near East, were engaged in a series of conflicts over territorial control in Mesopotamia, particularly in the period between 1514-1639, with a continued, but less tense, tension until the eighteenth century. The warfare was further fueled by sectarian and dogmatic differences, with Ottomans as a Sunni Muslim power and the Safavids leading the Shia Muslims. Islam played a key role in defining the Ottoman-Safavid relationship. The Islamic law or Sharīʿa basically prohibits internal wars among the Muslims unless a religious need emerges to enforce a sacred law, known as *fatwā*, or to check transgressions against it.[185]

However, the Turkish dominance over the power centers across the Ottoman Empire eventually raised a surge of outrage among the ruled communities, especially the Arabs who inhabited a main part of the empire and constituted a major population among its communities. Therefore, in a bid to absorb the growing discontent, the Ottoman authorities in the late nineteenth century offered positions of various degrees of importance to many elite and highly educated Arabs, and the natural leaders of Arab provinces and notable families in countries like Iraq and Syria became an integral part of the Ottoman system. Many members of such families joined the imperial civil and military services. Moreover, subsequent to the constitution's restoration in 1908, the Arabs became competent members of the political domain and the empire developed into a mainly Turco-Arab state. Yet the emergence of the Turkish national movement, amid the deterioration of the Ottoman Empire in various sectors, drove several communities away. With the outbreak of World War I, rifts and disputes between the Turks and Arabs intensified, eventually resulting in a rebellion by the Arabs against the rule of the Ottoman Empire. After its defeat in WWI, the empire witnessed an unprecedented wave of partitioning, opposed by Turkish nationalists who eventually launched the so-called Turkish War of Independence, abolishing the Ottoman Sultanate in 1922 and declaring the establishment of the Republic of Turkey in 1923.

Thus, the idea of national unity and the quest for territorial independence in the Muslim world have not emerged as important political concepts and agendas until the early twentieth century. The nationalist sentiments among the different communities increased amid dramatic developments across the Middle East throughout the first half of the twentieth century. These developments included an increased division between Arabs and Turks following the revolution of the *Young Turks* in 1908; the collapse of the Ottoman Empire after WWI and the establishment of the Republic of Turkey out of its ruins; the Persian opposition to Russian influence; the Egyptian resistance movement against the British domination; the imposition of French and British mandatory rule on major parts of the region; and the growing Jewish immigration into Palestine paralleled with a rising Zionist movement.

Nationalism is basically defined as a collective sentiment or identity binding individuals with historical commonality together within a certain territory, demarcating those who belong to it and others who do not, based on domestic political solidarity that is aimed at creating, legitimizing or challenging states.[186] As the concept originally arose in Europe and swept into the Middle East in later stages, it has been understood differently. During the first half of the twentieth century, two sorts of national concepts came to light in the Middle East. On the one hand, nationalism as manifesting itself on the basis of a joint relation with a specific piece of land, or territorial nationalism, like the Persian, Turkish, Lebanese, Egyptian and Syrian. On the other hand, nationalism linked to a population whose members share common cultural, ethnic, racial or linguistic identity, or popular nationalism, like in the case of Arab nationalism. Both concepts are sometimes combined, like in the case of the Kurds, a stateless nation unified by shared ethnic, cultural and linguistic traits that strives to establish its own national state on a territory they consider to be historically theirs.

The Arabs' dominance and leading role during the early Islamic history was one of the incentives behind their movement toward Arab nationalism, beside their exclusion from the inner power circle within the Ottoman Empire, and the increasing resistance movements against the Ottomans and later against the French and British mandatory rule during the first half of the twentieth century. Other factors, as pointed out by Antonius in his *The Arab Awakening*,[187] include the rediscovery of the Arabic language and its literature that moved the early Arab nationalists, who descended from different origins (Syrians, Lebanese, Iraqis, etc.) and different religious backgrounds (Muslims and

Christians), arguing that the Arabic language and literature revived the *Arab* consciousness and led to the re-emergence of a society in which Arabs can rule themselves and live together. Antonius adds to that the role of the ideas of the *Islamic modernism* movement and the contribution of the educated Christian class in Lebanon, Syria and Palestine. These factors combined are believed to have played a role in the emergence of Arab nationalism. There are two forces regarded as the founding fathers of the Arab nationalist movement. These comprise the Syrians, on the one hand, taking Damascus and Cairo as main bases for their activities; and the Hashimites, also known as the *Hashimite Sharifs of Mecca*, on the other hand, who had the Hejaz as their power center.

During the second half of the twentieth century, many Middle Eastern countries witnessed tensions between different ideas of nationalism, intermingled with socialism, neutralism and unity; and monarchic, hierarchical conception of nationalism based on a cautious approach to social issues, characterized by a pro-Western position in foreign policy and individualist in economic policy.[188] A nationalistic revolution occurred in each of Syria, Egypt, Iraq, Yemen, Sudan, Algeria and Tunisia, aimed at maintaining sovereignty and protecting popular interests—but the nationalist cause in most of these countries was later employed to serve dictatorships, leading to conflicts, corruption and policies of marginalization and exclusion toward minorities. Moreover, in countries like Turkey and Israel, the governments were able to accomplish a certain degree of internal unity with support of a prevalent common notion of society and pressure from an enemy. Yet, in both states matters of exclusion and suppression against particular local communities continue to take place until today. In Turkey, for example, the Turkish authorities deprived the Kurds of their basic civil and cultural rights and freedoms, and the mounting suppression led to a long-standing armed conflict. In 1978, the Kurdistan Workers Party (PKK) was established with the goal of fighting for the Kurdish rights in Turkey. Since 1984, the organization has been involved in an armed conflict with the Turkish authorities, which claimed thousands of lives amid heavy military campaigns by the army against Kurdish-majority towns southeast of the country. Furthermore, following a failed military coup in 2016, the government of Recep Tayyip Erdogan imposed an emergency law that implied the detention and prosecution of opposition politicians, including Kurdish parliamentarians despite their condemnation of the coup attempt, and ever since the situation continued to deteriorate in the Kurdish parts of Turkey. In Israel, Palestinians have suffered persecution, and the protests against the growing Israeli settlements were faced by a violent response. Armed resistance resulted in more violence and many civilian casualties. Today, the Israeli-Palestinian conflict is deemed to be a defining issue in the Middle East.

13. Sykes-Picot and the Development of National Borders

After the outbreak of WWI in the summer of 1914, with the Ottoman Empire joining the side of Germany in the war, representatives of Great Britain, France and Russia held a series of meetings to discuss the future of the territory controlled by the Ottoman Empire in Arabia, the Middle East and southern-central Europe. In March 1915, Russia and Britain signed a secret agreement, according to which the Russians would impose their control over the Ottoman capital of Constantinople, the Dardanelles and the Gallipoli peninsula. On the other hand, the British would claim control of other Ottoman territories, central Persia and Mesopotamia.[189] Over a year later, in May 1916, British representative Sir Mark Sykes and French representative François Georges-Picot reached another secret agreement to divide up a main part of the Ottoman territory into areas of influence. According to the terms of this secret convention, known as Sykes-Picot Agreement[190] or Asia Minor Agreement, France acquires Lebanon and the Syrian coast, and Great Britain takes control of central and southern Mesopotamia, and the provinces of Baghdad and Basra. Palestine, due to its religious importance as home to holy places which attracted the attention of other powers including Russia, would be under an international administration. The agreement also stipulated that the rest of the region –including Iraq's northern province of Mosul, modern-day Syria, and Jordan– would be run by local Arab leaders under British supervision in the south and French in the north. This undisclosed arrangement was later in 1917 published by the Soviet Russian government after the Bolshevik revolution led by Vladimir Lenin, along with other secret pacts of imperial Russia. Lenin considered the treaty an attempt by Britain and France to inherit the falling Ottoman Empire, calling it "the agreement of the colonial thieves". The Bolsheviks, under the leadership of Vladimir Lenin and Leon Trotsky, came across the text of the Sykes–Picot Agreement in one of the many archives of the Kremlin subsequent to the revolution. On November 23, 1917, they published the agreement's text in Pravda and Izvestia in a bid to embarrass the Allies about curving up the Middle East and making incompatible promises to Hussein and the Arabs as well as the Zionists. The local communities of the Middle East became aware of the Sykes-Picot Agreement only through its publication, which raised a certain degree of popular outrage and grudge toward Britain and France.

Thus, Sir Mark Sykes and François Georges-Picot unfolded a map of the Middle East and drew a line across the desert, from contemporary Iraq to the Mediterranean, carving up the region and creating alleged modern states –a process known as *a line in the sand*.[191] The Sykes-Picot's artificial borderline divided areas inhabited by Kurds and Arabs, Sunnis and Shias, Christians, Alawites and Druze. Ignoring the ethnic and religious diversity and complexities in the mapped region, the arrangement carelessly left behind many unsolved issues that later incited numerous conflicts and caused great tragedies.

The story of the Sykes-Picot Agreement, the surrounding circumstances and the associated developments have been conveyed by historians in different versions and from various perspectives. George Antonius stressed the contradictory nature of the British policy in the region at the time through three main points. Firstly, the *Hussein-McMahon Correspondence*, the well-known series of ten letters exchanged between the British High Commissioner to Egypt

Lieutenant Colonel Sir Henry McMahon and the Sharif of Mecca Hussein bin ʿAli in the period between July 1915 and March 1916, entails that the British Government provided Arab nationalists with definite undertakings in a bid to persuade them to revolt against the Ottoman Empire. Secondly, Great Britain made concessions to France in the Sykes-Picot convention which were discordant with the undertakings given to the Arab nationalists. Thirdly, in the 1917 Belfour Declaration, Britain provided the Zionists with undertakings which were no less inconsistent with those given to the Arabs.[192] However, according to historian Elie Kedourie, Great Britain did not give precise undertakings to the Arab nationalists. Kedourie emphasizes that the undertakings claimed by Arabs were no more than hopes conceived on the basis of poorly drafted letters, arguing that any such undertakings were not in any way incompatible with those given to France.[193] Furthermore, historian Isaiah Friedman maintains that Palestine was not part of any pledges given to the Arabs, and the Balfour Declaration was hence compatible with those undertakings.[194] According to Albert Hourani, when the British Government made the Sykes-Picot Agreement, it had the intention to reconcile the pledges given to Sharif Hussein with the interests of France in the region. Hourani further stresses the importance of understanding the circumstances within which the agreement was made, arguing that any ambiguity in the agreement cannot be attributed to its bad drafting, but to the conditions under which it was reached as a war-time agreement made in a hurry, under pressure and for immediate purposes.[195]

Nearly four years after reaching the Sykes-Picot Agreement, a mandate system was introduced and approved by Great Britain and France in the San Romeo conference in April 1920, which was mainly aimed at defining the destiny of the Middle East region. According to historian Kamal Salibi, among the main considerations taken into account at the time were the issues of oil and transportation.[196] Britain was facing mounting difficulties during WWI to seize control of Iraq, and the developments associated with the war had proven the strategic significance of oil. While the British were already in control of oil resources in Iran at the time, they were highly concerned that the Germans –major contributors to the Turkish Petroleum Company– would reach the oil fields of Iraq's Kirkuk. Under the developing mandate system, the oil fields were eventually completely controlled by the Allies, which led to the emergence of the Iraq Petroleum Company with British and French shares.

By splitting the region into two spheres of influence, the Sykes-Picot Agreement has changed the map of the Middle East forever, and numerous crises and conflicts that took place in the region over the past one hundred years have been considered as consequences of this agreement and the associated treaties. The Kurds are counted among the victims of the established borders. In 1920, with the Sèvres Treaty, the Sykes-Picot convention was signed into law, setting aside a part of post-Ottoman Turkey as a Kurdish territory, but Turkish nationalists protested against the decision and relocated tens of thousands of Turks into the Kurdish-populated areas southeast of Turkey in order to foil any Kurdish attempts toward establishing any form of autonomy. In 1923, the Allied Powers signed the Lausanne Treaty, which demarcated the borders of today's Turkey, and the northern borderlines of Syria and Iraq, leading to the separation of local ethnic groups, and practically eliminated the Kurdish aspiration of establishing a sovereign Kurdistan. Consequently, millions of Kurds were denied citizenship until the 1990s and have been in a decades-long conflict with the Turkish authorities, striving for their right to self-determination. In Syria, the Kurdish people have suffered suppression and persecution under the Baath regime, which denied them the right to practice their cultural and linguistic freedoms, beside depriving many of them of the right to citizenship for decades. The Kurds in Iraq suffered a genocide at the hands of the regime of Saddam Hussein in the late 1980s, beside numerous forced displacements internally and across the region. Iran's Kurds declared the establishment of a Kurdish government in 1946, but the move was faced by prompt and brutal oppression from the Iranian authorities, and the public executions of Kurdish activists have been taking place ever since. However, the Kurdish national movement has continued its activities in the region and was increasingly revived in the recent years. For instance, the Kurds in Iraq have enjoyed political, military, and economic prosperity in post-2003 Iraq, after decades of struggle against the former regime. In Syria, the Kurdish political movement increased their activities since President Bashar al-Assad came to power and replaced his father in 2000, organizing protests against the regime's suppression toward the Kurdish population. After the outbreak of the 2011 anti-Assad revolution, the Kurds emerged as a powerful military force and took control of Kurdish-majority cities and towns in northern Syria, where they established a semi-autonomous region known as Rojava [or Western Kurdistan]. While political disputes among Kurdish rivals in Syria and Iraq remained an internal concern, the Kurdish forces of the Peshmerga in Iraq and the Kurdish People's Protection Units (YPG) in Syria emerged as fierce fighters against ISIS and other extremist Islamist groups, entering an alliance with the Western coalition in the war on terrorism.

Looking back to earlier developments in the region, under the mandate system, France annexed parts of the Ottoman provinces and created the state of Lebanon in 1920, coupled with the establishment of two regional states –the Damascus State and the Aleppo State– and two sect-based states –the Jabal al-Druz State and the Alawite State. In 1932, the French responded to the national pressure and merged Damascus and Aleppo into the 'State of Syria', and later added to them the Jabal al-Druz and the Alawite states, to eventually demarcate the borders of the Syrian Republic. In cooperation with the French mandate authorities, Turkey seized control of Syria's Iskenderun province in 1939. France recognized the complete independence of Lebanon in 1944. Syria gained its independence from the French in 1946, amid a mounting pressure from the local nationalist political movement. Furthermore, after the end of World War I, the British-protected south-eastern parts of the Arabian Peninsula witnessed clashes between followers of the King of Hejaz Sharif Hussein and the Emir of Najd Abdul Aziz al-Saud. The conflict ended with al-Sauds taking control of the Hejaz, Medina, Jeddah and Yanbu, and subsequently the Kingdom of Saudi Arabia was founded in 1932. Meanwhile, Iraq emerged as a Hashemite monarchy under British protection in 1921, and the Kingdom of Iraq gained its independence in 1932, until its re-emergence as a republic following the downfall of the monarchy in 1958. Moreover, the British declared the independence of Egypt in 1922, but remained in control of its basic administration and foreign policy until 1952, when an Egyptian revolution by Arab nationalists overthrew the British-backed monarchy. Jordan emerged as the 'Hashimite Kingdom of Transjordan' under British protection in 1921, and it gained its independence in 1946. As for Palestine, after Britain ended its mandate over the country in 1948, the Jewish leadership immediately declared the establishment of the State of Israel, a move that ignited a long-term conflict in the Middle East. In the 1960s and

1970s, Britain gradually withdrew from the Arabian Peninsula: Kuwait gained independence in 1965, Aden in 1967, Oman in 1970, and in 1971 Qatar, Bahrain and the Emirates witnessed the withdrawal of the last batch of British troops.

It is worth-mentioning that the geographic area covered in today's reference to the Middle East also includes Arab-majority North African countries, namely Egypt, Sudan, Libya, Tunisia, Algeria and Morocco. The linguistic, religious and cultural ties between these countries and other Arab-majority states to the east of the region constitute a shared Arab identity that usually plays out in the political arena. More recently, the acronym MENA came into use as a reference to the Middle East and North Africa, a toponym deemed synonymous with the term the *Greater Middle East*. However, such terms remain Eurocentric by nature –basically introduced by colonial powers– and usually bear a relative geographic ambiguity, which led to the emergence of some conflicting definitions of the region.[197]

The concept of national identity in the Middle East grew with the emergence and development of national borders. Historically speaking, there was always an awareness of cultural identities among the region's communities, which became synonymous with people or nation amid the rise of national consciousness. However, the creation of nation-states in the Middle East led to the *minorization*[198] of many cultural communities, associated with issues of inequality, underrepresentation, marginalization, discrimination as well as exclusion. The predominance of cultural, linguistic or religious identity of a majority group over the national character of a country has resulted in undermining the diverse identities of minority groups, coupled with efforts to enforce assimilation as a condition to attain a certain degree of belonging and equality.

14. Post-Independence: States in Turmoil

In the Middle East, independence has brought about a state of unrest and instability across the newly established countries. There are several reasons for the instability that followed the emergence of independent states in the region, including the absence of the stabilizing power of an imperial rule; an inconsistency between the borderlines of the state and the boundaries of the prevalent national concept; the absence of a political tradition, which usually stimulates the army to assume control as the only neutral faction toward sectional interests; and the unfulfilled need to redefine the relations of the social components with each other and with the new governing force.[199] Thus, the post-independence states of the Middle East encountered inescapable complexities in the early stages, and the relevant stability that followed was not accomplished without costs.

One of the main pan-Arab nationalist movements that emerged as a reflection of the growing sense of nationalism across the region, coupled with mounting struggle and activism against British and French influence, was the Baath Party. The Baath Party was established in 1943 in Damascus by two Syrian schoolteachers who had studied at the Sorbonne in Paris during the 1920s, namely, Michel Aflaq, a Greek Orthodox Christian, and Salah al-Din al-Bitar, a Sunni Muslim. The party adopted its constitution in 1947. It merged with the Syrian Socialist Party in 1953, and together they founded the Arab Socialist Baath Party (*Ḥizb al-Baʿath al-ʿArabī al-Ishtirākī*). The Baath Party declared nonalignment and opposition to colonialism and imperialism as basic principles in its mission statement, allegedly taking inspiration from what it considered to be positive values of

Islam and expressed ambition to combat class divisions. The basic structure of the Baath Party was significantly centralized and largely authoritarian. Aflaq and al-Bitar envisioned the Baath Party as a modern revolutionary movement that would unite Arabs and liberate their lands from colonial control.[200] Its message of pan-Arab unity held a great appeal to the peoples inhabiting the territories of Syria, Iraq and Transjordan in the 1940s, and by the 1960s the Baath Party became a dominant player in the Syrian and Iraqi politics.

In Iraq, subsequent to the military coup that ousted the British-backed Hashimite monarchy, the process of decolonization coincided with the rise of militant movements, which caused an intensifying unrest in the country. This situation continued until 1963, when a socialist government, consisting of a coalition of members of the Baath Party and commanders of the nationalist army, took power. In 1968, the Baath Party became the sole ruling force in Iraq, and in 1979 prominent Baathist Saddam Hussein took over and stayed in power until the American invasion in 2003. During Saddam's rule, Iraq was engaged in wars with Iran from 1980 to 1988 and with Kuwait in 1990-91, known as the Gulf War which ended after intervention by a U.S.-led coalition. The Saddam era was also characterized by suppression and brutal persecution of internal opponents, such as the Kurds who suffered the Anfal genocide in 1986-89 and the Halabja chemical attack in 1988 which claimed thousands of civilian lives. The Sunni-led government under Saddam Hussein also oppressed the Shia majority in Iraq. However, the 2003 war didn't bring about the awaited stability and democracy in post-dictatorship Iraq. The country has ever since witnessed a Shia dominance over the central government in Baghdad, a deteriorating role of Sunni factions and a Kurdish tendency toward independence. Above all, the chaotic situation in Iraq has provided a fertile ground to extremism and eventually resulted in the emergence of the so-called Islamic State radical group.

Syria was recognized as an independent state in January 1944. However, the French military remained in the country, bombed Damascus in May 1945 and tried to arrest elected Syrian leaders. Under mounting pressure from Syrian nationalist groups as well as Great Britain, France withdrew its last troops on 17 April 1946. Over more than a decade following independence, Syria encountered a constant political instability, yet the economy saw a rapid development though. After gaining its full independence from the French, Syria adopted a republican form of government. However, the unity among Syrian leaders –who resisted the French troops until the latter's withdrawal– gradually disappeared. As the Alleppines and Damascenes started seeking control over commercial and political life, unprecedented forms of allegiances and groupings arose across Syria's provinces, the sectarian differences became more apparent than ever before, and the sectional interests played out between Arabs and Kurds, Alwaites and Sunnis, rural groups and urban populations, a secular young generation and a religious-minded older generation. The independent Syrian republic emerged under the presidency of Shukri al-Quwatli, supported by a fragile parliament without a strong leadership. The country faced its first crisis after a failed invasion into the newly established state of Israel in 1948, along with other Arab military forces, and the government faced a heavy wave of criticism in the local arena. In 1949, the army chief of staff Brigadier General Husni az-Zaim launched the first military coup in modern Syria, and took power after abolishing political parties. A few months later, az-Zaim was ousted through a countercoup led by General Sami al-Hinnawi, who returned the government to civilian politicians but kept the military guardianship to some extent. Then, a Syrian provisional government was formed under the leadership of Hashim al-Atassi, adopting a new electoral law that provided women with the right to vote for the first time. Decades before obtaining the right to vote, the Syrian women played a key role in the development of the society in the region. For instance, the first two girls' schools that were established in 1873 in Egypt had Syrian headmistresses, Rose and Cecile Najjar; the first indigenous woman doctor in the region, who graduated from Edinburg and started to practice in 1900, was of Syrian origin; and several female Syrian writers, including May Ziyada, emerged in an age when the literary salon was just beginning to exist.[201] Following al-Atassi's leadership, several leaders took turn on Syria's governance until the Arab Socialist Baath Party came to power in 1963. In the meantime, the Baathist Military Committee, which took control through a coup, established new terms of governance and monopolized the political life in the country. Several presidents were overthrown through the 1960s for alleged disloyalty to the Baath Party and claimed inability to lead the nation, until the arrival of notable Baathist and former Minister of Defense Hafiz al-Assad to power in 1971. Assad took control after another military coup under the banner *The Corrective Movement*.[202]

Meanwhile, Islamic activism grew in a parallel path to that of nationalism in the region, and both have occasionally overlapped. The Muslim Brotherhood (*Jamā'at al-Ikhwān al-Muslimīn*), a major reflection and product of Islamism or political Islam in the region, is considered a transnational Sunni Islamist organization established in 1928 in Egypt by Islamic scholar Hassan al-Banna and gained support across the Arab world. Activities of the Muslim Brotherhood reached Syria in the 1930s and the organization's Syrian branch was founded in 1945.

In the early years of independence, Syria's Muslim Brotherhood was deemed part of the legitimate opposition, and in 1961 it won ten seats in the parliamentary elections. However, soon after the 1963 coup that has resulted in the Baath Party taking power in Syria, the Muslim Brotherhood was banned.[203] The organization played a key role in the predominantly Sunni movement that opposed the secularist pan-Arab Baath Party, and its members eventually took up arms to fight against the regime of Assad the father in 1979, and the conflict developed in the early 1980s and ended with the military crushing the rebellion during the Hama uprising in 1982. The rebellion, led by the Sunni-based Muslim Brotherhood organization, started in Aleppo, and then its members concentrated their activities in Hama. However, the Assad regime responded promptly with an overwhelming military force, bombing the city of Hama and killing nearly 40,000 people between 1980 and 1982, mostly civilians. Since then, the movement has been banned in Syria and its membership has become a capital offense. However, the group re-emerged as a major faction of the Syrian opposition against Bashar al-Assad subsequent to the outbreak of the 2011 uprising, but its influence remained limited on the ground as most of its activities continued to take place in exile. Under Assad's rule, basically dominated by elite members of his Alawite sect, the Sunnis were largely excluded from power centers.

Furthermore, the Kurds, who constitute the largest non-Arab ethnic minority in Syria,[204] have suffered for decades under the Baathist authoritarian rule. In a bid to eliminate the Kurdish ambition to gain cultural and linguistic rights, the Syrian Baath authority targeted Kurdish-populated areas with an initiative known as the *Arab Belt* in 1963, which entailed Arabizing the names of Kurdish towns and villages in northern Syria, banning the Kurdish language, cultural and political activities, and subsequently hundreds of thousands of Kurds were arbitrarily denied the right to Syrian nationality in violation of international law. The *Arab Belt* is a project that entails Arabization policies against Syria's Kurds. In November 1963, Lieutenant Muhammad Talab al-Hilal, former chief of the Secret Services in the Kurdish-majority Hasakah province, published a study tackling the situation in the Jazira area in northeastern Syria in the form of a security report that was adopted by the authorities as a guide to action with regard to the Kurdish issue in the country. Hilal's report, known as *The Arab Belt Project*, denied the existence of the Kurdish people and considered them a population without history, civilization, language or ethnic origin, labelling the Kurds as enemies to Arab nationalism and comparing them –in terms of the threat they allegedly form– to Israeli Zionists. The *Arab Belt* suggested several measures to eliminate what Hilal considered *the Kurdish danger*, including forced displacement of Kurds from their lands; denial of education and employment possibilities; handing over 'wanted' Kurds to Turkey; launching an anti-Kurdish propaganda campaign; deportation of Kurdish religious *ʿulamāʾ* (clerics) and replacing them with Arabs; colonizing Kurdish lands by Arabs from other provinces and creating 'collective farms' for the new Arab settlers; implementing a 'divide-and-rule' policy against the Kurds; militarizing the 'northern Arab Belt' and deporting many Kurds from the region; denying anyone lacking knowledge of Arabic the right to vote or to hold office; and denying citizenship to any non-Arab wishing to live in the area.[205] In 2000, after Hafiz al-Assad's death, his son Bashar came to power. Although in the early years of his rule Bashar al-Assad promised the Syrians with a new progressive era on multiple levels, including the political domain, a few years later, particularly in March 2004, his regime suppressed Kurdish protests that called for equal citizenship. In March 2011, a popular uprising broke out calling for ousting the Assad regime, which later turned into a civil war, claiming hundreds of thousands of lives and causing the displacement of millions. The developments in Syria also paved the way for radical Islamist groups to rise and grow.

Lebanon's modern history since its independence in 1944 can be defined primarily in terms of the fluctuating politics shaped through the successive governments and leaders, who largely represented the diversity of the Lebanese society. Each sectarian community in Lebanon had renowned and leading families in the political arena. The Maronite Christians were represented by the Khuris, Shamuns, Shihabs, Franjiyahs and Jumayyils; the Sunni Muslims had the Sulhs, Karamis and Yafis; the Jumblatts, Yazbaks and Arslans represented the Druze; and the Shia Muslims had the Asads and Hamadahs.[206] The independent Lebanon emerged under the presidency of Bishara al-Khuri, who was criticized for his regime's narrow political structure, characterized by a strict sectarian framework. Under a popular pressure that took the form of a general strike, al-Khuri was forced to resign in 1952, and he was succeeded by Camille Shamun, another Maronite leader whose regime was later criticized for excluding non-Maronites from high ranking positions within governmental institutions. When the Suez Canal crisis broke out in 1956-58, Egyptian President Gamal Abdul Nasser emerged as a symbol of pan-Arabism, and in 1958 he merged Egypt and Syria to establish the United Arab Republic. These developments had a remarkable influence on Lebanese Muslims, who found in Nasser an inspiration to maintain and reinforce the Arab identity, unlike the Maronite Christians who sought better relations with the West to guarantee Lebanon's independence and stability. Rivalry increased among the Lebanese leaders, which forced the country into a state of turmoil. The country eventually descended into a civil war, and Shamun, who accused Lebanese Muslims of receiving Syrian support, which included Soviet arms, called on the United States to intervene under the pretext of seeking to maintain the country's independence. The crisis ended after the death of up to 4,000 people, mostly Muslims from Tripoli and Beirut, and the Chamber of Deputies elected the commander in chief of the Lebanese Army General Fuad Shihab as president. However, political unrest continued through the presidencies of Shihab, Charles Helou (1964-70), Suleiman Franjiyah (1970-76), Elias Sarkis (1976-82), Amin Gemayel (1982-88), and sometimes the rifts intensified to such a degree that left a leadership vacuum. One of the most prominent developments in Lebanon's modern history is the 1975-90 civil war, a multifaceted conflict where sectarian divide played a key role, devastating the country and causing over 120,000 fatalities. Furthermore, in the early years of the 21st century, Lebanon was destined to witness a series of political assassinations, the most prominent of which was the assassination of Prime Minister Rafic Hariri in 2005 in an explosion in Beirut. As prime minister of Lebanon (1992-89; 2000-04), Rafic Hariri played an instrumental and essential role in rebuilding the country after the devastating civil war and contributed to the growth of its economy. Hariri's assassination in 2005 caused political tensions between Lebanon and Syria. Many politicians and analysts accused the Syrian regime of orchestrating the assassination. Amid an escalating political unrest and under a mounting pressure from the international community, Syria withdrew its troops from Lebanon in April 2005, ending almost 29 years of occupation. Today, Lebanon continues to be an arena for regional interference, with Saudi Arabia holding strong ties to the Sunnis, and Syria and Iran supporting the Shia, particularly the Hezbollah militia.

Since the establishment of the State of Israel in 1948, an Arab-Israeli conflict broke out and turned into a major crisis in the Middle East. In May 1948, the neighboring Arab states launched a war on Israel, and the fighting continued until a cease-fire was reached one year later. In 1956, Israel was engaged in another war with Egypt which continued until 1967. A few years later, in 1973, the Egyptian and Syrian armies launched a heavy attack on Israel, but they were soon defeated and forced into a renewed cease-fire, and peace agreements were signed in its aftermath. In 1993, Israel and the Palestinian Liberation Organization reached an agreement, known as the Oslo Accord, which implied the establishment of a Palestinian self-rule in Gaza Strip and in the predominantly-Arab cities of the West Bank. However, peace has never found a solid ground in that part of the Middle East, and violent confrontations continued between the Arabs and the Israelis in years to come. The Palestinian issue remains unresolved, which makes lasting peace in the region unattainable.

Most of today's Middle Eastern states have encountered multiple challenges since independence and have constantly struggled to maintain sovereignty. Only a few countries in the region, particularly in the Gulf, enjoyed a certain degree of stability, which has remarkably contributed to the economic growth and the fulfillment of relatively higher living standards in comparison to other parts of the Middle East. Dictatorship, corruption and oppression found a fertile ground in many countries in the region, causing exclusion and marginalization of millions of citizens. The deteriorating economic conditions, kleptocracy and lack of freedoms sparked popular uprisings in several countries across the region in 2010-11, which became known as the *Arab Spring*.[207]

15. Arab Spring

After decades of dictatorship and tyranny, the MENA region was engulfed in an unprecedented outbreak of pro-democracy protests in 2010-11, when millions of people broke their silence to chant "the people want to bring down the regime". Long-standing dictatorships, oppression and corruption were among the main incentives for the outburst of what became known as the *Arab Spring*. The wave of revolts, which started in Tunisia and spread within weeks to Egypt, Libya, Yemen, Bahrain and Syria, called for freedom, political reform and social justice.

The self-immolation of Mohamed Bouazizi in December 2010 ignited a popular uprising known as the Jasmine Revolution in Tunisia, where a series of street demonstrations took place, precipitated by high unemployment, corruption, poor living conditions and lack of freedoms.[208] The armed intervention by the regime caused scores of civilian fatalities. In his last official speech after 23 years in power, Tunisian President Zine El Abdine Ben Ali stated that there would be "no life-long presidency." The ensuing protests led to his ouster 28 days later on 14 January 2011, when he officially resigned and fled to Saudi Arabia. Compared to other countries affected by the Arab Spring, Tunisia is deemed to be the only observable success story, with a new constitution and a certain degree of justice. However, human rights violations continued to take place in the country.

The Tunisian protests inspired similar movements throughout the region. The Egyptian revolution against the rule of Hosni Mubarak began as a campaign of non-violent civil resistance through marches, labor strikes, a series of demonstrations and acts of civil disobedience.

The state of emergency law, police brutality, lack of free elections, uncontrollable corruption and deteriorating living conditions were sufficient and persuasive reasons for millions of Egyptian protesters from a range of socio-economic and religious backgrounds to demand the downfall of Mubarak's regime. Despite its peaceful characteristic, the Egyptian revolution left hundreds of people dead and thousands injured following violent clashes between security forces and protesters. As pressure mounted on his regime, Mubarak, whose rule lasted for three decades, declared in his last speech that he wasn't intending to run for re-election. On 11 February 2011, following weeks of popular protests and an increasing pressure, Mubarak's resignation was announced, ending three decades of dictatorship. However, Egypt didn't take the direction its revolutionaries hoped for. In June 2012, Muslim Brotherhood's politician Mohamed Morsi won the first presidential elections in post-Mubarak Egypt. A year later, Morsi was removed by a military coup led by General Abdel Fattah el-Sisi in response to mounting pressure from liberal Egyptians.

The North African state of Libya was no exception to the anti-tyranny movements sweeping into the region, given its geographical location between Tunisia and Egypt. On 15 February 2011, protests against the dictatorship of Colonel Muammar Gaddafi, who ruled Libya for more than four decades, started to take place across the country. They soon turned into a full-fledged armed conflict after security forces fired on crowds of protesters. The movement escalated into a rebellion that spread throughout the country, with forces loyal to Gaddafi pitted against those seeking to oust his regime. Addressing the pro-democracy activists and rebels who were demanding him to step down, Gaddafi stated, "If I was an official president, I would throw my resignation letter in your faces. I'm a rebel myself, and I will never give up." The intervention of the United Nations Security Council played a significant role in weakening the rule of Gaddafi, and the Libyan National Transitional Council was established with the goal of achieving a democratic change in line with the aspirations of the Libyan people. After eight months of armed conflict, which claimed the lives of tens of thousands of Libyans, Gaddafi was captured and killed on 20 October 2011 by Libyan rebels as he tried to escape from the city of Sirte. The National Transitional Council then declared the liberation of Libya. However, the country was destined to suffer instability and unrest for years to come.

Over four decades, persecution and corruption were rife in Syria. Under the rule of the Assad family, the people of Syria suffered from tyrannical practices, where civil rights and political activists have been constantly exposed to brutal suppression. On 15 March 2011, Syrians decided to end their suffering; a peaceful uprising was declared against Assad's regime. The sacrifices that the Syrian people have made in their push against dictatorship have been described as 'unprecedented'. As the Syrian authorities hit back against the peaceful movement with an iron fist, the country descended into a long-term civil war, with various regional and international powers involved. Syria suffered one of the bloodiest armed conflicts in the 21st century, with atrocities and war crimes committed on a mass scale, causing hundreds of thousands of fatalities and the displacement of millions.

Although these popular movements haven't been as fruitful as many hoped, and despite the eventual infiltration and hijacking of the uprisings by radical Islamist groups and the survival of dictatorship in some cases, the Arab Spring became a new key chapter in the history of the modern Middle East. The revolutionary wave has undeniably brought about a significant and irreversible change to the region's societies and body politics. It has also caused a general change in the foreign policies of most of the region's states, and led to the emergence of new regional and international alignments. Furthermore, in the aftermath of the Arab Spring, sectarian tensions were considerably revived and remarkably increased across the Middle East. In Yemen and Bahrain, sectarian factions took advantage of the popular protesters and delegitimized legitimate popular demands through their sectarian discourse and the involvement of sectarian-guided political and military interventions from regional powers. With the downfall of several authoritarian regimes in the region, the previously suppressed communities started seeking more economic gains and political power, which resulted in unanticipated conflicts of interest. Another repercussion of the Arab Spring is the demographic change that occurred in some of the affected areas following forced displacements due to armed conflicts and escalation of violence. It has further proven the key role of media in moving the public opinion and stimulating people to take sides through uncovering oppressive authoritarian practices, promoting or slandering a certain party or agenda, or even inciting escalation.[209]

16. Political Islam and the Islamization of Popular Uprisings

Political Islam has its roots in the early stage of the Islamic history. Within a few months following the death of the Prophet Muhammad, different Islamic groups emerged and became involved in public affairs and political rivalry amid rising scholastic and sectarian divide.[210] Ever since, Muslim political theorists have been engaged in debates about the nature of political authority within the Islamic tradition and the proper way to be a Muslim.[211] Muslim thinkers of the 19th and 20th century stressed that the characteristic institution of modern Europe –democratic government, patriotic loyalty and legal reform– were permitted by Islam, only if Islam was accurately understood.[212]

Reformist Islamic thinkers believed that Islam was a *rational* religion that could be applied directly to modern life. They believed traditional-bound Muslim leaders had led the society astray and that religious thinking should instead be reformed and used as a vehicle for progress.[213] Nevertheless, such reformist thoughts about Islam as a rational religion should be viewed within the framework of the long-standing tradition of *tajdīd* (renewal) and *iṣlāḥ* (reform) in the Islamic history, reinforced by centuries-long debates about *ʿaql* (reasoning) and *naql* (transmission) as demonstrated through *ijtihād* (independent judgement) and a high-level philosophy. However, these debates haven't been as fruitful to develop methods of transition and the delegation of powers or tools to determine and preserve individual political and civil rights and freedoms. Throughout twelve centuries of Islam, the huge amount of debates hardly ever evolved into an independent Islamic political science, nor even did they reach the extent of developing tools to define and protect personal political rights, public liberties, transition and distribution of power. The modern concept of reinstalling Islam into public life and considering politics an authentic part of religion was developed by the 19th and 20th century thinkers, who were motivated by the provocation of direct contact with the West.[214] Moreover, Islam and Muslim scholars have been repeatedly used by rulers, political authorities or religious organizations to justify illegitimate policies and practices, and manipulate the *'umma* in a process often characterized by monopoly of power and exclusion of rivals.

One of the most conspicuous aspects of the Arab Spring is the rise of political Islam and Islamists as influential players. Prior to the recent Middle Eastern revolts, many prominent and influential Islamist figures were either in prison or in exile. While Islamists didn't play any mentionable role in the outbreak of these anti-dictatorship revolutionary movements in the region, Islamic parties and organizations are believed to have considerably hijacked these movements in their quest for power.[215] The rise of Islamism within the framework of the Arab Spring has raised suspicion and controversy about the alleged motivations and objectives of these uprisings, in terms of establishing democracy, accomplishing social justice, guaranteeing individual freedoms and pluralism, and the feasibility of realizing such goals.

Islamism, as a concept and phenomenon, refers to social and political expressions prevalent within Islamic societies, aimed at integrating and incorporating Islam into state affairs, politics, economics and legal systems. It is deemed a form of instrumentalization of Islam by certain individuals or organizations that seek political goals.[216] Under the slogan *Islam is the Solution*, which significantly reflects socio-political aspects of Islamism, the Muslim Brotherhood won the first presidential elections in post-Mubarak Egypt for the first time in the history of the movement since its establishment in 1928. The Muslim Brotherhood is deemed the first popular Islamist movement in the Arab world that spread across several countries since its establishment in Egypt, with a powerful rhetoric about solidarity with and belonging to the Muslim *'umma*. For decades, the organization's members have been repeatedly exposed to arrest and torture under secular regimes in Egypt, until they won the first presidential elections in the post-Mubarak era. However, after only one year in power, the organization was taken down by a military coup, its leaders and members were arrested and its activities were banned once again. Although their reign didn't last longer than one year, as they tried to Islamize the country on different levels before a military coup toppled them, the dramatic rise of the Muslim Brotherhood during the Arab Spring, following decades of forced inactivity, has shown Islamists as the main winners of the revolutionary movements in the Middle East.

In post-revolutionary Tunisia, the transitional government, which ruled from 2011 to 2014, included a majority block of Islamist politicians who, for the first time in Tunisia's post-independence history, gained a legal right to take part in running the country. Inspired by Egypt's Muslim Brotherhood, Rached Ghannouchi and other Tunisian intellectuals founded the Islamic Tendency Movement in 1981. A few years later, particularly in 1989, the newly established movement became Ennahda party. The party's leadership and members suffered suppression and persecution under the former regime of Zine El Abdine Ben Ali and his predecessor Habib Bourguiba. Ennahda's leader Ghannouchi was sentenced to jail under

Bourguiba, and later he lived in exile for nearly 20 years up until the outbreak of the Arab Spring, when he returned to Tunisia and his party resumed its political activities. While the ascendance of Ennahda raised concerns among many Tunisians, the party succeeded in becoming an important fixture in the Tunisian politics. When the secular Nidaa Tounes party won the 2014 elections, it could not form a government without establishing an alliance with Ennahda. Although this step initially caused controversy, Ennahda's willingness and determination to provide a successful example on political Islam guided the party toward moderation and reform.[217] According to some scholars, the legalization of political Islamism in Tunisia may hinder the influence of violent radicalism, lead to partnership in a democratic government, and could be a beginning to a possible democratic growth and sustainability in the region.[218] The rise of Ennahda party as a main Islamist political force in Tunisia raised fears among the seculars in the beginning. However, in 2016, the party adopted internal reforms that included the acknowledgement of the primacy of secular democracy over Islamic theocracy, announcing separation of religious activity from political activity. Ennahda's founder and leader Rached Ghannouchi, who once advocated a strict application of Islamic *Sharīʿa* law, said in May 2016, "Tunisia is now a democracy. The 2014 constitution has imposed limits on extreme secularism and extreme religion... We want religious activity to be completely independent from political activity. This is good for politicians because they would no longer be accused of manipulating religion for political means, and good for religion because it would not be held hostage to politics... We are going toward a party which specializes in political activities... We are leaving political Islam and entering democratic Islam. We are Muslim democrats who no longer claim to represent political Islam."[219] Hence, Ennahda made itself into an acceptable political force in Tunisia, the birthplace of the Arab Spring and its sole success story. Ennahda's criticism about Islamic militancy and violence, beside its pro-liberalist attitude, led some Islamists to question not only the commitment and attachment of the party's leadership to Islamism, but to Islam itself.

With the outbreak of the popular revolution against the regime of President Bashar al-Assad in Syria in March 2011, the Syrian Muslim Brotherhood became a main component of the Western-backed opposition. After 30 years in exile, leading members of the Syrian Muslim Brotherhood organization re-emerged as powerful figures within the opposition. They played an influential role in the formation of several political bodies in support of the rebellion against the Assad regime in its early stage. The Muslim Brotherhood contributed to the formation of the Syrian National Council, which was the first political body for opposition forces to be established subsequent to the outbreak of the 2011 uprising. Members of the Brotherhood were also among the founders of the Syrian National Coalition for Revolutionary Forces and the Opposition (SNC) in November 2012, which became the main umbrella for the political and armed opposition and their representative in the international arena. However, most of their activities remained constrained as they continued to operate from outside of Syria, taking Turkey as a main basis, except for some limited influence over armed rebels inside the country. The expansion of Islamist movements in Syria, the emergence of numerous armed groups with different loyalties, and the radicalization of several factions on the ground left the Muslim Brotherhood with a limited power in the later stages of the rebellion, which eventually descended into a civil war –and a proxy war to a certain degree. The growing power of extremist Islamist groups provided the Muslim Brotherhood with an opportunity to become a dominant force in the Western-backed Syrian opposition. The political pragmatism and the centrist ideological discourse of the Brotherhood's leadership contributed to the portrayal of the organization as a moderate Islamist group. Nevertheless, the rise of radical Islamist factions endangered the Brotherhood's aspiration to find a foothold inside Syria and led the organization to encounter unprecedented ideological challenges. Furthermore, despite the long political experience of its leading members, the Syrian Muslim Brotherhood failed in forming a real partnership with the liberal, secular factions of the opposition. One of the main reasons behind the movement's failure was its inability to establish trust with other opposition groups, as its long exile – enforced by the regime of Hafiz al-Assad since the early 1980s– created a state of hesitation and suspicion among different components of the Syrian society about the Brotherhood's undeclared agenda and the implicit aspirations of its leadership with respect to the ongoing crisis. Meanwhile, dozens of Islamist groups came into existence over the years of the Syrian crisis and were engaged in clashes with the regime as well as with each other, contributing to the escalation of violence in the war-ravaged country. Although some of these armed Islamist groups constantly claimed loyalty and commitment to the Syrian popular uprising, sectarianism and hostility toward rivals dominated their discourse. The involvement of sectarian Shia-based militias into the conflict on the side of the Assad regime, such as Hezbollah and the Quds Force, added to the complexity of the Syrian scenery, reinforcing the Islamization and sectarianization of the conflict. Besides, the state of instability and chaos, enhanced by a widespread security vacuum, led to the formation of a Syrian branch of al-Qaeda, namely al-Nusra

Front, and the conflict reached its darkest phase with the rise of the so-called Islamic State (ISIS) in mid-2014.

In order to gain an insight into the complex Syrian scenery with respect to the numerous sectarian-guided Islamist groups and their agendas, mentioning influential organizations active during the Syrian civil war seems inescapable. Among the opposition-linked Islamist rebel groups that emerged in Syria during the civil war were the Ahrar al-Sham, The Southern Front, Army of Islam, al-Rahman Legion, Levant Legion, Martyrs of Islam Brigade, Islamic Union of the Soldiers of the Levant, Sunna Lions, Islamic Freedom Brigade, and the Islamic Front. The main Salafi-Jihadi groups involved in the Syrian conflict included the Levant Liberation Committee, Anṣar al-Sham, Ghuraba' al-Sham, and Fatah al-Sham. At the top of extremist, hard-line Salafi-Jihadi groups were the Islamic State (ISIS) and al-Nusra Front (Jabhat al-Nuṣra). These different factions were often engaged in disputes and violent clashes against each other over power in regime-free areas of Syria. Some of these groups –ISIS excluded– were occasionally able to form alliances to fight other opposition groups or combat Kurdish forces or pro-regime troops. On the regime's side, there were several sectarian Shia-based militias involved in the conflict, including Hezbollah, Quds Force, Saberin Unit, Badr Organization, Abu Fadl al-Abbas, Asai'b Ahl al-Haq, Kata'ib Sayyid al-Shuhada', Kata'ib al-Imām ʿAli, and Zulfiqar Brigade. These Shia militias supported the Syrian Arab Army's military operations to retake areas lost to Sunni groups.

The dramatic growth of Islamist extremism has greatly affected the general image of Islamism, moderate Islamic movements included. However, Islamist extremism forms one single element within a multifaceted, broader and more complex picture. The cultural diversity within the Muslim societies and the different approaches to

Islamism led to the emergence of various movements throughout the Middle East, driven by different socio-political incentives and striving for discernible form of government, with a possibility of reform and adaptation in certain cases. One of such cases, as mentioned earlier, is Tunisia's Ennahda party, which represents one of the very few examples of Islamist movements to actually adapt and carry out reforms. Given its discourse and practices, the party adopted reforms and formed alliances with liberal parties in post-revolutionary Tunisia. Nevertheless, Ennahda was exposed to sharp criticism from other, local and regional, Islamist groups for its declared new position as a representative of 'democratic Islam', and its attachment to Islam was repeatedly questioned.

Part V

Sectarian Extremism

Crisis-stricken parts of the Middle East, particularly Syria and Iraq, reflect the dark outcome of a long chain of events and developments that have hit the region over decades on socio-political and religio-sectarian levels. Security vacuum, chaos and sectarian confrontations are believed to have allowed radical Sunni and Shia groups to emerge and expand at the cost of vulnerable communities that have fallen victim to the sectarian-guided extremist agenda of such groups. This part thoroughly scrutinizes the politico-sectarian roots of contemporary Islamist extremism. It tackles the multifaceted factors that have led to the rise and growth of some of the most atrocious, violent and ferocious sectarian-guided Islamist organizations in the heart of the Middle East, such as Sunni-based ISIS and Shia-based al-Hashd al-Shaabi. It also delves into the threat such extremist groups pose to the region through shedding light on the devastating consequences civilian populations have suffered at the hands of such organizations. Political, religious and sectarian dimensions of the expansion and growth of such groups are explored, their impact on local populations is investigated, and potential future implications for the region are examined.

17. Sectarianized Politics and Religionized Extremism: Syria and Iraq Under Scrutiny

In the heart of the Middle East, post-2003 Iraq and post-2011 Syria embody the outcome of failed attempts of democratization. Instead, sectarianized politics and religionized extremism have emerged as key consequences of the crises afflicting both countries. Syria and Iraq embody, to a certain degree, the dark outcome of a long chain of events and developments that have hit the region over decades on socio-political and religio-sectarian levels. This chapter explores the conflicts that have defined both countries in the early 21st century and ultimately led to the rise of the most powerful sectarian-guided extremist Islamist organizations, namely, ISIS and al-Hashd al-Shaabi.

In the aftermath of the 2003 war, Iraq descended into chaos and disorder. After the U.S.-led invasion toppled the regime of Saddam Hussein, a violent conflict started between rival groups that strived for power. The invasion of Iraq, which took place while the memory of the 9/11 attacks remained hot, was launched by the American-British alliance under the pretext of breaking potential ties between Saddam Hussein and al-Qaeda and eliminating alleged Iraqi mass destruction weapons, as well as removing what they perceived as the greatest source of unrest in the Middle East.[237] The U.S. assumptions on post-Saddam Iraq implied that the state would stay intact, local security services would preserve law and order, and that the Iraqi bureaucracy would continue to operate in running the state. However, these pre-war assumptions have been proven completely wrong by the developments that followed the removal of Saddam's regime, which basically resulted in the collapse of the state and a gradual slide into civil war caused by several factors, including security vacuum and a struggle for power among existing and emerging forces. Existing forces included opposition parties, mainly Shia and Kurdish, and remnants of the Baath Party; whereas the emerging forces included militias, such as al-Qaeda, ISIS and al-Hashd al-Shaabi, among others. Moreover, the erosion of the sovereignty of Iraq as a state and the elimination of key governmental institutions in post-2003 left a vacuum throughout political and social governance, leading people to retreat back into the sect or tribe in an attempt to reestablish an in-group identity and regain a certain degree of status in the new Iraq.[238] This resulted in a state of dramatically growing distrust and division among the components of the social fabric in Iraq, which was manifested later on in various forms, including armed struggle.

One of the main challenges facing post-dictatorship Iraq was the security vacuum. Subsequent to the invasion, the country has for years suffered from the absence of security forces capable of enforcing law and maintaining order. Meanwhile, the American troops focused most of their efforts on pursuing extremist insurgents in the rural parts of western Iraq, marginalizing densely populated cities that were encountering a large security vacuum.[239] The deteriorating situation led to the rise of organized crime, social elements hostile to each other amid a plague of ethnic and religious fear and insecurity, and sectarian militias seeking power and fighting for control over unstable areas. This has been evident in the case of ISIS taking control of Sunni-majority areas across Iraq amid a prompt collapse in the state security apparatus and an intensifying sectarian rivalry through later stages of the conflict. It was in this period that Muqtada al-Sadr established his sectarian Jaysh al-Mahdi militia to impose himself as a religious leader of Iraq's Shia, the Supreme Council of the Islamic Revolution in Iraq –an armed Shia force that has been based in Iran since the 1980s– re-entered Iraq, and the Iranian-trained Badr Brigades emerged as another powerful umbrella of Shia militias. The Sunnis, on the other hand, refused to stay inactive toward the American invasion and the dramatic growth of Shia power in Iraq. Under the leadership of Jordanian national Abu Musab al-Zarqawi, the Jamāʿat al-Tawḥīd wal-Jihad created its bases in the Sunni-majority parts of Iraq and recruited many local and regional jihadists, mostly affiliated with al-Qaeda, to combat the Americans and the Shiʿites. The sectarian militias carried out countless atrocities against civilians, including ethnic cleansing campaigns.[240]

Under the former regime of Saddam Hussein, the Sunni Arabs enjoyed a relatively greater political power and economic benefits in contrast to other communities in Iraq.[241] As Saddam's ethno-sectarian base, the Sunnis, who dominated the military and intelligence services, had been the regime's instrument in oppressing the Shia and the Kurds. The 2003 U.S. invasion was seen by many Sunnis as a threat, since the Americans demonstrated a determination to reestablish Iraq as a more equitable state than it had been under the Saddam regime, which basically meant reducing the Sunni share of the pie and increasing that of the Shia as a majority. However, handing over the new Iraq to sectarian Shia elements led to the persecution of the Sunnis in retaliation for the woes they had suffered under Saddam. The threat of being replaced by the Shia and the Kurds led the Sunni community to seek allies and any available support in order to resist exclusion from the power circle. Jihadist groups, with fighting skills and experience, weapons and financial resources, showed willingness to support the Sunni cause and fight the Americans as well as the Shia in Iraq. For the jihadists, the American troops were seen as *Crusaders* occupying a Muslim country, and fighting them was believed to be a duty. The alleged main cause to al-Zarqawi and his fellow militant jihadists was protecting Sunni Muslims and liberating their land from the so-called *Crusaders*. This while the historic sectarian tension with the Shia continued to play out, and in this case, they were seen as traitors to the Muslim community after showing support to the American invasion of Iraq. Although the Sunni tribal leaders rejected such Salafist groups in the beginning, their deteriorating situation eventually pushed them to submit and join a guerilla war against the Americans and establish militias to fight the Shia.

The emerging and growing militias sought military as well as political and economic power, taking over oil facilities and transportation routes in areas under their control, suppressing their opponents and rewarding supporters. Militia leaders became representatives of communities and were engaged in negotiations and elections on a state level.[242] Corruption flourished and sectarian divide deepened, turning Iraq into a failed state. The Shia-dominated government in Baghdad backed the incorporation of sectarian militiamen into the state security services and the military, inciting intensification of Sunni guerilla struggle, incubated by many voiceless people within the Sunni community across the country. Additionally, the increased Iranian support to the Iraqi Shia groups, and Tehran's mounting interference into Baghdad's politics, further inflamed the sectarian tension.

The Kurds, as a separate nation with their own cultural, linguistic, ethnic and historical identity, never desired to be part of Iraq, Turkey, Syria or Iran. Since 1918, the Kurds have been struggling to reach autonomy and establish their own state.[243] In comparison with their peers in other parts of 'Great Kurdistan',[244] Iraq's Kurds have been successful in accomplishing self-rule and developing their own economy. In the period between 1991-2003, the Kurds ruled a semi-autonomous region in northern Iraq. They counted on the American invasion to provide them with an opportunity to finally realize independence, but the U.S. insistence on the necessity to maintain Iraq's territorial unity under the pretext of preventing the outbreak of a civil war deprived the Kurds of the right to independence and forced them to join a coalition with Shia and Sunni factions in Baghdad. However, despite their de facto partnership with the Iraqi Central Government, the Kurds continued to rule themselves and achieved a considerable economic growth, beside proving their capability in maintaining security and civil peace within the borders of the Kurdistan Region while the rest of Iraq was sinking into a devastating sectarian conflict.[245] Furthermore, when the war on ISIS started in 2014, the Kurdish Peshmerga forces emerged as a powerful ally to the U.S.-led International Coalition in combatting the radical group.[246]

The formation of the Iraqi Security Forces (ISF) in 2007 was supposed to bring about more stability and civil peace, but the sectarian inclination remained dominant among the political blocks and overshadowed public life across the country. The significant Shia dominance over the Iraqi government and its policies led to the marginalization, and sometimes exclusion, of the Sunnis.[247] This while the relation between the Kurdistan Regional Government in Erbil and the Iraqi Central Government in Baghdad remarkably deteriorated over several outstanding issues, including the governance of the so-called disputed areas[248] –which fall outside the Kurdish borders but allegedly belong to Kurdistan– and economic matters such as the distribution of oil returns and Kurdistan Region's constitutionally mandated share of the federal budget which had been suspended for years by the central government.[249] These factors stimulated the Kurds –who began to enjoy an unprecedented military and security power– to revive their call for independence and struggle for separation from Iraq.

The joint military operations by competing Iraqi factions against the ISIS radical group, which began in the summer of 2014 in cooperation and coordination with a global coalition, gave many Iraqis a glimpse of hope to reach a new social contract and rebuild the country on the rubble of counter-terrorism efforts. ISIS constituted a threat to the various components of the Iraqi society, including the Shia, the Kurds, the ethno-religious minorities as well as the Sunnis themselves, through its brutal practices and innumerable atrocities. However, the roots of the sectarian divide appeared much deeper and greater than an urgent need for unity and reconciliation, as the 'war on terrorism' was exploited by different groups in a way that ignited further escalation of tension and struggle for power throughout Iraq.

In Syria, where the ruling Assad family and the Baath Party have for decades employed the concept of nationalism in the service of monopolizing power and a forced sanctification of the leadership, opposition groups remained largely paralyzed, unable to take any actual steps toward reforms, constitutional change or devolution of power in the country. Moreover, corruption has eaten up government institutions, amid the absence of freedoms and basic human rights, causing a growing public outrage. As the 2010-11 revolutionary movements succeeded in ousting dictatorship in Tunisia and Egypt, many Syrians were seeking a spark to start a similar uprising against Assad's rule. The day Mubarak stepped down in Egypt gave Syrians a glimpse of hope.

The Syrian President Bashar al-Assad acknowledged in January 2011 that there have been economic hardships for many Syrians and that political reform had been slow, but he was confident that his country was not in a state to undergo an anti-regime uprising similar to Tunisia and Egypt, arguing that his administration's policies were principally aligned with the fundamental aspirations of the Syrian people.[220] However, amid ongoing unrest in the region, a group of children in Syria's southern city of Daraa drew a few fearless graffiti on the walls of their school, saying, "People want to overthrow the regime...You [Assad] are next."[221] As the children were arrested and tortured, an uprising broke out and thousands started to take to the street across the country, calling for an end to the repressive authoritarian practices of the Assad regime, which have been taking place since Bashar's father Hafiz al-Assad came to power in 1971.[222] The authorities resorted to violence in a bid to end the protests, but that policy failed to hinder the storm of public anger; on the contrary, the crisis escalated and the numbers of protesters grew dramatically in a matter of days. The decades-long stagnation in Syria's social and political life, reflected in a large-scale persecution and economic woes, were factors that raised popular outrage against the authorities after more than four decades of silence, and rebellion became inevitable. Undoubtedly, the general environment in the region regarding other ongoing popular movements, beside other internal factors, played a role in motivating Syrians to take to the street and protest against their regime. In addition, global warming was also deemed one of the reasons that sparked the 2011 uprising in Syria, as a severe drought plagued Syria since 2007, pushing over 1.5 million people to leave the countryside and move into cities, which led to increased poverty and social unrest.[223]

In fact, Syrians were already familiar with the repressive practices of the security apparatus, especially after witnessing the suppression of the Muslim Brotherhood-led Hama rebellion in the 1980s and the Kurdish uprising of 2004. At the beginning of the 2011 uprising, young activists led the demonstrations, and social media played a remarkable role in the coordination of the popular movement on the ground. The active role of media activists enabled the documentation of the daily developments, which increased the importance of 'citizen journalism'.[224] Amid an increasing scale of protests, the regime started to cut off communications and besiege neighborhoods and towns that had become strongholds for anti-regime protesters. At the time, the Syrians appeared determined and aspiring to write a new chapter in Syria's history through founding a pluralistic and democratic system. However, the excessive use of force by the authorities to suppress the demonstrations, which swept into most of the country's major cities in a matter of months, claimed many lives and stimulated dozens of soldiers to desert the ranks of the regime's military forces. In July 2011, the defectors announced the formation of the Free Syrian Army (FSA), to become the first armed wing of the revolution. The FSA was established under the pretext of protecting peaceful demonstrators and supporting the cause of overthrowing the government and promoting democratic and pluralistic principles. Nevertheless, the armament increased across the country and various rebel groups emerged. Hence, Syria began to slide into a long-term civil war that eventually resulted in devastating consequences.[225]

During the early stage of the uprising, Syrian protesters strongly condemned sectarianism, called for unity against dictatorship and stressed the need for a democratic change. The opposition accused the Assad government of inducing minority groups into supporting its forces against the uprising. On the other hand, President Assad in his public statements constantly sought to portray the opposition forces as Sunni extremists equivalent to al-Qaeda, and as participators in foreign conspiracies against his country.[226] As the uprising descended into a civil war, it has acquired a sectarian overtone. The overwhelming majority of rebel fighters were Sunni Muslims, engaged in battles against predominantly Alawite troops and Shiʿite militias. The sectarian split was reflected in banners raised by parties to conflict in Syria, with anti-regime groups emphasizing their Sunni identity and pro-regime forces displaying their Shia-Alawite affiliation on different occasions, especially on the battleground. This sectarian dimension was also reflected in the alliances that emerged between local armed forces and regional actors, with Shiʿite Iran supporting the Alawite Assad regime and Sunni Saudi Arabia, Qatar and Turkey supporting different rebel groups.[227]

As the conflict exacerbated, sectarian divisions hardened and rifts emerged and intensified between armed opposition factions that shared control over different parts of the country. The FSA itself weakened amid increasing divisions that led to the rise of numerous rebel groups with an Islamist overtone, which paved the way for the emergence of the al-Qaeda-affiliated al-Nusra Front and the so-called Islamic State or ISIS. Meanwhile, the Kurds created their own armed force, namely, the Kurdish People's Protection Units (YPG), and seized control of the Kurdish-majority parts of northern Syria. The Kurdish units concentrated their fight against ISIS and other Islamist groups, and developed their ranks by including Arab and Christian fighters under the umbrella of the Syrian Democratic Forces (SDF), which then became a key ally to the U.S.-led coalition in the war on ISIS.[228]

While rebel groups continued to mainly rely on light-to-medium weapons, pro-regime troops possessed a capable air force and various heavy weapons, including a chemical arsenal. The imbalance of military power between the parties to conflict in Syria, beside the continuous heavy military support by Russia and Iran to the Assad regime, enabled the latter to regain control over major parts of the country, including the key city of Aleppo. The Syrian regime forces also launched several chemical attacks on opposition-held areas, causing many casualties.[229] Political efforts weren't as fruitful to put an end to the conflict in its early years, and the rebellious movement against the regime declined gradually with the start of a global war on terror in Syria and abroad. The political opposition remained deeply divided, as rival blocks continued to battle for supremacy. The main political opposition body was the Syrian National Coalition (SNC), but the fact that it was formed and remained based in exile kept its legitimacy dubious and its influence remained limited on the ground in Syria. At the United Nations Security Council, Russia vetoed at least eight Western-backed resolutions on Syria, which prevented the fall of the Assad regime. Several short-term cease-fire agreements had been reached, but failed in implementation to stop the bloodshed or lead to a sustainable truce between the regime and the armed opposition forces. While the international community remained for years paralyzed toward finding a solution, the civil war in Syria caused a mass destruction to the country's infrastructure, the death of nearly half a million people, forced disappearance of hundreds of thousands, and forced displacement of half of the country's population, with millions of people seeking asylum in other countries. Syria then became one of the most dangerous places in the world.[230]

Civil war is considered the prevalent form of armed conflict in the contemporary international system, as most of the post-Cold War deadly conflicts have been domestic rather than interstate.[231]

Nonetheless, many of these civil wars, like in the Syrian case, cannot be seen as purely internal or domestic. The Syrian crisis has been greatly influenced by regional developments at the beginning, and its decline into a civil war led to the rise and development of a set of loyalties and alliances among internal, regional and international actors. The government of President Bashar al-Assad received a remarkable support –financial and military– from Iran, as a strategic regional ally, and Russia, as a key long-standing international ally, beside manpower reinforcement from sectarian (Shiʿite) militias like the Lebanese Hezbollah and the Iraqi Abu Fadl al-Abbas and al-Hashd al-Shaabi.[232] On the other hand, factions of the Syrian political opposition and the armed rebel groups –referred to as 'revolutionary forces'– formed separate bodies in correspondence with their diverse regional supporters and financiers such as Saudi Arabia, Qatar and Turkey, beside the western-led Friends of Syria Group on an international level.[233] Consequently, the conflict took the form of a proxy war that drew in different regional and world powers. The war at times also spilled over into Lebanon, showing a regional dimension of the Syrian crisis. Lebanon witnessed sporadic clashes between some Syrian rebel factions and pro-Assad militias such as Hezbollah. Syria-related clashes occurred occasionally on the Lebanese soil in the period between 2011-2017.[234] Damascus was further exposed to several Israeli airstrikes that targeted regime army bases, convoys and shipments of weapons.[235] Syria and Israel are purportedly at war since 1948, but the borderline remained quite since 1973 until the outbreak of the Syrian civil war. Besides, Turkey intervened militarily into northern Syria and targeted Kurdish-held areas in an attempt to prevent the establishment of a Kurdish self-rule or self-administration along its southern border, but its operations had been limited due to an American military presence alongside the Kurdish-led SDF troops, who jointly fought against ISIS in the group's de facto capital of Raqqa and other parts of northern Syria. After driving ISIS militants out of several areas in northern Syria, the Kurds announced the establishment of a self-rule in 2015 to run Kurdish-majority areas of northern Syria under the banner of "Federation of Northern Syria-Rojava". This has ignited an aggressive Turkish response for fear of a similar move by Turkey's Kurds, and the Turkish military then repeatedly bombed Syria's Kurdish areas in a bid to deter the alleged threat. Eventually, amid a declining American presence in northern Syria, the Turkish military and allied Syrian rebels took over a couple of predominantly Kurdish towns north of Syria under the pretext of eliminating threats to Turkish national security.[236] Furthermore, the emergence of radical Islamist groups, such as ISIS, led to the involvement of many jihadists from different parts of the world, who joined the Syrian conflict under the pretext of defending fellow Sunni Muslims against the Alawite regime of Assad and allied Shiʿite militias. This multifaceted intervention from numerous regional and international actors indicates the transnational characteristic of the Syrian civil war.

18. Beyond Sunni and Shia: Politico-Sectarian Roots of Contemporary Islamist Extremism

Unlike other "-isms" which have a semantic kernel that partly explains the use of a concept, extremism has no such a core that could provide guidance as to its meaning.[250] Extremism could take a political or a religious form, namely, 'political extremism' or 'religious extremism', and it is manifested by non-violent or violent activities. The term *extremism* is defined as the rejection, in thought or action, of democratic pluralism, and its operational heart is the suppression of difference and dissent and the elimination of the marketplace of ideas.[251] Extremism is also described as a set of activities -which involve beliefs, feelings, attitudes, strategies and actions- of a character far removed from the ordinary.[252] It is viewed as a quality that is radical in opinion, characterized by intolerance toward opposing interests and is the key motivation for terrorist behavior.[253] Extremists may cross the line through their willingness to engage in violent activities in order to accomplish their goals. Crossing the line turns extremists into terrorists who usually develop honorable and dignified arguments in a bid to rationalize and justify their violent acts toward people, religions or nations. According to Backes, the definition of extremism as a concept remains relativistic, yet extremists share a clear notion of what they absolutely oppose and struggle against, including pluralism, orientation toward common good of all people, self-determination by the majority of the people and the generally binding legal rules.[254] Furthermore, Schmid maintains that humans "have a tendency to think that others should also think like they do and therefore tend to assume that their own position is shared by the majority of other 'reasonable' individuals."[255] Thus, it may occur that those deemed to be extremists consider others as "extremist," like in the case of the al-Qaeda leader Ayman al-Zawahiri who once condemned ISIS as being "too extreme."[256]

In order to rise and establish itself, extremism undoubtedly requires a fertile ground. Iraq and Syria emerged in the first two decades of the 21st century as major incubators to extremist Islamist groups in the Middle East. In the aftermath of the 2003 war, Iraq suffered from a widespread chaos and security vacuum, coupled with intensifying sectarian rifts, which erupted at a governmental level and later reached the very core of the society. These were key factors that led to the rise of sectarian Shia militias such as al-Hashd al-Shaabi and the radical Sunni ISIS group. Meanwhile, as the Syrian uprising of 2011 descended into a civil war, extremist organizations like al-Qaeda and ISIS found a sufficient foothold and joined the conflict under the pretext of protecting fellow Muslims. The rise of religious extremism considerably deprived the Syrian and Iraqi people of their legitimate aspirations in establishing a pluralistic form of government based on democratic principles and willing to demonstrate respect to basic human rights. The anti-tyranny revolutionary era in these two countries was largely infiltrated and hijacked by some radical movements that sought to forcibly impose their extremist agenda on exhausted populations in war-ravaged areas.

Religious radicalism (*al-Taṭarruf al-Dīni*) is defined as a mode of thought and action that basically implicates the rejection of surrounding cultural values and embodiments perceived as nonindigenous or inauthentic to the religious tradition, which consequently entails defense of a tradition believed to be under siege.[257] The underlying impetus to the emergence and growth of radical Islamist activism is the failed secular modernization projects in the Middle East.[258] Radical Islamist ideology equips adherents with considerable strengths, and, at the same time, constitutes a source of constraints. Ideology is considered a crucial determinant of the ability of radical Islamist organizations to mobilize support, provide an alternative to the ideological superiority and control of the ruling class in the society, and to seize power. Radicalism, according to Richards, sprang up in the form of a political response to the deteriorating and deepening social, political, economic, and cultural crises in the Muslim World.[259] Besides, a rejectionist discourse to the West, democracy, secularism and liberalism seemingly has been employed by radical Islamist groups to incite a state of grudge and outrage among the already desperate Muslim youth and ultimately drag them into an alleged rebellion against local as well as international actors and ideologies claimed to be behind their miseries and provide them with a supposedly holy cause to fight for. Thus, the rise of radical Islam in the Middle East can be attributed to a multitude of factors, including government policy failure, rapid demographic growth, high unemployment and increasing poverty, which alienated a considerable proportion of the Muslim youth and opened the path to radical Islamist groups to emerge and expand. Radical Islamists were driven by various incentives, such as the search for alleged identity and recognition, an optimist aspiration of reaching an eventual transformation from marginalization to power, opposition to secular ideologies and frustration toward ruling regimes accused of apostasy and corruption. Moreover, war-ravaged countries like Syria and Iraq, where security vacuum and chaos have prevailed for years, have served as breeding grounds for radical Islamists to establish themselves.

The Islamic State –also known as Daesh, ISIS, ISIL or IS– is deemed to be the most powerful radical Islamist group in world history.[260] The significantly powerful image demonstrated by and portrayed about the group stems from the remarkable combination of features that are deemed to be unprecedented to exist in a single Islamic militia. This strong combination involves ideology, military power, ruthless violence, financial astuteness and a strategic social media campaign.[261] In order to better understand the development of the group into a powerful self-proclaimed caliphate, exploring its origins seems inescapable. The group arose from the remnants of al-Qaeda in Iraq, also known as AQI, an offshoot of al-Qaeda organization founded by Jordanian national Abu Musab al-Zarqawi in 2004. Al-Zarqawi initially founded the *Jamaʿat al-Tawḥid wal-Jihād* group in 1999. In 2004, he pledged allegiance to al-Qaeda leader Osama bin Laden. Subsequently, his group became known as AQI or al-Qaeda in Iraq. Both al-Qaeda and ISIS belong to the same family, namely Salafi-Jihadism (*al-Salafiyya al-Jihādiyya*), and share a similar worldview. The Salafi-Jihadi ideology, which rejects human-made laws, entails the replacement of state sovereignty with Allah's rule through the establishment of Qur'ānic-based states. This is deemed central to the worldview of all Salafi-Jihadis.[262] Yet, the origins of ISIS could be traced to the late 1980s, when al-Zarqawi headed to Afghanistan to join the Mujāhidīn[263] in the fight against the invading Soviet troops. In 2000, al-Zarqawi set up a training camp for jihadist fighters in Afghanistan with financial support from al-Qaeda, a step that enabled him to develop a recruitment network which attracted fighters whose backgrounds were mostly in line with his own: Muslim youth with low education and fragile theological knowledge of the Qur'ān, often radicalized in prison.[264] While his resources were considerably insignificant when he arrived in Iraq to establish a branch of al-Qaeda there, the intensifying sectarian clashes provided al-Zarqawi with an opportunity to get supporters and attain the required resources in order to establish and strengthen his radical organization.

The U.S.-led invasion of Iraq and the subsequent social turmoil resulted in the dismantling of governmental institutions and the formation of a political system that was largely based on *muḥāṣaṣa* or the distribution of power among communal, ethnic and tribal groups. Deteriorating socio-economic conditions in predominantly-Sunni parts of Iraq post-2003 is considered among the main factors that have pushed many Sunnis into cooperating with rising pro-Sunni militias for the sake of regaining some of the power they had lost subsequent to the fall of Saddam's regime. The sectarian-based political system and the tensions attributed to it are seen as a product of the destruction of the Iraqi state which followed the 2003 invasion. Therefore, Iraq can be viewed as a unique instance of how foreign intervention and failing state institutions and services paved the way to a condition of divisive discontent that was eventually exploited by ideologues such as al-Zarqawi. One of the key institutions that was dismantled subsequent to Saddam's removal was the military, which entailed the expulsion of tens of thousands of Sunni officers from their posts. Consequently, a state of resentment and rancor prevailed among the Sunni population in Iraq. Many Baathists, who were excluded from state services in post-2003 Iraq, were approached and recruited by al-Zarqawi's network. These new recruits, some of whom enjoyed remarkable military knowledge and experience that in some cases extended to the time of the Iraq-Iran war, would later hold high-ranking positions in the ranks of ISIS. However, the Baathists and al-Zarqawi basically had very little in common, except having a common enemy.[265] Initially, they resorted to him for weapons and military support, while he used them to provoke and spread chaos and to overthrow the U.S.-appointed government in Baghdad.

The Sunni insurgency in Iraq broke out with a few thousands of ex-Baathists fighting against the U.S. occupation. Thus, it was far from being an Islamic revolt in its early stage. However, al-Zarqawi's arrival to Iraq and his rapid popularity among anti-U.S. fighters on the ground weakened the Baathists and persuaded many to follow him. Meanwhile, Nouri al-Maliki, who then occupied the position of Prime Minister in the post-Saddam government, insisted on disregarding calls for inclusion and, simultaneously, pursued sectarian-driven policies, which contributed to the escalation of the sectarian divide and helped al-Zarqawi play on the feelings of excluded Sunnis. The latter then established AQI with the blessing of Osama bin Laden, who supported the idea of launching a collective war against Shia Muslims alongside the already mounting struggle against the Americans in Iraq. Al-Zarqawi sought a sectarian strategy that targeted the Shia population and its religious centers, having in mind that a Sunni-Shia sectarian civil war could eventually force the U.S. troops to withdraw. The leader of AQI believed that once Iraq's territorial unity had collapsed and the country turned into separate sectarian enclaves, he would have the advantage to become the emir of the Sunni-populated territory, and the region would turn into a breeding ground for the rise of a new generation of jihadists. Nevertheless, Abu Musab al-Zarqawi was killed in a U.S. airstrike on 7 June 2006, and he was replaced by Abu Ayyub al-Masri. A couple of months later, al-Qaeda in Iraq (AQI) merged with other armed groups and formed what became known as the Islamic State in Iraq (ISI), but maintained tentative ties with al-Qaeda. Al-Masri announced the establishment of

ISI on 15 October 2006, with Abu Omar al-Baghdadi as its leader.[266] The emerging ISI group was reportedly responsible for approximately 70 percent of the suicide attacks carried out in 2007 in Iraq.[267] As the U.S. troops extended their military campaign to hunt down ISI militants, the group was driven from Baghdad and many of its members were then concentrated in Mosul. The American military operations led to the death of prominent jihadists in the group and, by 2008, over 2000 ISI members were killed and nearly 8,800 were detained.[268]

Al-Maliki's authoritarian regime and his insistence to refrain from addressing the increasing sectarian divide and the deteriorating security conditions across the country added to the complexity of the Iraqi landscape.[269] After taking office in 2006, al-Maliki started a security consolidation and took control of Iraq's military troops, intelligence and security apparatus, special operations units and state ministries. This enabled the rising Shiʿite Prime Minister to target Sunni groups and overcome any coup attempts. Under al-Maliki, Iraq basically descended into a spiral of sectarian confrontations amid a state of uncertainty. Sullivan maintains that Iraq's political and military powers were "highly centralized in the Prime Minister Maliki's personal office. The national unity government, which was formed in the wake of the 2010 parliamentary elections, has given way to a de-facto majoritarian government in which Maliki has a monopoly on the institutions of the state."[270] Such practices evidently had significantly serious implications for Iraq in the years that followed. The U.S.-instituted process of *de-Baathification* was largely politicized by Nouri al-Maliki, who refused to integrate the Sunnis into state services, whether civilian or military, and excluded Sunni politicians for criticizing his regime.[271] The process of *de-Baathification* mainly entailed the elimination of the remnants of the Saddam Hussein regime and any elements of the then ruling Baath Party. The process was aimed at creating the basis for a democratic transition in Iraq. By 2009, al-Maliki government's excessive sectarian policies and practices toward the Sunnis led to mounting sectarian tensions, and ISI did not hesitate to intensify its suicide attacks in Baghdad and other cities and towns across Iraq, mostly Shia-populated. As a result, the popularity of and support for ISI considerably increased among Sunni tribal groups. This while the U.S. and allied Iraqi forces boosted their cooperation and coordination to combat Sunni insurgents and eliminate ISI leaders, an effort that eventually resulted in the killing of Abu Omar al-Baghdadi and Abu Ayyub al-Masri in April 2010. Subsequently, ISI found itself a new leader known as Abu Bakr al-Baghdadi, a man who would take al-Zarqawi's unfulfilled ambition further to the extreme. While al-Zarqawi sought an emirate, al-Baghdadi pursued –and considerably succeeded in– the reestablishment of an alleged caliphate, a long-standing goal and an ultimate aspiration among jihadists. According to Sekulow *et al.*, under the leadership of al-Baghdadi, ISIS has gone further than any other jihadist group to make that radical dream or reviving and reestabilishing the caliphate a present reality.[272] Within less than a decade, al-Baghdadi had gone "from quiet, pious obscurity to becoming the leader of one of the most feared" jihadist groups in history, yet people who knew him closely confirm that "he has always disliked the limelight and would never have pushed himself forward as a leader."[273]

After a little more than a year in the leadership of ISI, al-Baghdadi took the first step toward expanding his group's power through sending jihadist operatives from Iraq into Syria in July 2011—as the country was descending into civil war. One of the key figures among these militant operatives was Abu Muhammad al-Joulani, who, in early

2012, formed a Syrian branch of al-Qaeda, known as al-Nusra Front. While his operatives started to get engaged in the Syrian conflict, al-Baghdadi launched an unprecedented armed campaign under the banner "Breaking the Walls"[274] which targeted state institutions and included some eight prison breaks in Iraq in the period between July 2012-July 2013.[275] The ISI-led prison breaks freed many jihadists, who had been imprisoned by the Iraqi authorities on the background of participating in various AQI-led attacks against the state. The campaign gave al-Baghdadi much credit among the jihadists and showed him as a strong and influential leader whose capabilities cannot be underestimated. Although ISI was funding the operations of al-Joulani-led al-Nusra Front in Syria,[276] al-Baghdadi formed his own cell there to represent ISI directly and to guarantee his share of the pie in case any of future rifts with jihadists operating under al-Joulani's command. In March 2013, the Syrian regime troops were driven out of Raqqa, and the city fell to several anti-Assad groups, including Syrian opposition fighters, al-Nusra Front and ISI. While these ideologically different factions[277] shared control over Raqqa in the beginning, ISI began to bring in more military reinforcements from Iraq in a bid to consolidate power over the city and to expand its territory through opening new fighting fronts in Syria. In mid-April, al-Baghdadi moved into Syria's Raqqa and announced that ISI merged with al-Nusra Front to form the so-called Islamic State in Iraq and Syria (ISIS), which would unite jihadists in Iraq and Syria both militarily and territorially. However, al-Nusra's al-Joulani condemned the announcement and rejected an alliance with al-Baghdadi, stressing his group's allegiance to al-Qaeda. The ISIS leadership then considered al-Joulani "traitorous" and called al-Qaeda and its leader Ayman al-Zawahiri "a joke", beside accusing al-Qaeda of shifting its ideology and abandoning *tawḥīd* (monotheism) and *jihād*.[278] Al-Joulani's refusal to subordinate himself to al-Baghdadi and his newly founded group caused a major split among the jihadists, who had to either stress their loyalty to al-Qaeda and continue to fight in the ranks of al-Nusra Front, or pledge allegiance to al-Baghdadi and join his rising ISIS group. The consequences of the split surfaced in August 2013, when ISIS launched a major armed operation against al-Nusra Front and other Syrian Islamist rebel groups, such as Ahrar al-Sham (Aḥrar al-Shām) and Liwa' al-Tawhid (Liwā' al-Tawḥīd), in Raqqa and Aleppo.

Meanwhile, ISIS was expanding in Iraq amid ongoing social frustration agitated by the failing state services and a considerably dysfunctional political system, and the group was able to capture large territories by December 2013, including the Sunni-majority city of Fallujah and parts of Ramadi in the central province of al-Anbar.[279] The destruction of state services and the subsequent social turmoil triggered a deep sectarian divide between Sunni Muslims and Shia Muslims and propelled the rise of ISIS "from an inconsequential non-state actor to an Islamic state", and Iraq's dysfunctional and broken political system, which suffered from increasing factionalism, provided the group with "ideological nourishment."[280] Thus, ISIS exploited the situation in favor of its agenda through promoting itself as a protector to the marginalized Sunnis, and took Sunni-populated areas as strongholds for its operations.

In Syria, the increased military and logistical support from Shia powers like Iran and Hezbollah to the Assad regime was largely condemned and frequently and emphatically referred to by ISIS in an attempt to support its narrative of defending and protecting Sunni Muslims against a Shia domination. Thus, like in the case of Iraq, the sectarian dimension of the conflict in Syria was remarkably exploited by ISIS. Meanwhile, after a few months of heavy fighting against al-Nusra Front and Syrian rebel groups, ISIS eventually seized control of Raqqa city in January 2014, and declared it a capital of its self-proclaimed Islamic emirate. The so-called *emirate* was the initial form of proclamation claimed by ISIS in territories taken over by its militants, before the group officially claimed the establishment of a *caliphate* in June 2014. A few months later, the radical group took over the city of Mosul in Iraq's northwestern Nineveh province following a major offensive. ISIS then expanded its territories by seizing control of more areas across Syria and Iraq, including Tikrit and Deir ez-Zor, beside taking over key oil facilities—which would constitute a crucial resource for the group to fund its operations. The group's weapons arsenal was also growing to include U.S.-manufactured arms seized from Iraqi troops, machine guns and anti-tank rockets captured during clashes with Syrian rebel groups, as well as a certain quantity of chemical weapons obtained after capturing a chemical facility in Iraq.[281]

At the time, al-Baghdadi believed that his group's power had reached such a level that could enable him and his followers to finally reap the fruits of their alleged *jihād*. In a speech at the Grand al-Nuri Mosque in Mosul city, on 29 June 2014, Abu Bakr al-Baghdadi stated that his group was rebranding itself as the *Islamic State* (al-Dawla al-Islāmīya), announced the establishment of an alleged *caliphate* (Khilāfah) and proclaimed himself as *caliph* (Khalīfah) or the ruler of all Muslims. Although al-Baghdadi's self-proclaimed caliphate received a wave of criticism from leaders of renowned extremist groups, such as al-Qaeda and Taliban,[282] ISIS succeeded in attracting numerous jihadists from all over the world. The rapid advance on the ground further enabled ISIS to systematically dismantle the border between Syria and Iraq, in order to facilitate its operations on both sides of the borderline. It was then when the radical group announced the destruction of the Sykes-Picot border: "Allah facilitated that it [ISIS] step over the Sykes-Picot borders in its jihād."[283] In order to enhance its power in controlled territories and to legitimize its alleged caliphate, ISIS founded public institutions –including religious, judicial, educational, security, infrastructure and humanitarian– to reflect its vision and strategy at political and military levels in order to demonstrate its governance capacities. In a study about governance within the ISIS's self-proclaimed caliphate, Caris and Reynolds maintain that the group's project was not a mere empty rhetoric: "The idea of the caliphate that rests within a controlled territory is a core part of ISIS's political vision. The ISIS grand strategy to realize this vision involves first establishing control of terrain through military conquest and then reinforcing this control through governance. Available evidence indicates that ISIS has indeed demonstrated the capacity to govern both rural and urban areas in Syria that it controls. Through the integration of military and political campaigns, particularly in the provincial capital of Raqqa, ISIS has built a holistic system of governance."[284] Moreover, the group was able to diversify its sources of revenue in order to guarantee a considerably uninterrupted management of internal affairs in the controlled areas as well as its military operations that were aimed at expanding its territorial presence. ISIS basically relied on natural resources, foreign donations, taxes and fees, sale of antiquities, kidnapping for ransom, looting, confiscation and fine as key financial resources.[285] Nevertheless, in order to impose its rule over populations inhabiting areas under its control, ISIS committed numerous atrocities toward entire communities –such as the Yezidis who suffered forced displacement, mass killings and sex slavery at the hands of ISIS militants– or individuals who were accused of "apostasy" or other indictments for opposing the group or violating its strict rules.

Through its capable media outlets, ISIS produced and released many footages that depicted public beheadings, floggings, mass executions, and other forms of brutal practices in a bid to deliver and maintain an image of strength and ruthlessness toward its internal opponents and external enemies. The group also claimed responsibility for several terror attacks that targeted densely-populated locations in the West. Representing the most extreme manifestation of *Salafi-Jihadism*, ISIS received support from Salafi-Jihadis across the world, who hoped that its self-proclaimed caliphate would bring about a strict rule of Islamic *Sharīʿa*,[286] especially when the group made rapid advances against rivals and claimed gains that were deemed unprecedented among Salafi-Jihadi-guided radical groups. Thus, even though ISIS's power declined and its territories shrunk by end of 2017, the effects of its discourse and practices on the local level –in terms of sectarianism– and its influential role in the arena of global *Jihadism* in the period between 2014-2017 are believed to have long-term consequences.

While ISIS undoubtedly constitutes an instance of radical Sunnism, al-Hashd al-Shaabi remarkably represents Shiʿism in its extremist form. The rise and growth of both organizations reflect a deeply-rooted sectarian schism within the Muslim society, which has evidently ignited long-standing tensions in the region. As each group was seeking glorious triumph, territorial expansion and prevalence of dogmatically-guided agendas, the civilian populations on both sides of the battleground had to pay an inescapable price and endure unbearable conditions.[287] Both Sunni- and Shia-populated areas, as well as territories inhabited by minority communities, were targeted by such sectarian forces, which committed boundless atrocities.

When ISIS declared its caliphate following the capture of major cities such as Mosul, Fallujah and Tikrit, and vowed to march further to Baghdad, the Iraqi army and security forces appeared incapable of impeding the radical group's progress, and many Iraqi soldiers deserted or fled the battleground.[288] Following the ignominious collapse of the Iraqi army in the face of ISIS in June 2014, several Shia militias unified ranks to form al-Hashd al-Shaabi and fight under its umbrella in order to fill the vacuum and contribute to the defense of the capital Baghdad and the protection of the Shia-populated areas and worship centers across Iraq. The formation came in response to an edict or *fatwā* by Iraq's supreme Shia religious cleric Ayatollah Ali al-Sistani, who urged all capable men to assist in protecting the country, the population and the holy shrines, which he deemed to be a duty in the face of the existential threat posed by ISIS. Despite al-Sistani's relatively careful language in his edict, which basically stressed a national rather than sectarian duty to confront the jihadists of ISIS, his call has been interpreted in a sectarian context, and the developments on the ground eventually took the form of an unavoidable Shia-Sunni struggle. In his statement, Grand Ayatollah al-Sistani said: "Iraq and the Iraqi people are facing great danger, the terrorists [of ISIS] are not aiming to control just several provinces, they said clearly, they are targeting all other provinces including Baghdad, Karbala and Najaf. So, the responsibility to face them and fight them is the responsibility of all, not one sect or one party. The responsibility now is saving Iraq, saving our country, saving the holy places of Iraq from these sects."[289] Nevertheless, by mentioning the imminent threat to Karbala and Najaf, two holy Shia cities that are home to sacred shrines and hold a historical importance for the Shia sect, it may not come as a surprise that al-Sistani's edict has been interpreted in a sectarian context and eventually used by Shia militias as a source of inspiration to unite under the umbrella of the subsequently founded al-Hashd al-Shaabi to combat the Sunni extremists of ISIS and their alleged corroborators.

Interestingly, al-Hashd al-Shaabi included within its ranks Shia militiamen from various movements, who apparently decided to overcome their partisan differences for the sake of protecting the sect and its symbols. Among the foundational factions of al-Hashd were the pre-existing Shia armed groups that were previously active on the Iraqi soil in the period between 2003-2011 and continued to exist due to a remarkable Iranian support, such as Asaib Ahl al-Haq, Badr Organization and Kataib Hezbollah. Another kind of forces that joined the ranks of al-Hashd were the armed wings of sectarian Shia political parties in Iraq, which were already involved in the post-2003 civil war, such as al-Mahdi Army and Liwa' al-Shabaab al-Rasali –affiliated with the prominent Shia cleric Muqtada al-Sadr. Moreover, in response to Sistani's *fatwā*, new militias emerged comprising Shia volunteers from southern Iraq, mainly from Karbala and Najaf, and joined al-Hashd.[290] The growing recruitment network helped the emerging organization to gain an increased popularity and expand its power rapidly. Undoubtedly, the monopoly of power in Baghdad by Prime Minister Nouri al-Maliki, who appointed Shia officers to hold the most significant command positions within the army and security divisions,[291] enabled such Shia militias to grow and enjoy unprecedented freedom of movement and armament with a large Iranian support. Noteworthy, some factions within al-Hashd al-Shaabi pledged allegiance to al-Maliki and remained loyal to him as a member of al-Daʿwa Party, even after he resigned the office of Prime Minister under popular pressure in August 2014. It is also worth mentioning that Iran's support to al-Hashd al-Shaabi and its involvement in the already raging sectarian divide in Iraq did not remain restricted to the supply of arms, but developed further into organizing training programs and providing strategic planning to the militias operating on the ground, in a bid to boost their position and enable them to accomplish more military gains. Qassem Suleimani, then the commander of the Quds Force of the Iranian Revolutionary Guards Corpse (IRGC), guided several al-Hashd operations on the ground, along with other experienced Iranian military commanders.[292] Developing into a major force in the fight against ISIS in Iraq, by 2016 al-Hashd had already included over 60 armed factions under its umbrella and the number of its fighters exceeded 150,000.[293]

Through the numerous military campaigns it led across Iraq, al-Hashd has proven to be a crucial force in the war on ISIS and played a key role in preventing a further territorial expansion by the group. Al-Hashd, in cooperation with the Iraqi security forces, Kurdish Peshmerga and the U.S.-led coalition, were able to impede ISIS's advance and eventually brought the group to the brink of defeat through late 2017.[294] However, the confrontations transcended the battleground to reach the civilian population. Al-Hashd blamed the Sunnis for the rise and expansion of ISIS, accusing them of providing a fertile ground and a social incubator to the militants of the group. On 1 April 2015, al-Hashd militiamen took control of Tikrit after expelling ISIS from the city. In the aftermath of the alleged 'liberation' of the Sunni-populated city, the people of Tikrit reportedly suffered from revenge acts by militants of al-Hashd al-Shaabi.[295] The city turned into a scene of violence and looting, summary executions of unarmed civilians, and hundreds of houses were burned down. The atrocities were justified by al-Hashd through allegations of potential collaboration between the affected people and ISIS. Moreover, during the battle for the Sunni-majority city of Fallujah in mid-2016, the Shia paramilitary militias besieged the city and prevented food supplies from reaching civilians there as an act of collective punishment to the Sunni population inside the then ISIS-held Fallujah, which led to the starvation of dozens.[296] Until the city was fully retaken from ISIS on 30 June 2016, the human cost was deemed devastating.[297] Al-Hashd has been accused of exploiting the battle for sectarian purposes.[298] While many houses were demolished during the armed operations, hundreds of Sunni civilians were arrested and tortured –some of them were even beheaded and their corpses were desecrated– under the pretense that they have supported ISIS, and al-Hashd militiamen were blamed for committing acts of arson, crimes and human rights violations based on sectarian incentives.[299] Comparable incidents were reported in Mosul[300] and its environs during anti-ISIS operations and following the announced 'liberation' of the city on 9 July 2017, as Shia militiamen were accused of using Western-supplied arms to facilitate the forced disappearance of thousands of Sunni civilians, torture and extrajudicial executions, ethnic cleansing campaigns as well as wanton destruction of private property of Sunni families.[301] Hence, al-Hashd militiamen became a source of fear and dread for the Sunni population throughout Iraq. Such sectarian-based atrocities may be seen as a reflection of deeply-rooted hostility and grudge among Shia militiamen toward Sunni rivals, which substantially transcends a mere interim conflict between two radical groups such as al-Hashd al-Shaabi and ISIS. Power vacuum and uncertainty are considered as the main reasons for the rise and growth of al-Hashd al-Shaabi as well as ISIS, as these conditions often allow for the emergence of such militias to assume authority and impose their power on local populations and even gain a national recognition, like in the case of the Shia militias in Iraq.[302]

As al-Hashd al-Shaabi became an irrefutably strong force on the Iraqi soil, the central government under the leadership of Prime Minister Haidar al-Abadi had no other option than institutionalizing this powerful Shia group. Al-Maliki's legacy of unstable state institutions and widespread unrest –which resulted in the rise of sectarian militias in the first place– could neither be denied nor easily resolved by al-Abadi's administration.[303] Nevertheless, when Shia politician al-Abadi took office in September 2014, the already growing al-Hashd al-Shaabi drew his attention and was seen as a potential ally to the state in the then intensifying fight against ISIS. It is noteworthy that al-Hashd possessed several key characteristics that rendered the organization an acceptable force in the eyes of al-Abadi's government, including its significant military capacities and its members' fighting skills compared to the then collapsing Iraqi army; its remarkable ability to mobilize popular support among Iraq's Shia majority; its strong opposition to ISIS and willingness to combat Sunni jihadists by all means; being a Shia organization which could facilitate coordination between its leadership and the Shia-led central government; and its affiliation with Iran—major supporter of post-2003 Shia-dominated government in Baghdad. Indeed, regardless of its extremist sectarian nature, al-Hashd cooperated with other state services in the war on ISIS and coordinated its ground operations with the Iraqi Central Government—which made al-Hashd an indirect ally of the U.S.-led coalition in counter-terrorism efforts. Subsequently, al-Abadi, who was previously reluctant to reveal the full-scale cooperation between his government forces and al-Hashd al-Shaabi, declared in September 2015 that the group was part of the state's official forces, and openly legitimized it.[304] In a bid to manage and regulate its complex relationship with al-Hashd amid ISIS's decline, the Iraqi government took several steps, including recognizing al-Hashd al-Shaabi as a legitimate national anti-terrorism force operating under the Iraqi Prime Minister's National Security Council, beside maintaining al-Hashd's prestige and autonomy as an independent unit, and adopting a resolution under the Iraqi Council of Ministers to provide financial support to al-Hashd and salaries to its fighters.[305] The recognition of al-Hashd al-Shaabi as a legitimate force and rewarding it financially, beside institutionalizing the group and including it under state services, indicates the sectarian framework within which the Iraqi government principally operates. Taking into consideration the widespread violations of human rights and atrocities committed by al-Hashd al-Shaabi, the group could be seen as no less a threat to the social coexistence in Iraq and the region than ISIS.

While al-Hashd al-Shaabi focused its efforts on the mobilization of sectarian-guided Shia militiamen on a local and regional scale, ISIS's recruitment activities went further beyond such borders to reach radicalized recruits throughout the globe. Since its establishment and increasingly subsequent to announcing a self-proclaimed caliphate, ISIS was able to attract thousands of foreigners to its ranks in Syria and Iraq. The group made an undeniably remarkable success in terms of recruitment. ISIS recruiters began to operate at a global level and succeeded in inducting many foreign nationals into the group's ranks. ISIS considerably depended on its ability, through social media and the widespread recruitment cells, to demonstrate an image of being the most effective jihadist group across the world.

ISIS was often described as the strongest, most powerful, richest and most influential jihadist group ever. Making a comparison between ISIS and al-Qaeda, Sekulow points out, "If we have feared and fought al-Qaeda, consider the following facts about ISIS: ISIS is more brutal than al-Qaeda, so brutal that al-Qaeda tries to persuade ISIS to change its tactics; ISIS is the world's richest terrorist group; ISIS controls more firepower and territory than any jihadist organization in history."[306] In terms of recruitment in Islamic countries, initial approaches were more often made "via an intermediary or recruiter, but in the West, most said they had either directly messaged someone via Twitter or Facebook, or had been contacted by a friend, relative or acquaintance already inside Islamic State, to initiate their own 'migration' and to receive practical advice and logistical instructions."[307] Given the fact that a great number of recruits who emigrated to ISIS-controlled areas originate from non-Muslim countries, the group's recruitment process has mainly taken place online or by digital means. Even for those recruited by intermediaries or recruitment cells, the digital channels exploited by the group have played a key role in attracting potential recruits before making a final decision to join the so-called caliphate or seek a way toward joining the group. Hence, ISIS has made a remarkably extensive use of social media and launched competent, multi-lingual media outlets to increase the effect of its propaganda and present itself as a well-organized, rich and powerful force that is eligible to lead the Islamic jihād (*jihād Islāmī*) and bring about an unprecedented triumph to the allegedly oppressed Muslims.

Making a significant use of advanced technology to promote its radical version of Islam, ISIS was able to expand its arena of impact and influence to such a degree that has never earlier been accomplished by any other hardline organization. According to experts, digital media outlets run by ISIS became remarkable propaganda tools for the group to attract undeniably great numbers of recruits from different parts of the world. Moreover, the group's use of Twitter and other social media platforms helped circulate messages that held the power of inciting so-called lone wolves to launch domestic attacks across countries deemed to be enemies of the ISIS's self-proclaimed caliphate. ISIS's propaganda was described by the FBI Director as "unusually well done... broadcasting in something like 23 languages."[308] In order to attract recruits, ISIS employed several themes in its presentation of itself, including, but not limited to, rebranding itself into a caliphate as a utopian social space for Muslims; pledging allegiance to a caliph who is portrayed as a rightful ruler of all Muslims; raising sense of belonging among the mujāhidīn; presuming an alleged merciful redemption for each and every recruit who emigrate to the caliphate; emphasizing the greatness of martyrdom and the promised divine reward for those sacrificing themselves for the sake of the caliphate; presenting its courts as executors of divine justice; and promoting *jihād* as a righteous warfare against enemies of the caliphate.[309] Through such themes, ISIS was largely able to play on the emotions of a fairly considerable number of young men and women, and radicalize them to eventually join its ranks. Studies show that a majority of ISIS would-be members or sympathizers are youngsters of whom 89 percent are active online and over 70 percent use social media networks on a daily basis, and each spends an average of 19.2 hours a week online.[310] By January 2016, up to 30,000 foreign recruits from over 85 countries had already joined ISIS in Syria and Iraq. Major countries of origin of ISIS foreign recruits dragged into the conflict in Syria and Iraq respectively include Tunisia, Saudi Arabia, Jordan, Morocco, France, Russia, Lebanon, Turkey, Libya, Germany, UK, Uzbekistan, Pakistan, Belgium, Turkmenistan, Egypt, Bosnia, China, Netherlands and Australia, among others.[311] The majority of these recruits were men aged 15-35, mostly vulnerable, culturally isolated and marginalized individuals who had various incentives to join ISIS, such as status seeking, identity seeking or revenge seeking.[312] Attracting such a relatively large number of foreign recruits from dozens of countries across the world within a matter of couple of years is in itself a demonstration of the significant success of ISIS's propaganda and an affirmation of the cross-border influence and effectiveness of its discourse.[313]

The group took a careful recruitment approach through its multifaceted discourse to attract as many people as possible to its areas of control through calling not only for would-be fighters to join its battlefields, but also anyone who is willing to serve the caliphate within his/her area of expertise. ISIS sought –through its sophisticated propaganda– to entice potential jihadi wives and professionals such as engineers, doctors, media workers, and accountants in its endeavor to develop a new society under the banner of its so-called caliphate.[314] The ISIS threat raised widespread concerns among Western societies and enormously captured the attention of the public, as the group's propaganda machine continued to broadcast footages of young citizens of Western countries pledging loyalty to the group's leadership and heading to Syria and Iraq to join ISIS's ranks in the fight for the alleged caliphate. While some of these recruits shared the ethnic linkage of the local populations living under ISIS, many of them did not.[315] Nevertheless, the self-proclaimed caliphate seemed inclusive enough to accept any new recruit willing to serve under its black flag regardless of his or her ethnic affiliation, coming from an Islamic background or being a recent convert. Speaking of an alleged golden era of Muslim honor and dignity following the formation of the so-called caliphate, ISIS's late leader and self-proclaimed caliph Abu Bakr al-Baghdadi, in an audio speech broadcasted on 1 July 2014, said: *"O Muslims everywhere, glad tidings to you and expect good. Raise your head high, for today – by Allah's grace – you have a state and khilāfah, which will return your dignity, might, rights, and leadership. It is a state where the Arab and non-Arab, the white man and black man, the easterner and westerner are all brothers. It is a khilāfah that gathered the Caucasian, Indian, Chinese, Shāmī, Iraqi, Yemeni, Egyptian, Maghribī, American, French, German, and Australian. Allah brought their hearts together, and thus, they became brothers by His grace, loving each other for the sake of Allah, standing in a single trench, defending and guarding each other, and sacrificing themselves for one another. Their blood mixed and became one, under a single flag and goal, in one pavilion, enjoying this blessing, the blessing of faithful brotherhood. If kings were to taste this blessing, they would abandon their kingdoms and fight over this grace. So, all praise and thanks are due to Allah."*[316] Thus, al-Baghdadi tried through his speech to encourage Muslims from all over the world to emigrate to the then newly established caliphate which, according to him, would regain them their dignity and preserve their rights in a utopian-like social space, characterized by brotherhood among the mujāhidīn, regardless of their ethnic backgrounds or countries of origin. The death of al-Baghdadi in an American raid in northwestern Syria, on 27 October 2019, did not hinder the group's propaganda machine from proceeding with its activities. ISIS has implemented a multifaceted recruitment process in an attempt to reinforce its military ranks, increase its jihadi operations, enhance its institutions within areas under its control and give legitimacy to its de facto state among the Muslims. The recruitment process included online activities through social media, chat rooms and video indoctrination. Such channels enabled ISIS to promote its message and attract many new recruits, mostly on an individual basis. Yet the group also sought –and relatively succeeded in– the implementation of collective recruitment campaigns, mainly through messages delivered to crowds by religious leaders and conservative mosques.

Therefore, the process of indoctrination, radicalization and eventual recruitment took place personally as well as via the cyberspace, where the directed messages employed Qur'ānic verses, narrations of the Prophet, importance of jihād against the enemies of the Islamic caliphate, an urgency to assist Muslims suffering in war-ravaged countries like Iraq and Syria, and the obligation to regain dignity and might as Muslims. In order to demonstrate its cross-border influence and ability to target its enemies[317] through its widespread jihadi cells, ISIS launched a series of terrifying attacks[318] in the West that claimed dozens of lives and raised serious security concerns in key Western cities. Most of the attacks that hit Europe were launched by European nationals of Muslim origins who were radicalized and recruited by ISIS.[319] Amid ISIS's decline on the ground in Syria and Iraq after suffering heavy losses at the hands of the U.S.-led coalition and allied local troops, European officials voiced concerns about returning jihadists and how to deal with them, considering the potential threat they pose to their home countries.[320]

Conclusion

Thus, the rise and growth of sectarian Islamist militant organizations can be seen as a fruit of the emerging radical interpretations of the conception of *jihād*, the evolution of the movement of *Islamism* in accordance with the surrounding developments, and the historical sectarian divide that has been enormously utilized as a source of inspiration by such groups to seek exclusionary and violent tactics against the perceived *others*. The tactics, targets and arenas of operation pursued by such groups in the recent years indicate the dramatic evolution of the movement of *Jihadism*. Such a development constitutes an unprecedented transformation of the basic idea of *jihād* into a radical concept upon which some of the most fanatic and atrocious organizations are based in terms of thought, ideology, discourse and course of action. Besides, globalization and the digital age surface at the heart of the propaganda and recruitment campaigns launched by such radical groups to attract as many members to their ranks and sympathizers to their alleged cause as possible, and *jihād* has been hereby exploited as a brand to provide a religious legitimacy to their cause and emotionally manipulate the recipients of their increasingly ideological discourse. As a consequence, the cultural diversity that once enriched the Middle East on multiple levels, and the historical coexistence among the region's various communities, have been threatened and jeopardized by a few sectarian extremist groups, whose atrocities reached every single social component with different religious, doctrinal or ideological tenets. Ethnic and religious minorities have become a target to radical groups, and sedition was ignited and reinforced by the extremist discourse of sectarian organizations in the region. In addition, people from different social components have been suppressed for their critical position toward radical groups –whose oppressive practices and atrocities undermined public liberties and deprived people of their basic civil rights.

On the path of striving to impose and enforce an *Islamic system*, many non-adherents and opponents have been victimized, especially over the past two decades in crisis-afflicted parts of the Middle East, which basically illustrates the exclusionary nature of such an agenda, in contrast to what its pioneers claimed to be an inclusive system. The preferential and tendentious foundations upon which such a system is fundamentally built, especially when it comes to man-made laws, systems and currents of thought, can be viewed as an indication of the theocratic totalitarianism Islamist militant organizations tend to accomplish, and a reflection of how essentially unappreciative of diversity the system they strive for seems to be.

Crisis-stricken parts of the Middle East, particularly Syria and Iraq, reflect the dark outcome of a long chain of events and developments that have hit the region over decades on socio-political and religio-sectarian levels. Foreign interventions that led to the creation of nation-states without taking cultural, religious, sectarian and ethnic diversity in the region into consideration, beside failed attempts of democratization, have led to endless conflicts over disputed territories and forms of government, and eventually resulted in major political crises that the region is still encountering today. Security vacuum, chaos and sectarian confrontations are believed to have allowed radical groups to emerge and expand at the cost of vulnerable communities that have fallen victim to the sectarian-guided extremist agenda of such groups. While new radical Islamist groups continue to emerge, the extremist ideology to which most of such groups subscribe seems to remain intact and growing in impact, and new technologies appear to play a crucial role in the acceleration of spreading the message and goals of such ideologies across the globe to incite and inspire more activities among potential militants.

Religionized and sectarianized policies by governing authorities in various parts of the Middle East, and the associated practices of marginalization, discrimination, exclusion, misrepresentation and othering, ultimately produce and feed extremism, incite rancor and hostility among different components of the society, and allow radical groups a sufficient foothold to rise and thrive. The recent multifaceted developments in the Middle East, as discussed throughout this volume, hold serious implications for the future of the region and its populations, and the world as a whole in this era of globalization. The arduous journey of searching for efficient approaches to dismantle the extremist sectarian-guided ideology of radical Islamist groups, and methods to deter its threat, begins with understanding and comprehending the fundamental elements of such an ideology, the conditions that led to its emergence in the first place, and the agenda its adherents tend to realize, and the pages of this volume constitute an attempt in this direction.

Note on Transliteration

The topics covered within the framework of this volume necessitate the employment of various Arabic terms. These terms are mainly transliterated by the author in accordance with the conventions of the International Journal of Middle East Studies with diacritic markings. There are, however, some exceptions. The Arabic alphabetic system comprises twenty-eight letters, of which fifteen are consonants, phonetically comparable to the English *b*, *d*, *f*, *h*, *j*, *k*, *l*, *m*, *n*, *r*, *s*, *t*, *w*, *y* and *z*. Three other consonants in Arabic reflect particular sounds as in the English *sh* and both the voiced and voiceless *th*, which are orthographically represented by a combination of two letters. Besides, there are four unfamiliar consonants that emerge in Arabic describable as the emphatic parallels of the English sounds *d*, *s*, *t* and the voiced *dh*. Another two consonants sound as the voiced and voiceless French *r*, while the remaining four consonants are to be considered as entirely unfamiliar, including the glottal stop. In the case of the familiar fifteen Arabic consonants that hold phonological features comparable to that of English sounds, explicit Latin parallel graphemes are used. Whereas various symbols are employed while transcribing the other unfamiliar consonants. Hence, the unique Arabic letters transcribed throughout this volume include: glottal stop [']; voiceless interdental fricative [th]; voiced palato-alveolar sibilant [j]; voiceless pharyngeal constricted fricative [ḥ]; voiceless velar fricative [kh]; voiced interdental fricative [dh]; voiceless palatal sibilant [sh]; voiceless emphatic post-dental fricative [ṣ]; voiced emphatic post-dental stop [ḍ]; voiceless emphatic post-dental stop [ṭ]; voiced emphatic post-interdental fricative [ẓ]; voiced pharyngeal fricative [ʿ]; voiced uvular fricative [gh]; long open front unrounded [ā]; long close back rounded [ū]; long close front unrounded [ī]. Nonetheless, certain terms, such as the Arabic names of organizations or acronyms, and particular concepts, which are derived from Arabic and transcribed into a comprehensive and straightforward Latin form, do not fall under this transliteration system for their already prevalent use and commonness.

Glossary

ʿAdl

Justice; fair and equal division; justice handed out by a sovereign or a *qāḍī*. According to the *Muʿtazilites*, *ʿadl* refers to divine justice. These moralist rationalists emphasized that humans have free will land that therefore God cannot be held responsible for evil.

'Ahl al-Bayt

Members of the household of the Prophet Muhammad. The term is commonly used to refer to the descendants of the Prophet's daughter Fatima and her husband ʿAli ibn Abi Talib (the prophet's cousin and son-in-law), as the only ones qualified to become Imāms.

'Ahl al-ḥall wal-ʿaqd

Elite scholars and clerical authorities who loose and bind. Refers to the representatives of the *'umma* who come together to arrive at a consensus of the community with regard to a religio-political question.

'Ahl al-Kitāb

People of the Book or Possessors of Scripture. This expression from the Qur'ān refers to the Christians and the Jews who are deemed to be the first to have received the monotheist revelation upon which Islam is established.

'Ahl al-Sunna wal-Jamāʿa

People of tradition; followers of the traditions of the Prophet Muhammad; upholders of the Sunna and the community.

Akhlāqīyāt al-Islām

Ethical principles of the Islamic faith and tradition.

Alawite/ʿAlawiyya

Minority sect within Shia Islam whose followers consider the duties of Islam as symbolic rather than applied obligations. The deification of ʿAli is the basic doctrine of the Alawite faith. The Alawites interpret the Pillars of Islam (the five duties required of every Muslim) as symbols, and therefore do not practice these Islamic duties, and many of their practices are secret. They consider themselves as moderate Shiʿites. As the roots of Alawism lie in the teachings of Muhammad ibn Nusayr an-Namiri, who was a Basran contemporary of the tenth Shiʿite Imām, the group is frequently referred to as *Nuṣayriyya* or *Namiriyya*.

Al-'Amr bil-maʿrūf wal-nahī ʿan al-munkar

Islamic call to command good and forbid evil; the ordering of the good (which is commended) and the prohibition of the bad (which is reprehensible); to promote virtue. It is considered to be a formula that constitutes one of the cornerstones of social and economic morality in Islam, referring to the basic principles of *ḥisba* (accountability).

Al-aʿmāl bi-l-jawāriḥ

Reflection of confidence in faith through activities with the limbs; an aspect of *'īmān* (faith).

Al-'Arkān al-Khamsa

Notorious five duties incumbent on each Muslim. These include the Muslim profession of faith (*al-Shahāda*), prayer (*Ṣalāt*), the distribution of alms to the poor (*Zakāt*), the fasting of Ramadan (*Ṣawm*), and the pilgrimage to Mecca for those financially and physically capable (*Ḥajj*).

ʿAmalu l-qalb bil-niyya wal-ʿazm

Spiritual intention and determination.

ʿAmalu l-isān bid-daʿwa wal-bayān

Communication for the sake of invitation and clarification.

ʿAmalu l-ʿql bir-raʾī wal-tadbīr

Intellectual opinions and planning.

ʿAmalu l-badan bil-qitāl

Physical effort in combat.

ʾAqalliyya

Minority.

ʿAqīda

Doctrinal creed. Refers to an article of faith. The *ʿaqīda* constitutes the foundation of *ʾīmān* or faith. It is one of the essential components of the Islamic belief system.

Al-ʿAql wal-naql

Reasoning and transmission.

ʾArkān al-Islām

Notorious pillars of Islam or the five duties incumbent on each Muslim. These include the Muslim profession of faith (*al-Shahāda*), prayer (*Ṣalāt*), the distribution of alms to the poor (*Zakāt*), the fasting of Ramadan (*Ṣawm*), and the pilgrimage to Mecca for those financially and physically capable (*Ḥajj*).

ʿAṣabiyya

Group feeling. According to Ibn Khaldun, the concept of *ʿaṣabiyya* basically entails a process of developing group relations and ties as a key factor for empowering a community and ensuring the survival of its identity and basic values against any outside danger.

ʾAṣḥāb al-bāṭin

People of internal reality. The Ṣūfī vision of greater jihād as being the "root" of the general concept of jihād and assigned to *ʾaṣḥāb al-bāṭin*.

'Ashurā'

Ritualistic remembrance of the death of ʿAli's younger son Hussein, who was murdered during a battle with Sunni forces in Iraq's Karbala in 680. The Shiʿites believe that the tale of Hussein's martyrdom holds moral lessons for the community, and it considerably reinforced and strengthened Shia religious beliefs and practices.

Bāṭin

Esoteric aspect; hidden meaning of the *Qur'ān*, the search for which constitutes the foundation of the esoteric exegesis pursued by the Shiʿites and the followers of *Ṣufism*.

Bayʿa

Oath of allegiance; swearing allegiance by Sunni Muslims to the Caliph, thus conferring on him the legitimacy of his power.

Bidʿa

Heretical or deviant doctrinal innovation. It implicates a prohibited and sinful religious innovation. The term is used in religious law (*fiqh*) to describe any practice, doctrine or belief contrary to the earliest form of Islam.

Dār al-Ḥarb

House of war; Territory of war that basically consists of lands that are not yet conquered by Muslims. These are inhabited either by the "People of the Book", namely Jews and Christians, or polytheists. These territories must be conquered by Muslims by means of war (*ḥarb*) with no possibility of peace (*ṣulḥ*).

Dār al-Islām

House of Islam; Islamic-controlled territory; lands conquered by Muslims and subjected to the religious and social laws of the Sharīʿa.

Daʿwa

Politico-religious call, mission. Refers to the call to conversion to Islam; the invitation of non-Muslims to convert to Islam.

Dawla

State or empire.

Dhikr

Frequent mention and remembrance of God. It refers to the repetition of the name of God or of his Beautiful Names (*Asmā' Allah al-Ḥusna*).

Dīn

Faith or religion.

Faqīh (pl. fuqahā')

Jurist. According to the Shia, the *faqīh* enjoys all the prerogatives and rights required for governing the *'umma*.

Farḍ (pl. farā'iḍ)

Prescription or obligation; religious, social or moral duty.

Farḍ ʿayn

Individual duty; obligation and duty of every individual member of the Muslim community.

Farḍ kifāya

Collective duty that could be performed by a group of volunteers who are willing and determined to perform the duty on behalf of the entire community.

Fasād

Corruption, depravity, perversion and disorder that the community of Muslims should shun.

Fatwā (pl. fatāwā)

Non-binding juristic opinion; Judicial advice or legal opinion on a point of Islamic law (*Sharīʿa*) given by a qualified jurist in response to a question concerning a current case or contemporary issue.

Fiqh

Islamic jurisprudence. There are various types of jurisprudence in Islam. Therefore, the word *fiqh* is often accompanied by a suffix, like in *fiqh al-muwāzanāt* (the jurisprudence of balances, measuring the relative benefits and harms of a specific practice or action).

Fī ʿuqri dārih

On their own soil; in their own territory.

Al-Firqa al-Nājiya

The saved denomination. Refers to the way the Salafis define themselves. The *ḥadīth* refers to an anticipated divide within the Muslim community, marked by the rise of different currents, mostly deviant, except for one group of Muhammad's followers who will remain pure in their belief and practice Islam in accordance with God's Order and will thus eventually prevail.

First Fitna

First Muslim civil war that broke out during the Rāshidun Caliphate in 656 and continued until 661. The First Fitna led to the establishment of the Umayyad dynasty.

Fitna (pl. fitan)

Disorder; spreading schism; inciting divide. See *First Fitna.*

Ghayba

Refers to the occultation of the Twelfth Imām Muhammad al-Mahdi. According to Twelver Shiʿism (*Itna ʿAsharis*), Imām al-Mahdi, also known as the 'Awaited Imām' or 'Hidden Imām', has disappeared from a cave below a mosque in 874 and will reappear at the end of time to bring absolute justice and peace to the world.

Ḥadd (pl. ḥudūd)

Legal sentence; punishment; limit; boundary. The term is used in the *Qur'ān* in reference to restrictive prescriptions that are divine in origin.

Ḥadīth

Narratives of the Prophet's words and actions; collections of teachings, sayings, actions and traditions attributed to the Prophet Muhammad. The *ḥadīths* are collected in volumes, the most famous of which are: Bukhari, Muslim, Tirmidhi and Daud.

Ḥajj

Pilgrimage to Mecca for those financially and physically capable. *Ḥajj* is the fifth pillar of Islam.

Ḥākimiyya

Dominion of God and His law; God's might and rule. It basically refers to securing God's sovereignty in the political system.

Ḥalāl

Permissible.

Ḥall (pl. ḥulūl)

Solution.

Ḥanafī

Ḥanafism; a Sunni school of Islamic law founded by Abu Hanifa in 767 A.D. in Iraq. The *Ḥanafī* is deemed the oldest school of Islamic law. It was the dominant school of law in the Ottoman Empire. The Sunni legal schools place reliance on analogy in formulating verdicts and judgements, incorporating narrations and teachings of the Prophet Muhammad and his companions, known as the *Ḥadīth*, into their jurisprudential interpretations and verdicts differently. *Ḥanafism* follows the principle of *istiḥsān* (search for the best solution) and increasingly employing *ra'y* (personal reflection). *Ḥanafism* espoused views that are deemed to be less strict than those of other schools of Islamic law.

Ḥanbalī

Ḥanbalism; a Sunni legal and theological school founded by Imām Ahmed ibn Ḥanbal in 855. It formulates verdicts and judgements based on narrations and teachings of the Prophet Muhammad and his companions. *Ḥanbalism* is noted for its literalism, and this school of jurisprudence is represented today by *Wahhabism*. *Ḥanbalism* was associated with the rise and development of a traditionalist tendency accused of *tashbīh* (anthropomorphism).

Ḥarām

Forbidden or illicit.

Ḥarb Muqaddasa

Holy war.

Hawā

Caprice, vagary or passion. Refers to doctrinal errors or deviations. The term also refers to doctrinal errors or deviations.

Hijra

Emigration of the Prophet Muhammad and the first Muslims from Mecca to Medina. The date, established by the first caliph Abu Bakr as 16 July 622, marks the beginning of the Muslim era and its calendar. The term *hijra* is also used by Muslims who leave a hostile land for a region where they settle until they are fully equipped and ready to return as conquerors. Such a *hijra* is claimed to be inspired by that of Muhammad.

Ḥisba

Accountability within the framework of the Islamic call to command good and forbid evil.

Ḥizb (pl. aḥzāb)

Party, group or faction.

Ḥujja

Proof; argument.

Ḥukm (pl. 'aḥkām)

Islamic rulings, based on jurisprudence (*fiqh*).

'Iftā'

Issuing a judicial advice or legal opinion on a point of Islamic law (*Sharī'a*) given by a qualified jurist in response to a question concerning a contemporary issue.

Al-'Ījābiyya

Positive orientation.

Ijmā'

Consensus.

Ijtihād

Independent judgement; independent juristic reasoning by a competent scholar who employs spiritual sources to deduce a legal ruling.

'Ilm (pl. 'ulūm)

Knowledge.

'Imām

Guide or leader. A title that, according to the Shia, indicates leadership and signifies blood relation to the Prophet. 'Ali's descendants (*'Imāms*) undertook the leadership of the Shia community. Serving as a political and spiritual leader, each Imām appointed a successor and passed down spiritual knowledge to the following leader, according to the Shia doctrine.

'Imāmah

Imamate or the leadership of the infallible Shia Imāms.

'Īmān

Faith or belief in Islam. The concept is typically tied to the acceptance of six core articles of the Islamic faith: God, prophets, angels, divine books, the day of judgement, and predestination.

Al-'Īmān wal-'amal

Belief and practice.

'Iṣlāḥ

Reformation. It also refers to the movement of *Reformism* that emerged in Egypt at the end of the nineteenth century with the objective of giving new life to Islam by means of returning to the original form and to the ideas of the ancients (*salaf*). The pioneers of the Islamic reformist movement sought to accomplish these objective in different way. Jamal al-Din al-Afghani opposed British imperialism in Egypt and India, rejecting the influence of western materialism; Muhammad 'Abduh set about modernizing the educational system at al-Azhar and reforming the legal organization; and Rashid Rida established the journal of al-Manar to advocate the restoration of the caliphate –which was abolished in Turkey in 1924– and called for the reopening of the door of *ijtihād* (independent juristic reasoning) in order to change particular aspects of *fiqh* (religious jurisprudence).

'Iṣma

Impeccability, faultlessness and infallibility. For Twelver (*Ithna 'Ashari*) and Sevener (*'Ismā'īli*) Shi'ites, *'Alid imāms* are believed to be impeccable (*ma'ṣūmūn).*

'Ismāʿīli

Also known as the *Sevener Shiʿism*. It constitutes the second largest sect among the Shiʿites. The *'Ismāʿīli* sect emerged in the eighth century and its followers only recognize the first seven Imāms. The seventh Imām was named Ismail, thus the sect derived its name from his (Ismailis) and his position in the sequence of ʿAli's successors (Sevener). The Ismailis are historically known for pursuing territorial and military power and have founded strong states that took an active part in the Islamic history. The *'Ismāʿīlis* are also referred to as the followers of the hidden meaning of the *Qur'ān* or *Bāṭiniyya*.

Isteʿdād

Refers to being fully willing to engage in jihād and sacrifice for the cause of God.

Istiḥlāl

Advocating the permissibility of a certain behavior or action; rendering a particular action permissible through argument based on the interpretation of a certain religious text.

Istiṣlāḥ

Principle or method employed within the framework of religious jurisprudence (*fiqh*) which implicates taking into consideration the general interest (*maṣlaḥa*). This method was favored by the followers of *Mālikism* for the sake of resolving practical problems posed by the application of the Islamic law (*Sharīʿa*).

Ithna ʿAshari

Also known as *Twelver Shiʿism*. It constitutes the largest sect of Shiʿites. The *Ithna ʿAsharis* believe that the Prophet's spiritual authority and religious leadership were passed on to twelve of his descendants, beginning with ʿAli, Hasan and Hussein. They believe that the 12th Imām, Muhammad al-Mahdi, known as the Awaited Imām or Hidden Imām, has disappeared from a cave below a mosque in 874 and will reappear at the end of time to bring absolute justice and peace to the world.

Al-Iʿtiqād bi-l-qalb

Acknowledgement of faith in the heart; an aspect of *'īmān* (faith).

Jahl

Ignorance.

Jāhiliyya

Pre-Islamic days of ignorance; lack of enlightenment; lack of knowledge.

Jihād

Struggle for a noble cause or striving for the cause of God.

Al-Jihād al-'Akbar

The *greater jihād* which, according to the Ṣūfī doctrine, entails an internal spiritual struggle in the path of God against worldly trials.

Al-Jihād al-'Aṣghar

The *lesser jihād*. It refers to an external struggle for the sake of Islam, including fighting for God's cause on the battlefield or any form of physical action in defense of Islam.

Jihād al-Dafʿ

Defensive struggle.

Jihād al-Jazā'

Military jihād. It is primarily assigned to kings and emirs of Muslims. *Jihād al-Jazā'* is deemed a mere branch of the greater jihād.

Jihād al-Ṭalab

Proactive or offensive struggle.

Jihād bil-ḥujja

Jihād with argument.

Jihād bil-lisān

Jihād of the tongue.

Jihād bil-qalb

Jihād of the heart.

Jihād bil-sayf

Jihād of the sword.

Jihād bil-yad (bil-ḥaraka)

Jihād of the hand; activism.

Jihād fī sabīl Allāh

Striving in the path of God.

Jihād Madani

Refers to the employment of force and military fighting alongside *Daʿwa*, which is stressed by Ibn Taymiyya as the best form of and true jihād for its potential efficiency. In order to support his claim, Ibn Taymiyya quotes the *Qur'ānic* verse: "You are the best nation produced for mankind. You enjoin what is right and forbid what is wrong and believe in Allah. If only the People of the Book (*'Ahl al-Kitāb*) had believed, it would have been better for them. Among them are believers, but most of them are defiantly disobedient."

Jihād Makki

Refers to struggle with *ʿilm* or knowledge, as symbolized by the Prophet's *Daʿwa* or call to Islam in Mecca, which comes in the form of *jihād bil-ḥujja* (jihād with argument). Hence, *jihād makkī* implies the call for obeying the Islamic teachings and abiding by the *Sharīʿa* among the Muslims and the invitation to Islam among the non-Muslims. This type of jihād is referred to by several modern scholars as inward jihād and jihād against the lower self.

Jizya

Refers to the tax imposed on non-Muslim People of the Book (*'Ahl al-Kitāb*) residing in a Muslim-controlled area. The concept of *Jizya* basically implicates calling on non-Muslims to either convert to Islam or pay the *Jizya*. Those who fail to submit to one of these conditions will eventually have no choice but to fight for their lives.

Juhd

Effort.

Kāfir (pl. kuffār)

Infidel; unbeliever; apostate.

Khawārij

Rebellious sect that emerged during the *First Fitna*, operating in accordance with the belief that any authority they considered as illegitimate and not abiding by God's dominion had to be overthrown for judgement belongs to God alone. The *Khawārij* (*Khārijites*) arose in opposition to both ʿAli and Moʿawiya upon the occasion of the arbitration following the Battle of Ṣiffīn (657). They had been part of ʿAli's army, but once the question of the Caliphate was said to be decided by means of negotiation, they, over twelve thousand members, decided to leave (*Kharajū*), believing that such a matter cannot be compromised, since the decision was God's alone. They were referred to as "old believers", given their puritanism or nostalgia to the Caliphate of ʿUmar. The *Khārijites* deemed the upheavals of the Muslim politics as a fall from perfection. They were also against the Arab patronage over non-Arab converts to Islam. The *Khārijites* were mostly public reciters of the Qur'ān (*qurrā'*). They believed in the obligation of revolting against any leader who has sinned. According to the *Khārijite* doctrine, major sins are deemed to be beyond salvation and in violation with the basic condition of being a believer, making a sinner *de facto* an apostate, without remedy. They believed that if a Muslim sinned, then he could not possess a perfect state of soul, and therefore was not really a Muslim or has even turned against Islam. To sin proved one's inward apostasy, and, hence, a sinner could be put to death. The *Khārijites* went so far as to consider all but themselves unbelievers and traitors of Islam.

'Al-Khulafā' 'al-Rāshidūn

The four rightly-guided Caliphs or successors of the Prophet Muhammad; Abu Bakr al-Siddiq (632-634), ʿUmar ibn Khattab (634-644), ʿUthman ibn Affan (644-656), and ʿAli ibn Abi Talib (656-661).

Kufr

Infidelity or disbelief.

Kufr Aṣghar

Lesser unbelief or involvement in an insignificant sin. It mainly occurs due to ignorance (*jahl*) or misinterpretation of religious and jurisprudential texts, and it does not necessarily place the one involved outside the faith.

Kufr Akbar

Greater unbelief or involvement in a grave sin. It occurs while the one involved is fully aware of the fundamental principles of the faith and has correct and clear interpretations at his or her disposal, and it leads to labelling him or her as *kāfir* and consequently to *'iqāmat al-ḥadd* (carrying out punishment). The involvement in *kufr akbar* often concerns questions relating to *tawḥīd al-rubūbiyya* (the oneness of the dominion of God). It emerges as a result of *iʿtiqād* (belief) in the concerned behavior or action, an attempt to render that behavior permissible (*istiḥlāl*), or a conscious effort (*juhd*) to demonstrate one's rejection of Islam.

Luṭf

Benevolence.

Maʿād

Judgement Day.

Madhhab (pl. madhāhib)

Refers to a school of jurisprudential thought. There are four jurisprudential schools in normative Sunni Islam. These include the *Ḥanafī*, *Shāfʿī*, *Mālikī* and *Ḥanbalī*.

Mālikī

Mālikism; a Sunni school of jurisprudence founded by Mālik ibn Anas in 795 in the Arabian Peninsula. *Mālikism* placed a great emphasis on the importance of the tradition (*Ḥadīth*). It made great efforts to find solutions to particular problems of importance to the *al-maṣlaḥa al-ʿāmma* (general/public interest) by means of the method of *istiṣlāḥ* (principle of taking into consideration the general interest).

Manhaj (pl. manāhij)

Methodology employed to accomplish a particular virtue or ideal.

Mashrūʿ

Refers to legitimate and justified actions based on Islamic teachings and values.

Maṣlaḥa

Interest.

Mawla

Master or spiritual leader to whom a group of people adhere.

Muʿāmalāt

Dealings or social rules that make up the second part of any treatise on religious law (*fiqh*) and following the acts of worship (*ʿibādāt*).

Mujaddid

Reviver of Islam.

Mujāhid (pl. mujāhidūn)

Struggler for the cause of God.

Mujtahid

Supreme religious scholar.

Muḥāṣaṣa

The distribution of power among communal, ethnic and tribal groups.

Munāfiq (pl. munāfiqūn)

Hypocrite.

Mushrik (pl. mushrikūn)

Polytheist.

Murji'a

Murji'ites, from *irjā'* (postponement or deferment); a sect of early Islam that may be termed *quietists*. The *Murji'a* believed that serious sins are offset by faith and that punishment for them is not everlasting. Hence, they withheld condemnation and judgement of sinners in this world. This position has led to political univolvement. The *Murji'ites* are believed to have emerged in reaction to the extremism of the Khārijites, who attribute to sin a definitive nature, labelling the sinner as unbeliever and requiring immediate punishment. The *Murji'a* is also considered to be a school of theology that refused to exclude from the community those who were found guilty of grave sins. They justified this attitude with the reference to *qadar* (divine decree) which determined human actions.

Muʿtazila

Muʿtazilites, from *iʿtizāl* (distancing oneself or withdrawing); an influential school of theology and a politico-religious movement characterized by the role it gave to *ʿaql* (reason) in the interpretation of doctrine. The *Muʿtazila* believed in *tawḥīd* (oneness of God), *ʿadl* (divine justice) implying human free will, divine reward and punishment implying the impossibility of any form of *Shafāʿa* (intercession) on *yawm al-dīn* (Day of Judgement), and the obligation to promote virtue (*al-'amr bil-maʿrūf wal-nahi 'an al-munkar*). One of the key beliefs of the *Muʿtazila* implicates an intermediate position (*manzila bayna-l-manzilatayn*) of the sinful Muslim, according to which a sinner is considered to be neither a believer nor an infidel, but somewhere between the two positions. Hence, their *iʿtizāl* stems from the fact that they tended to distance themselves from passing an absolute judgement on any Muslim involved in a grave sin. The *Muʿtazila* emerged out of, or inserted itself into, the controversies of the civil war that broke out during ʿAli's Caliphate and the absolute black-and-white condemnatory views of the *Khārijites*.

Muwaḥḥid (pl. Muwaḥḥidūn)

Monotheist.

Naql

Transmission.

Nifāq

Hypocrisy.

Niyya

Refers to having the right intention before declaring or being engaged in *jihād*.

Niẓām Islāmi

Islamic system; *Sharīʿa*-based political order.

Nubuwwa

Muhammad's messengership.

Al-Qaḍā' wal-Qadar

Divine will and predestination. It constitutes one of the six articles of *'īmān*.

Al-qawl bi-l-isān

Voicing internal faith by the tongue; an aspect of *'īmān*.

Qatl

Murder.

Qawānīn waḍʿiyya

Man-made laws that are deemed inferior to divine laws or the *Sharīʿa*.

Qitāl

Fighting or engagement in armed combat.

Qiyās

Reasoning by analogy.

Rāfiḍa (pl. rawāfiḍ)

Rejectionists. *Rāfiḍa* is a pejorative term for Shia. The Sunnis, who constitute the vast majority within the Muslim community today, endorse and approve the first four Caliphs, including ʿAli, as *'al-Khulafā' 'al-Rāshidūn* or the Rightly-Guided successors of the Prophet. This while the Shiʿites insist on the idea that ʿAli and his descendants were the sole rightful successors instead. Taking such a position with respect to the succession of the Prophet has resulted in branding them as *rāfiḍa* or rejectionists.

Al-Rabbaniyya

Divinity.

Ridda

Apostasy. The term was first used to stigmatize the rebellion of the Arab tribes who, following the death of the Prophet Muhammad, refused to obey the first caliph Abu Bakr and who were vigorously opposed. It later came to mean any form of departure by a Muslim from the beliefs and practices of Islam. The *Ridda* is punishable by death based on legal sentence (*ḥadd*).

Ṣaḥāba

Companions of the Prophet Muhammad. They are considered the earliest converts to Islam.

Ṣaḥwa (pl. Ṣaḥawāt)

Awakening. It refers to a chain of various revivalist movements in the Gulf, the Levant and North Africa.

Ṣalāt

Prayer. *Ṣalāt* is the second pillar of Islam.

Al-Salaf al-Ṣāliḥ

Pious predecessors. These include the Prophet's contemporary companions (*al-Ṣaḥāba*), the last of whom died around the year 690; the generation that followed and known as *tābiʿīn*, lived until 750; and the third generation referred to as *tābiʿ tābiʿīn*, the last of whom died around 810. These three generations are viewed as the founders of and participants in a golden era of authenticated, attested and orthodox Islam. This arises in a ḥadīth of the Prophet in which he tackles the characteristics of the finest Muslims as "Of the generation to which I belong, then of the second generation, then of the third generation."

Salafiyya

Salafism movement. The movement fundamentally entails the revival and maintenance of the version of Islam specifically as understood and practiced by the *al-salaf al-ṣāliḥ*.

Saqīfa

The term *Saqīfa* is derived from the name of a place known at the time as *Saqīfat Bani-Saʿidah*, where the Anṣar gathered subsequent to the Prophet's death to discuss his succession. In Arabic, the term *Saqīfa* means roof, ceiling or arch under which issues of general communal concern were discussed.

Ṣawm

Fasting Ramadan. Ṣawm is the fourth pillar of Islam.

Shafāʿa

Intercession on behalf of sinful Muslims. The act of Shafāʿa is not possible according to the *Qur'ān*. However, according to the ḥadīth it can be exercised by Muhammad on the Day of Judgement (*yaum al-dīn*).

Shāfʿī

Shāfiʿism; a Sunni school of jurisprudence, founded by Muhammad ibn Idris al-Shāfʿi in 819. It was established alongside *Mālikism* and *Ḥanafism* in the ninth century. *Shāfiʿism* was mainly characterized by the constant attempts to provide a precise definition of the functioning of *qiyās* (reasoning by analogy).

Shahāda

Muslim profession or proclamation of faith. It consists of the recitation of the formula: *Lā illāha illā Allāh wa-Muḥammad rasūl Allāh* (There is no god but God and Muhammad is the messenger of God). *The Shahāda* is the first pillar of Islam. It is also employed as a witness of the "martyr". The same term is used in reference to *martyrdom* for a holy or noble cause.

Shahīd (pl. shuhadā')

Witness of Islam or martyr. Refers to the one who died on *jihād*. According to the Qur'ān, everyone who dies as a shahīd will be rewarded with Paradise.

Sharīʿa

Islamic law; Islamic legal system derived from the *Qur'ān*, Sunni and supplementary sources of *fiqh* (jurisprudence). It refers to the set of rules and laws revealed by God to Muhammad, that are to be applied to the social and religious life of the Muslim community (*'umma*).

Sharr

Evil.

Shiʿat ʿAli

Party of ʿAli; the followers of ʿAli ibn Abi Talib, the fourth rightly-guided Caliph and the Prophet's son-in-law.

Shirk

Polytheism; denying the unitary oneness of God or denying God altogether.

Shia

Derived from *Shiʿat ʿAli* or the party of ʿAli ibn Abi Talib, the fourth rightly-guided Caliph and the Prophet's son-in-law. The Shia or Shiʿites believe in the principle of *ʾImāmah* (Imamate) or the leadership of the infallible Shia Imāms. Unlike the Sunnis, who emphasize the importance of reaching consensus concerning political matters, the Shiʿites insist on the idea that ʿAli and his descendants –as part of the household of the Prophet– were the sole rightful successors of Muhammad. Taking such a position with respect to the succession of the Prophet has resulted in branding them as *rāfiḍa* or rejectionists, which has become a pejorative term for Shia. ʿAli's descendants (*ʾImāms*) undertook the leadership of the Shia community. Serving as a political and spiritual leader, each Imām appointed a successor and passed down spiritual knowledge to the following leader, according to the Shia doctrine. *Shiʿism* defines itself as an essentially esoteric and initiatory doctrine that does not uncover itself easily. In a tradition traced back to several Shiʿite Imāms, it is stated, "Our teaching is secret, it is a secret about a secret. It includes an exoteric (*ẓāhir*), esoteric (*bāṭin*), and esoteric of the esoteric (*bāṭin al-bāṭin*) dimension."

Shumūl

Comprehensiveness; inclusiveness.

Ṣūfi

Follower, member or representative of *Ṣūfism*, a mystical movement in Islam. It derives its name from the word *Ṣūf* (wool), referring to the woolen garment worn by these mystics. *Ṣūfism* emerged in the eighth century. The *Ṣūfis* initially preached asceticism and advocated the renunciation of wordly goods; their poverty enabled them to reach true submission to God, *Islām*, in accordance with the *Sharīʿa*. Later on, they emphasized the struggle against human passions with the assistance of *qalb* (heart), and they sought ecstasy through union with God on the basis of what they considered to be a reciprocal love between God and humankind, as mentioned in the *Qur'ān*. *Ṣūfī* schools defined and explained the different stages (*manzila*) of this mystical journey (*ṭarīqa*). Gradually, the popularity of *Ṣūfī* masters grew within the society, and they came to possess a position of sanctity that led them to confer blessings (*baraka*). *Ṣūfism* was mostly practiced individually until the eleventh century. From then on, *Ṣūfīs* began to come together in fraternities led by a *shaykh* to perform their rituals collectively. These rituals are primarily focused on living a religious life without getting involved in any form of theoretical conflict with the demands of the religious law and, by doing so, they tended to increase their impact and influence over the society. The *Ṣūfīs* perform some ritualistic practices, such as *shafāʿa* (intercession) and *dhikr* (frequent mention and remembrance of God), both of which are considered by many orthodox Muslims, such as the Salafis, as certain forms of heretical innovation (*bidʿa*).

Sunna

The teachings, sayings, actions and experiences of the Prophet Muhammad. The Sunna forms a source of law beside the *Qur'ān*. The Sunna are recorded in the *ḥadīth*. The Sunnis, who constitute the vast majority within the Muslim community today, endorse and approve the first four Caliphs, including ʿAli, as *ʿal-Khulafāʾ ʾal-Rāshidūn* or the Rightly-Guided successors of the Prophet, as well as those who followed. The followers of the Sunna and of the community, called Sunnīs or *'Ahl al-Sunna wal-Jamāʿa*, found themselves in conflict with the Shia over certain political and spiritual matters, such as the succession of the Prophet Muhammad. This conflict is reflected in the concepts of "Sunni Caliphate" and "Shia Imamate". Sunnism is represented by four schools of law (*madhāhib*), including the *Ḥanafī*, *Shāfiʿī*, *Mālikī* and *Ḥanbalī*, that remained faithful to the tradition of the community.

Tābiʿīn

Followers or adherers. Refers to the generation which followed the *Ṣaḥāba* (companions of the Prophet Muhammad), one of the three generations that constitutes the *al-salaf al-ṣāliḥ*.

Tābiʿ tābiʿīn

Refers to the generation that followed the *tābiʿīn*, and the last of the three generations that form *al-salaf al-ṣāliḥ*.

Ṭāghūt (pl. ṭawāghīt)

Idolatry. It refers to all kinds of notions and conceptions that seem to replace God, deviate a believer from His worship and eventually endanger *tawḥīd* or monotheism—the cornerstone of the whole religion.

Al-Ṭā'ifa al-Manṣūra

The sole triumphant group of Muslims. Refers to the way the Salafis define themselves. The Salafi doctrine supports this claim by a *ḥadīth* in which the Prophet Muhammad is reported as saying, "A group of my followers will remain victorious till Allah's Order [the Hour] comes upon them while they are still victorious."

Ṭā'ifiyya

Sectarianism; sectarian-based social stratification, schism and divide; discrimination based on ethno-sectarian identity.

Taḥrīm

Forbidding. It refers to the act of forbidding all practices that emerge in violation of the basic Islamic teachings, beliefs and values.

Tajdīd

Renewal or revival in matters of religion.

Takfīr

Denouncing someone as apostate or infidel (*kāfir*). It refers to the practice of excommunication toward fellow Muslims, banishing them from the faith, labelling them as infidels (*kuffār*) and combatting them by all means possible.

Taqlīd

Imitation. Refers to the attitude of the *ʿulamā'*, specifically jurists and *fuqahā'*, who insist on imitating the ancients (*salaf*) by avoiding and rejecting any kind of innovation (*bidʿa*).

Ṭarīqa

Mystical method or journey that consists of different stages.

Taṭarruf

Radicalism or extremism.

Tawāzun

Balance; moderation.

Tawḥīd

Monotheism; the unitary oneness of God. The concept of *tawḥīd* constitutes the chief and fundamental aspect of Islam. It also forms the single most important factor in Salafism.

Tawḥīd al-'asmā' wa-l-ṣifāt

The oneness of the names and characteristics of God.

Tawḥīd al-ḥākimiyya

The oneness of the sovereignty of God.

Tawḥīd al-rubūbiyya

The oneness of the dominion of God.

Tawḥīd al-ulūhiyya

The oneness of the divinity.

Thabāt

Stability of performance.

'Ulamā' (s.ʿālim)

Religious scholars; clerical authorities.

'Umma

Islamic community.

ʿUnf

Violence or aggression.

'Uṣūl (s. 'aṣl)

Refers to the primary sources of jurisprudence.

Wahhabiyya

Wahhabism movement; orthodox methodology employed to realize salafi-guided form of government and practices among the society based on the Sharīʿa. Wahhabism mainly implicates a return to the basic values and teachings of Islam, and striving for the purification of the faith from any forms of theological additions or philosophical speculations. Introduced by Muhammad ibn Abd al-Wahhab (1703-1792), the followers of this manhaj are frequently referred to as Wahhabis, and the works and legacy of ibn Abd al-Wahhab are considered to be highly influential among and of great impact on contemporary Salafis worldwide. Ibn Abd al-Wahhab provided what some scholars consider to be a narrow definition of ʿtrue faithʾ, as it mainly focuses on the founder's teachings that have ultimately introduced the principles of takfīr (denouncing fellow Muslims as apostates) and jihād against the kuffār (infidels). Wahhabism is deemed to be the most extreme manifestation of radical Sunni Islam. Ibn Abd al-Wahhab's extremely conservative thoughts stem from the fact that he was remarkably influenced by the teachings of the strictly orthodox and traditionalist Ḥanbalī school of law, and particularly by the works and thoughts of the Ḥanbalī-based legal philosopher Ibn Taymiyya. This has led scholars on Islamism to associate Salafism with the legacy of both Ibn Taymiyya and Muhammad ibn Abd al-Wahhab, who are seen as primary architects of today's Salafism.

Al-walā' wa-l-barā'

Loyalty and disavowal; to love and hate for the sake of Allah.

Wal-tuzimat fīh ḥudūd Allāh

Refers to actions that are taken within the boundaries of God's teachings.

Al-Wāqiʿiyya

Realism.

Wa-ṣaḥḥat fīh an-niyya

Refers to actions that are based on right and justifiable intentions.

Waṣiyya

Commandment; testament.

Waṣiyyat 'Ali

Commandment of ʿAli ibn Abi Talib as the rightful successor of the Prophet Muhammad. According to the Shia, Muhammad had on several occasions referred to ʿAli and his male descendants as his righteous successors. One of these occasions, which has been mentioned in authentic and authoritative Shia and Sunni sources, has been interpreted by the Shia as a formal approval and authorization of ʿAli's right to succession by the Prophet. While on his way back from his last pilgrimage to Mecca, on the eighteenth day of the month Dhul-ḥijja of the eleventh year of his *Hijra* in 632 A.D., at a place called Ghadīr of Khumm, the Prophet Muhammad reportedly made a crucial declaration, stating: "He for whom I was the master, should hence have ʿAli as his master (*fa-hādha ʿAlīyun mawlāh man kuntu mawlāh*)." For the Shia, the alleged circumstances that took place at the Ghadīr of Khumm, referred to as *Waṣiyyat ʿAli*, constituted the single significant piece of evidence on the basis of which they legitimized the succession of ʿAli and his descendants.

Wilāya

Guardianship.

Wilāyat al-Faqīh

Guardianship of the theologian.

Yaqīn

Certainty.

Yawm al-Dīn

Judgement Day.

Ẓāhir

Exoteric aspect.

Zakāt

Distribution of alms to the poor. *Zakāt* is the third pillar of Islam.

Ẓann

Conjectural thought.

Zaydis

Minority sect of Shia Islam. The Zaydis only recognize the first five Imāms and differ about the identity of the fifth. The first five Imāms of the orthodox Shia include ʿAli ibn Abi Talib, his sons Hasan and Hussein, Hussein's son ʿAli Zayn al-Abidin and the latter's son Muhammad al-Baqir. However, the Zaydis, also known as Zaydiyyah, preferred the younger son of Zayn al-Abidin, Zayd, over his brother al-Baqir, as their Imām. This came after Zayd led a revolt against Caliph Hisham and was massacred, while his older brother al-Baqir didn't show any interest in politics. The Zaydis reject the idea of the infallibility of Imāms and deny the concept of the awaited Imām.

Ẓulm

Injustice; oppression; inequity.

Appendix
Influential Islamic Thinkers

Taqi al-Din Ahmad Ibn Taymiyya

In a climate characterized by political uncertainty and fragmentation, Ibn Taymiyya was born in 1263 in the city of Harran in southeastern Turkey. His family fled to Damascus, Syria, in 1269, amid the advance of the Mongols into the region. He settled along with his family in the Ḥanbalī quarter of Damascus. Ibn Taymiyya received his principal education at the Sukkariyya Ḥanbalī madrasa, where his father was serving as a director. By this he followed the footsteps of his parental grandfather Majd al-Dīn b. Taymiyya (d. 1255) and his uncle Fakhr al-Dīn b. Taymiyyah (d. 1225), both of whom were distinguished authorities of the Ḥanbalī school. Ibn Taymiyya later succeeded his father as director of the Sukkariyya madrasa and, one year later, in 1285, he began teaching *tafsīr* (Qu'ānic exegesis) at the notorious Umayyad Mosque in Damascus. Several years later, he began teaching Ḥanbalī law and jurisprudence at the Ḥanbaliyya madrasa in Damascus. Ibn Taymiyya's authoritative lessons attracted a growing circle of scholars, and he gained a great respect among the intellectuals of his time for his impressive training in law and his well-grounded knowledge of *ḥadīth* and *tafsīr*. In 1299, he wrote one of his most notorious statements of creed, *al-Fatwā al-Ḥamawiyya*. He got increasingly engaged into politics amid intensifying attacks by the Mongols against Damascus in 1300. In the following few years, Ibn Taymiyya played a political as well as a military role during the Mongol invasion of Damascus. He was a spokesman of the resistance party in Damascus, which enabled him to negotiate the release of many prisoners and reach a peace agreement with the Mongols to ensure the safety of the inhabitants of Damascus. Ibn Taymiyya also participated in two Mamluk-led campaigns against the Shia of Kasrawan, in 1300 and 1305, after they were accused of collaborating with both the Mongols and the crusaders. He also fought at the battle of Shaqhab in 1303 against a third Mongol invasion. Ibn Taymiyya then returned to writing and participation in scholarly debates. His opposition to and criticism about mysticism in general, and Ṣūfism in particular, indicated an orthodox overtone on his part, as manifested in his second statement of creed *al-ʿAqīda al-Wāsiṭiyya*. He was then banished to Cairo, where he was convicted of propagating anthropomorphic views, and he was consequently imprisoned for eighteen months at the citadel of Cairo. Ibn Taymiyya condemned different beliefs and practices which he labelled as *bidʿa* (reprehensible innovation), including the practice of *tawassul/istighātha* (supplication for divine assistance through the intermediary of the Prophet or a high-ranking spiritual leader, known as *walī*). He condemned such practices as forms of *shirk* (idolatry). Such views led to his arrest and imprisonment once again. After spending several months in a cell, Ibn Taymiyya was released and exiled from Cairo to Alexandria, where he was again placed in prison. Upon his release one year later, he returned to Cairo and started teaching and writing for approximately three years, before a new Mongol invasion into Damascus prompted him to return to Syria. Under a new governor of Damascus, Ibn Taymiyya was promoted to the rank of professor. His teachings were then organized and popularized by his famous and influential student Ibn Qayyim al-Jawziyya (d. 1350). Ibn Taymiyya's vast corpus of writings reflects a great familiarity with various major schools of thought, including philosophy and theology. He is viewed by scholars as a bold and formidable debater, a public intellectual par excellence with an unmatched degree of knowledge and understanding about the social and political realities of his time. He won numerous admirers due to his sharp intellect, his boldness in defending his views, and his high moral integrity. Nonetheless, the controversial nature of some of his views, coupled with his insistence to defend them, has gained him many significant opponents as well. During his sixty-five years of life, Ibn Taymiyya was summoned to trial nine times, imprisoned six times on separate occasions for a total period of over six years, ordered to refrain from giving *fatwās* (legal opinions), and exiled twice, first from Damascus to Cairo, and then from Cairo to Alexandria. Delving into Ibn Taymiyya's extensive works on various subjects reveals that he was a remarkably prolific writer who penned a couple of hundreds of works spanning hundreds of volumes. His works on exegesis and its principles include: *Muqaddima fī uṣūl al-tafsīr* (*Introduction to the Principles of Tafsīr*); a full-volume commentary on the phrase "and none knows its *taʾwīl* save God"; a treatise on the phrase "in it [the Qurʾān] are *muḥkam* verses"; a treatise on the phrase "a Book whose verses have been made firm (*uḥkimat*)"; a fifty-leaf treatise on the all-important verse "There is none like unto Him"; and an eighty-leaf treatise on the terms "literal" (*ḥaqīqa*) and "figurative" (*majāz*), reflecting his understanding of language and interpretation. Looking into Ibn Taymiyya's works on theological topics (*uṣūl al-dīn*), *Asmāʾ muʾallafāt* lists 165 separate writings of various lengths and genres, the most famous of which are *Kitāb al-ʾĪmān* (*Book of Faith*); *Darʾ taʿāruḍ al-ʿaql wa-l-naql; Bayān talbīs al-Jahmiyya fī taʾsīs bidaʿihim al-kalāmiyya* (Elucidating the deceit of the Jahmiyya in laying the bases of their theological innovations); *Kitāb Minhāj al-sunna* (The way of the Sunna), in refutation of Shīʿism; the seven-volume *al-Jawāb al-ṣaḥīḥ li-*

man baddala dīn al-Masīḥ (The correct response to those who altered the religion of the Messiah), in refutation of Christian trinitarian theology; and the work *Iqtiḍā᾿ al-ṣirāṭ al-mustaqīm li-mukhālafat aṣḥāb al-jaḥīm* (On the obligation of remaining distinct from the people of the fire). Other theological treatises of a general nature penned by Ibn Taymiyya include *al-ʿAqīda al-Wāsiṭiyya, al-Qāʿida al-Murrākushiyya* (on the question of the divine attributes), and a fifty-leaf treatise on the creed of the Ashʿarīs, the Māturīdīs, and the non-Māturīdī Ḥanafīs. Ibn Taymiyya also wrote several treatises that touch upon questions of epistemology or rational methods of argumentation. These include: a 100-leaf *qāʿida* (treatise) on the notion that every rational argument adduced by an innovator (mubtadiʿ) proves the invalidity of his position; a full-volume work on knowledge that is firmly established (*al-ʿilm al-muḥkam*); a three-volume work refuting the position that definitive (scriptural) indicants (*adilla qaṭʿiyya*) do not yield certainty (*yaqīn*); a treatise on the superiority of the knowledge of the early community (the *salaf*) over those who succeeded them (the *khalaf*); and a treatise on the perceived contradiction between the texts of revelation and consensus (*ijmāʿ*). Ibn Taymiyya's works on purely philosophical themes include: a refutation of Ibn Sīnā's *al-Aḍḥawiyya fī al-maʿād*, which denies physical resurrection after death (one of many extensive philosophical discursions found throughout the *Darʾ*); a volume on the "*tawḥīd*" of the philosophers following in the way of Ibn Sīnā; a work entitled *al-Radd ʿalā falsafat Ibn Rushd*; a short volume on universals; a "large volume" refuting the philosophers' assertion of the eternity of the world; and, finally, the aforementioned all-out attack on Greek logic, *Kitāb al-Radd ʿalā al-manṭiqiyyīn*. These works, among others, indicate Ibn Taymiyya's rich thought and intellect, and illustrate the reason behind the multifaceted interest of many scholars in exploring his voluminous writings.[321] He was frequently arrested due to the views he advocated in his writings, and he insisted to continue writing even during his detention. In 1326, Ibn Taymiyya was arrested and placed in a cell at the citadel of Damascus, where he spent two years, due to his treatise *al-Risāla fī ziyārat al-qubūr wa-l-istinjād bi-l-maqbūr* (Treatise on the visitation of graves and seeking aid from the buried), in which he attacked the practice of visiting the graves of righteous people (*awliyā*ʾ) for the purpose of making tawassul through them. He continued to write from his cell, producing several works, including a treatise in which he expounded his critical standpoint toward visiting and praying at the graves of the *awliyā*ʾ. He was then deprived of ink, pen and papers. A few months after being denied the means to write, Ibn Taymiyya passed away in his cell at the citadel of Damascus on 26 September 1328. Controversy over Ibn Taymiyya's legacy has persisted to the present time.

Muhammad Ibn Abd al-Wahhab

Theologian and founder of the Wahhabi movement, Ibn Abd al-Wahhab was born in 1703 in the city of ʻUyaynah, Arabia (now Saudi Arabia) to a family of Islamic judges and scholars. While the adherents of the movement he established used to call themselves *Muwaḥḥidūn* (monotheists), the movement was labelled by its opponents at the time as *Wahhabiyya* (Wahhabism), a term that has ever since continued to be used to describe the movement based on the teachings of Ibn Abd al-Wahhab –which implicate a return to the principles of Islam as practiced by its early forebears (*al-salaf*). After completing his formal education in Arabia's holy city of Medina, Ibn Abd al-Wahhab travelled and taught in several places across the region, including four years of teaching in Iraq's Basra. In 1736, he moved to Iran where he taught theology for a few years. During these years, he increasingly criticized the ideas and doctrines of Ṣūfism. Upon his return to his native city 'Uyaynah, Ibn Abd al-Wahhab wrote his famous *Kitāb al-Tawḥīd* (Book of the Oneness [of God]), which has become the main text and the fundamental source for the Wahhabi doctrine. As a strictly conservative theologian and Ḥanbalī jurist, Ibn Abd al-Wahhab opposed *taqlīd* (adherence to tradition) and promoted instead a strict adherence to traditional Islamic law. He proclaimed the necessity of ignoring medieval interpretations of Islam and only rely on the *Qur'ān* and the *ḥadith*. He also denounced requests for intercession from anyone other than God or assigning authority to anyone other than God. His plans for socioreligious reform within the *'umma* were primarily based on the doctrine of *tawḥīd*. The significant emphasis placed on the key concept of *tawḥīd* in Ibn Abd al-Wahhab's teachings led his followers and adherents to distinguish and characterize themselves as *Muwaḥḥidūn*. He began teaching extremely revolutionary ideas and preaching conservative religious reformation. At the core of his teachings, the impact of the Ḥanbalī scholar Ibn Taymiyya seemed obvious. Ibn Taymiyya's call for the purification of Islam by means of expelling any practices that involve innovations, speculative theology, mysticism, shrine cults and saint worship were reiterated by Ibn Abd al-Wahhab. According to the ideologue of Wahhabism, the *Qur'ān* and the *Sunna* (traditions of the Prophet Muhammad) are deemed to be the sole legitimate sources doctrine (*uṣūl al-fiqh*), and any form of deviation from these two sources, including traditions and practices not originally rooted in either the *Qur'ān* or the *ḥadith*, were strongly rejected and branded as *bidʿa* (heretical innovations). Another key feature of his teachings is the condemnation of any form of tendency toward an intermediary between the faithful and God, considering such a practice as *shirk* (polytheism).[322] Preaching and propagating such revolutionary ideas and extreme measures under the pretext of purifying the faith and safeguarding the very spirit of the *'umma* led to a widespread controversy across 'Uyaynah. In 1744, as a result of the controversy he caused, Ibn Abd al-Wahhab was eventually expelled from his hometown 'Uyaynah. Then, he headed to al-Dirʿiyyah and he settled there. Al- Dirʿiyyah was then the capital of the ruler of Najd, prince Muhammad Ibn Saud, the founder of the Saud dynasty that continue to rule Saudi Arabia today. Ibn Saud formed an alliance with Ibn Abd al-Wahhab. Based on mutual oaths of loyalty, the alliance between the prince and the theologian promptly began to thrive in terms of military success, conquest and expansion. The alliance has also led to a further spread and impact of Wahhabism in the region. Amid the expansionist campaign by Ibn Saud's son Abd al-Aziz I (reigned 1765-1803), who worked in harmony with Ibn Abd al-Wahhabi, Wahhabism was made the dominant force in Arabia. From 1800, the Wahhabis gradually took control of the civil administration of the country that continued to expand under the Saud dynasty. Ibn Abd al-Wahhab himself died in 1792, but his teachings continued to influence many people in the region and his doctrines attracted a growing circle of adherents and followers throughout the 19th and 20th centuries into this day. Many contemporary conservatives, as well as Islamists, claim inspiration from the doctrines introduced by Ibn Abd al-Wahhab.

Jamal al-Din al-Afghani

Al-Afghani was born in October-November 1838 in Asadabad, in Iran's northwestern province of Qazvin. Hen then moved to Tehran before attending higher education in Iraq in the 1850s. Al-Afghani travelled through India in the period between 1856 and 1858, where he came to realize the dangers of Western domination in the East, after witnessing the Indian Mutiny against the British colonial rule. He visited Cairo in 1869, and he headed afterwards to Istanbul and stayed there until 1871. He later returned to Cairo and lived there until 1879. During this period, and due to his sharp intellect, he was awarded by the Egyptian government as a teacher at al-Azhar. Al-Afghani was admired by many of his students for his teaching skills in philosophy, theology, logic, mysticism and jurisprudence. His students became leaders of the Egyptian political and intellectual landscape. Due to his later involvement in political activism and his anti-Western fiery speeches, he was eventually arrested and deported to Jeddah in the Hijaz in 1879. He then travelled to India, where he published several remarkable books, including *al-Radd 'ala al-Dahriyyin* (The Refutation of the Materialists). In 1882, al-Afghani moved to Paris, where he, together with his former student Muhammad ʿAbduh, published the notoriously influential newspaper *al-'Urwa al-Wuthqa* (The Firmest Bond). Although the mass circulated newspaper lasted merely for seven months, it had a remarkable influence among intellectuals across the region. In 1885, al-Afghani travelled further to England, where he tried to influence the British public opinion and convince them to put an end to the British rule in Egypt. He also visited Russia, where he called for a greater opposition against the British. Shortly afterwards, he travelled to Persia, where he tried to inspire the removal of the Shah. In 1892, al-Afghani was invited to Istanbul by 'Abd al-Hamid II, the Ottoman Sultan. His critical position concerning the situation of the Muslims across the Empire resulted in his placement under house arrest, where his ability to write and speak was enormously restricted. He died from cancer in 1897.[323]

Muhammad ʿAbduh

ʿAbduh was born in 1849 in the village of Shanra in the Egyptian Gharbiyya province. He attended al-Azhar in 1869, where he studied Ṣūfism and philosophy, and graduated in 1871. He joined a group of enthusiast scholars gathered around al-Afghani, and he was drawn together with his teacher into local politics. ʻAbduh later became editor of the government gazette *al-Waqaʻi al-Masriyya*, and member of the Council of Higher Education in Cairo. Amid a growing nationalist movement in Egypt, ʻAbduh became more involved into anti-colonial activities and frequently criticized the foreign intervention in Egypt. ʿAbduh was a committed pan-Islamism political activist until 1879, and then he turned into a highly devoted nationalist until 1882, the year when he was eventually exiled after calling for an armed rebellion against the British. He then reverted back to pan-Islamism. ʿAbduh stayed one year in Beirut, and afterwards moved to Paris to join al-Afghani, where they together published 18 issues of the influential newspaper *al-ʻUrwa al-Wuthqa* from March to October 1884. In 1888, ʿAbduh was allowed to return to Egypt, where he surprisingly turned back to nationalism once again, and he then became a member of Egypt's colonial establishment and religious institution. Unlike his committed teacher al-Afghani, ʿAbduh followed the prevailing winds and adapted himself into supporting strong leadership, regardless of the colonial influence. ʿAbduh became a *qadi* (judge) in religious and national courts. He was portrayed by many as a popular Islamic reformer at the time. ʿAbduh believed that the most efficient solution for Egypt's malaise was educational and religious reform. He contributed to the reformation movement of al-Azhar from 1895 until shortly prior to his death. ʿAbduh was appointed Mufti of Egypt in 1899. He died on the 11th of July, 1905.[324]

Muhammad Rashid Rida

Rida was born in 1865 in the Syrian town of al-Qalamun. He initially received a traditional education in al-Qalamun's Qur'anic school, and later he attended a national Islamic school in Tripoli. Rida graduated in 1892 and worked as a journalist for several years. Reading *al-'Urwa al-Wuthqa* led Rida into fascinating the ideas of al-Afghani and ʿAbduh and the *salafiyya* movement they initiated. In 1897, Rida moved to Cairo in order to join ʿAbduh and to eventually collaborate with him. One year later, Rida launched the *salafi* journal *al-Manar.* ʿAbduh advised Rida to avoid any involvement in politics and to rather focus on reform through education. *Al-Manar* emerged as one of the most influential and authoritative journals concerning Islamic reform throughout its 37 years of continuous publishing. It provided its readers with articles on a variety of topics, including religion, politics and science, beside disseminating legal opinions (*fatwā*, pl. *fatāwa*) and reviewed published works on religious and educational reform. Rida was among the first Islamic thinkers to warn about the threat of modern nationalism to the Islamic culture and identity. He also criticized Islamic clerics for the abuse of power and doctrinal errors. Although he initially embraced al-Afghani's radical position against the West, Rida later took a conciliatory path. Yet, some of his radical views continued to surface, like when he labeled the notorious Taha Husayn as an apostate for the latter's literary work *Fi al-Shi'r al-Jahili.* After the collapse of the Ottoman Empire, Rida called for the establishment of a new caliphate, and he tirelessly demanded the revival of the Sharīʿa. He criticized the Zionist colonization of Palestine and attacked the British involvement in Arab affairs. Rida and his journal *al-Manar* were celebrated for the influential conservative interpretation of Islam and adopting the Wahhabi *manhaj.* He died in Cairo on the 22nd of August 1935.[325]

Abu al-Ala Mawdudi

Mawdudi was born on September 25, 1903, in India's central state of Maharashtra, particularly in Aurangabad. He grew up in an aristocratic religious family. Mawdudi received a traditional education in his early years, and worked as a journalist for several years. In the period between 1919 and 1924, Mawdudi joined the pan-Islamic Khilafat movement that supported the Ottoman caliphate and struggled to end British rule in India. He later moved to Delhi and joined a group of Islamic scholars there, where he became an editor of the *Muslim* newspaper. He was known then for his pan-Islamic overtone and anti-nationalism position. His condemnation of the nationalists increased following the collapse of the Ottoman caliphate. During these years he specialized in the *Ḥanafī* legal tradition and received a diploma in religious training in 1926. He emphasized the need to preserve the Islamic faith against any influences and demanded Muslims to protect their religious identity. Mawdudi's teachings and speeches were collectively published in the influential groundbreaking treatise *al-Jihād fi al-Islam* (Jihād in Islam), which allowed him to emerge among major Islamic scholars and leave an undeniable impact among the intellectuals of his time across the region. He also wrote a series of Qu'ānic interpretations under the title *Tafhim al-Qur'an* (Understanding the Qur'ān), a project that he started in 1942. Mawdudi founded a pan-Islamic political party in India in 1941, known as *Jama'at Islami* (The Islamic Party). Subsequent to the India-Pakistan partition in 1947, Mawdudi's party started campaigning for the establishment of an Islamic state to replace the secular nationalist one and called for a greater role of Islam in the emerging Pakistani state. He was arrested several times for his increasingly influential activism and agitation against Pakistan's secular government, including in 1948, 1950, 1954,

1964 and 1967. Mawdudi launched his final political campaign in 1970, but his party lost the elections. He then left politics once and for all, and focused on writing. He died on the 22nd of September 1979. More than a million of his admirers attended his funeral in Lahore.[326]

Hassan al-Banna

On October 17, 1906, al-Banna was born in the town of Mahmudiyya, in the Egyptian province of Beheira. His father, Shaykh Ahmed 'Abd al-Rahman, was an independent Islamic scholar and a local imam in Mahmudiyya. Al-Banna was influenced by his father since a young age. He was also influenced by his teacher Shaykh Muhammad Zahran, the head of the local Ṣūfī branch known as Hasafiyya, as well as by the nationalist revolution of 1919. He studied at the Primary Teacher's Training School in Damanhur until 1923, and then he moved to Cairo and attended Dar al-'Ulum there. Al-Banna subscribed to the social and political unity, and the *salafiyya* doctrines. Yet, unlike his forbears al-Afghani, ʿAbduh and Rida, he established a permanent organization to attain the goals that for his forebears remained merely an ambition on paper. Al-Banna joined his first Islamic organization, the Society for Moral Behavior, when he was 12 years old. He later founded the Hasafiyya Benevolence Society. As a student at Dar al-'Ulum in Cairo, al-Banna joined the Association of Muslim Youth. Following his graduation in 1927, he started teaching in the city of Isma'iliyya. In 1928, al-Banna established the Society of Muslim Brothers, which then became known as the Muslim Brotherhood. Initially, the party was considerably focused on raising awareness about the situation of Egyptian workers under British rule, where numerous cases of discrimination and exploitation were reported. The Brotherhood gradually grew, and hundreds of branches were established across Egypt. By 1938, over 300 branches were founded throughout the country, and thousands of new members joined its ranks. In 1948, the organization grew dramatically to include over one million members. Al-Banna started propagating the Brotherhood's message in 1932 through various newspapers and journals, as well as through sermons and public readings. The main objectives of the Brotherhood, that were propagated by means of various activities, included strengthening unity among the members of the *'umma*, teaching Islamic values, reviving Islamic activism and modernizing Islam. Al-Banna's organization soon began to establish various kinds of affiliated institutions, including educational programs, schools, clinics, hospitals, pharmacies, mosque construction and *zakāt* (alms) committees. Al-Banna established ties with al-Azhar and the Parliament in order to protect his organization and ensure the continuity of its activities. Although he warned the members of the Brotherhood against violence, the increasing pressure led the organization to adopt some radical tactics to accomplish its goals. During a mass demonstration in Cairo in October 1937 in support of Palestinian rebellion against the British and Zionists, dozens of Brothers were arrested for the first time due to their political activities. By 1939, the Brotherhood became a key player in Egypt's national politics. In 1940, the first divide within the Muslim Brotherhood broke out between the advocates of nonviolence and those who sought violent tactics against the government and the imperialist powers, which eventually led to the establishment of the radical group Shabab Muhammad that broke away from the Brotherhood. Al-Banna continued to advocate nonviolence. Yet, this could not prevent some branches within the Brotherhood to eventually get involved in violent activities, including the Secret Apparatus of the organization. Despite al-Banna's advocacy of nonviolence and his attempt to mainly focus on social justice, the outbreak of the Palestinian revolt in 1936 triggered him to call for bold anti-colonial activities and engagement in armed combat if necessary. In November 1948, the Egyptian police seized documents that pointed to violent plans by the Secret Apparatus, which led to the arrest of al-Banna, but he was soon released. However, when Cairo's chief of police was killed by a bomb in December of that year, the brotherhood was banned by a government decree. After the increased involvement of his organization in violent confrontations with the authorities, al-Banna had to pay the ultimate price. On February 12, 1949, he was shot several times in the chest by a gunman in front of one of the offices of the Muslim Youth, and he died the same evening.[327] His organization remained active to this day.

Sayyid Qutb

Sayyid Qutb is frequently described as one of the most radical Islamic thinkers of the 20th century, and the impact of his intellectual works among contemporary Islamists led some to portray him as "the philosopher of Islamic terror."[328] Yet, labelling him merely as such tends to neglect his extensive intellectual contribution to Arabic literature as an author and poet, and to theological interpretation as an Islamic theorist and educator. Qutb was born on October 9, 1906, in the village of Musha in Asyut province, in Egypt's southern region of Sa'id. He first attended the governmental *madrasa* school, then the traditional religious *kuttab*, and he afterwards returned to the *madrasa* for its broader curriculum. By the age of 10 Qutb had already memorized the entire Qur'ān, demonstrating a high level of commitment. His remarkable dedication to reading was nurtured throughout his life. In 1921, he moved to Cairo where he joined the Wafd Party, attracted by its anti-British agenda. At the time, he had no ambition to explore religious politics. He started writing and publishing poems in local literary magazines. From 1925 to 1928, Qutb attended the preliminary training school Madrasat al-Mu‘allimin al-Awwaliya in Cairo. He then attended Dar al-‘Ulum and graduated in 1933 with a license in Arabic Language and Literature. Following his graduation, Qutb joined the Egyptian Ministry of Education and started to teach for several years at different schools in Cairo, Dumyat and Bani Swayf. Disappointed by the government's treaty agreements with the British, Qutb joined the nationalist Sa‘dist Party in 1937. In 1940, he was appointed an inspector at the General Culture Administration and then moved to the Translation and Statistics Administration, before returning to the Culture Administration where he remained working from 1945 to 1948. Beside his full-time employment, writing and reviewing, Qutb also became chief editor of Cairo's two major journals *al-Fikr al-Jadīd* (New Thought) and *al-‘Ālam al-‘Arabī* (the Arab World). Qutb received a scholarship from the Ministry of Education to the United States, where he stayed from 1948 to 1950 and became acquainted with its education curricula. After his return to Egypt, he resumed his work as an inspector at the Education Ministry, and then moved to the Office of Technical Research and Projects. He then joined the Muslim Brotherhood. In 1952, Qutb resigned his ministerial post after protesting what he considered to be non-Islamic educational policies pursued by the new government. His great passion for literature led him to join the liberal al-Diwan school of writers with an ambition to be regarded among the ranks of Cairo's prominent literary figures and intellectuals, including ‘Abbas Mahmud al-‘Aqqad, Taha Husayn, Muhammad Husayn Haykal and Ahmad Amin. At the time, Qutb was already emerging as a prolific writer, eventually publishing over

130 poems, more than 500 articles and essays, and nine books. Qutb initially considered himself a nationalist and modern secularist. He promoted principles such as justice, equality and freedom. He was anti-imperialist, advocating Egyptian independence. Although he remained an influential literary critic and writer, Qutb's attention was gradually redirected toward social and political issues in Egypt, which eventually marked his transition from secularism to Islamism. By the end of 1930s, he already started to question his earlier involvement in liberal politics and his endorsement of secular principles. He then gradually distanced himself from his colleagues who embraced modernism, and he began to explore Islamic themes. At first, just like many of his Egyptian peers, he viewed Islam as a civilizational artifact and heritage. Later, he began to emphasize the idea that Islam, as a distinct religion, provides unique solutions to the calamities suffered by the society. For him, Islam provides the most convenient and satisfying way of life, as extensively explored in his book *Social Justice in Islam*. This indicated his growing discomfort with modernity and modernization. Qutb's visit to the United States convinced him of the corruption of Western secularism and modernity. His denunciation of the West and imperial powers increased dramatically, and he started to attack countries like the U.S., France, England and Holland for their so-called bankruptcy and corruption on political and moral levels. He lashed out at these Western powers for opposing the liberty of Muslim countries, calling on Arabs and Muslims to rise up against Western domination. Furthermore, he strongly condemned national governments for collaborating with the West and adopting its corrupt policies. He also criticized and denounced the media, *'ulama*, literati and intellectuals, considering them apologists, hypocrites, opportunists and mercenaries. According to Qutb, the Muslims were

in a malaise due to increasing impact of nationalism, secularism and materialism, which he condemned as loyalties to other than God. He considered the West and those living by its corrupt standards as being stuck in *jāhiliyya* (ignorance), and he called for the establishment of *ḥākimiyya* (God's dominion) as a condition to save the society from ignorance. According to Qutb, in order to move from *jāhiliyya* to *ḥākimiyya*, *jihād* was needed as a *manhaj* (method). This perspective, on which Qutb wrote extensively, reflects his radicalization as inflamed by surrounding circumstances and personal experiences. When the Muslim Brotherhood was charged with the assassination attempt on the life of the Egyptian President Jamal 'Abd al-Nassir in 1954, many members and officials of the Brotherhood, including Qutb, were arrested, tried and imprisoned. While in prison, Qutb wrote his magnum opus, 30-part, six-volume commentary on the Qur'ān, *In the Shade of the Qur'an* (*Fi Zilāl al-Qur'ān*), which is considered his most significant intellectual undertaking, written under the brutal conditions of the Liman Tura prison. Witnessing the brutal torturing of the Brothers at the hands of prison officers ignited outrage and unprecedented grudge inside Qutb, whose tendency toward militancy appeared to grow. As time went on, he became more conservative, radical and militant. He expressed much of this outrage in his well-known book *Signposts on the Road* (*Ma'ālim fi al-Tarīq*), which he wrote while in prison. *Signposts* was published in 1964, just before Qutb's release following the dramatic deterioration of his health. His release came after the Iraqi President 'Abd al-Salam 'Arif, who was close to 'Abd al-Nassir and also sympathetic to the Muslim Brotherhood, intervened during a visit to Egypt on Qutb's behalf. Just six months after his release, Qutb was re-arrested and imprisoned on charges of treason. His very words in *Signposts on the Road* were used against him during his trial. Qutb was sentenced by a military court to death by hanging. He was executed on August 29, 1966. He was the first Islamist to be executed by the state. The government then issued an official ban on the distribution of his books. However, this has backlashed and led to the spread of his ideas across the region.

Notes

1 Sectarianism (*al-Ta'ifiyah*) was frequently brought forward by the media and political analysists during the coverage of the Iraqi and Syrian conflicts as a key aspect of the political rifts and armed tensions. This sectarian dimension was demonstrated and reinforced by parties to conflict through their discourse and declared agendas with the objective of gaining popular support from their communities and drawing a boundary between them and their alleged enemies.

2 "It is a common complaint that sectarianism is an under theorised concept, although there have been attempts to define its features." (Higgins and Brewer 2003: 2).

3 Liechty and Clegg, *Moving Beyond Sectarianism: Religion, Conflict and Reconciliation in Northern Ireland*. 102.

4 ibid, 103.

5 Brewer, *Sectarianism and racism, and their parallels and differences*. 359.

6 Higgins and Brewer, *The Roots of Sectarianism in Northern Ireland*. 2.

7 Makdisi, *The Culture of Sectarianism: Community, History, and Violence in Ninteenth-Century Ottoman Lebanon*. 7.

8 ibid, 6.

9 Mabon and Royle, *The Origins of ISIS: The Collapse of Nations and Revolution in the Middle East*. 55.

10 Champion, *The Paradoxical Kingdom: Saudi Arabia and the Momentum of Reform*. 64.

11 Mabon and Royle, *The Origins of ISIS: The Collapse of Nations and Revolution in the Middle East*. 54.

12 Jarman, *Defining Sectarianism and Sectarian Hate Crime*. 7.

13 Fattah and Caso, *A Brief History of Iraq*. 68.

14 The *Saqīfa* is derived from the name of a place known at the time as *Saqīfat Bani-Saʿidah*, where the *Anṣar* gathered subsequent to the Prophet's death to discuss his succession. In Arabic, the term *Saqīfa* means roof, ceiling or arch under which issues of general communal concern were discussed.

15 El-Hirbi, *Parable and Politics in Early Islamic History: The Rashidun Caliphs*. 3.

16 Sachedina, *Islamic Messianism: The Idea of the Mahdi in Twelver Shiʿism*. 21.

17 Enayat, *Modern Islamic Political Thought: The Response of the Shi'i and Sunni Muslims to the Twentieth Century*. 4.

18 Sanders, *Ritual, Politics, and the City in Fatimid Cairo*. 122.

19 Cornell, *Voices of Islam*. 114.

20 Sardar and Davies, *The No-nonsense Guide to Islam*. 52.

21 Fadl, *Reasoning with God: Reclaiming Shari'a in the Modern Age*. 421.

22 Legitimate in the sense of being the grandsons of the Prophet Muhammad (descendants of his daughter Fatima and her husband ʿAli) and thus of the direct bloodline of the Prophet. According to the Shia, Allah has ordained that the spiritual leader of Islam and the Muslim community must be of the direct bloodline of the Prophet.

23 Redha, *Al-Hasan and Al-Hussein: The Two Grandsons of the Messenger of Allah*. 45.

24 Hasan ibn ʿAli passed away in Medina in the year 49 Hijra, ten years after Moʿawiya's Caliphate, and he was buried in al-Baqe'. According to several historical accounts, Hasan was poisoned by his wife Ja'ada, and died after forty days of sickness. The poisoning of Hasan reportedly took place within the framework of an alleged conspiracy by Moʿawiya or his son Yazid to keep the Caliphate for himself. However, the story remained unconfirmed (Redha, 1999).

25 Abdul-Raof, *Theological Approaches to Qur'anic Exegesis: A Practical Comparative-Contrastive Analysis*. 38.

26 Badamchi, *Post-Islamist Political Theory: Iranian Intellectuals and Political Liberalism in Dialogue*. 188.

27 Arjomand and Brown, *The Rule of Law, Islam, and Constitutional Politics in Egypt and Iran*. 105.

28 This was demonstrated through the joint efforts by several Muslim-majority countries to condemn the emergence of ISIS and combat its alleged Caliphate. Nevertheless, this does not undermine the fact that some undeclared policies with sectarian overtone have been for long pursued by certain Muslim states in the Middle East, such as that of Saudi Arabia –as a Sunni power– and Iran –as a Shia power. Thus, although pan-sectarian powers remain to exist in the region, the extremely radical forms of sectarianism are being condemned at an official level.

29 Hassan, *The Sectarianism of the Islamic State: Ideological Roots and Political Conflict*. 51.

30 Blanchard, *Islam: Sunnis and Shiʿites*. 3.

31 Brunner, *Sunnis and Shiʿites in Modern Islam: Politics, Rapprochement and the Role of Al-Azhar*. 25.
32 Malbouisson, *Focus on Islamic Issues*. 16.
33 Moezzi, *The Spirituality of Shi'i Islam*. xiv.
34 The Ismailis founded states, cities and institutions, and had reportedly contributed to the traditions of scholarship in Islam and were known as elite members of the educational and arts communities with intellectual achievements throughout the Islamic history. Today, they live as a religious minority in the region.
35 Malbouisson, *Focus on Islamic Issues*. 19.
36 Blanchard, *Islam: Sunnis and Shiʿites*. 5.
37 Moaddel and Karabenick, *Religious Fundamentalism in the Middle East*. 94.
38 Stefon, *Islamic Beliefs and Practices*. 134.
39 Brunner, *Sunnis and Shiʿites in Modern Islam: Politics, Rapprochement and the Role of Al-Azhar*. 26.
40 Hashemi and Postel, *Sectarianization: Mapping the New Politics of the Middle East*. 2.
41 Dixon, *Beyond Sectarianism in the Middle East: Comparative Perspectives on Group Conflict*. 11.
42 These developments also ignited Shia-led attacks on Sunni areas in Iraq, where ethnic cleansing campaigns at the hands of al-Hashd al-Shaabi militiamen were reported. See Human Rights Watch's report on abuses by Shia militiamen in Sunni areas near Mosul: https://www.hrw.org/news/2017/02/16/ iraq-looting-destruction-forces-fighting-isis.
43 Bonine *et al.*, *Is There a Middle East? The Evolution of a Geopolitical Concept*. 14.
44 Payind and McClimans, *Keys to Understanding the Middle East*. 21.
45 Including, but no limited to, the Egyptian civilization, Mezopotamia, the Medes, Sumeria, Babylonia and Assyria. See *A History of the Middle East* by Saul Friedman (2006) and *The Multiple Identities of the Middle East* by Bernard Lewis (2001).
46 In many cities across the Middle East, a multicultural society can be found. Despite the eruption of many conflicts and civil wars, various communities with different religious and ethnic backgrounds continued to share territories and have a joint destiny, and coexist regardless of the surrounding circumstances.
47 Joseph, *Language and Identity: National, Ethnic, Religious*. 16.

48 Aramaic was the native tongue of Jesus Christ.
49 See '*Approaches to Arabic Dialects*' by Manfred Woidich (2004).
50 Versteegh, *The Arabic Language, Second Edition*. 42.
51 Kreyenbroek and Sperl, *The Kurds: A Contemporary Overview*. 53.
52 The statistics mentioned are based on a comparative research across multiple sources, since none provides an officially certified or academically reliable statistics on the speakers of each of these languages. Several sources were used in order to provide this brief mapping of the linguistic diversity in the Middle East, including the *Middle East Studies Center* at the Ohio State University, Yasir Suleiman's *Language and Identity in the Middle East and North Africa* (2013), *Bilingualism in the Middle East and North Africa* by Judith Rosenhouse and Mira Goral (2004), among others.
53 Gunderson, *Religions of the Middle East*. 5.
54 Longva, and Roald, *Religious Minorities in the Middle East: Domination, Self-Empowerment, Accommodation*. 4.
55 This mapping is based on a comparative research throughout several sources, including a demographic study by the Pew Research Center (Retrieved from: http://www.pewforum.org/ 2015/04/02/middle-east-north-africa/); socio-political charts on Middle Eastern populations by the WGBH Educational Foundation (Retrieved from: http://www.pbs.org/wgbh/global connections/mideast/maps/demotext.html); and a demographic study by the Center for Educational Technologies at the Wheeling Jesuit University (Retrieved from: http://www.cotf. edu/earthinfo/meast/mepeo.html).
56 Balakian, *Raphael Lemkin, Cultural Destruction, and the Armenian Genocide*. 57.
57 Shoup, *Ethnic Groups of Africa and the Middle East: An Encyclopedia*. 133.
58 Kia, *The Persian Empire: A Historical Encyclopedia*. 185.
59 This is uttered in the Yezidi Statement of Faith, "*Min sha'datīya 'īmānā xwa, Bi nāvē xwadē ū Tāwūsē Malak dāya – I attest that my faith is given, In the names of god and Tāwsê Malak*." See Asatrian, G. and Arakelova, V. (2014). *The Religion of the Peacock Angel: The Yezidis and their Spirit World*. 10.
60 Croucher, *Global Perspectives on Intercultural Communication*. 359.
61 Hitti, *The Arabs: A Short History*. 5.
62 The Arab League was founded in Cairo in 1945 by Egypt, Iraq, Syria, Saudi Arabia, Palestine, Lebanon, Transjordan and Yemen. The

membership increased during the second half of the twentieth century to include 22 member states in total.

63 Stokes *et al.*, *Encyclopedia of the Peoples of Africa and the Middle East*. 616.
64 Lambton, *Social Change in Persia in the Nineteenth Century*. 150.
65 These four parts together form the so-called *Great Kurdistan*, the unattained independent Kurdish state. Chaliand, *A People without a Country: The Kurds and Kurdistan*. 4.
66 Mapping the Middle Eastern communities undoubtedly requires an in-depth research into such a broad domain, which, however, goes beyond the framework of this volume. Any shortage in mentioning or elaborating on a specific group or community should thus be seen within the framework of relevance to the topic at hand and the limits demarcated by the core objective of this study.
67 Abdulmajid, *Religious Diversity and Conflict in the Middle East*. 2.
68 Maher, *Salafi-Jihadim: The History of an Idea*. 31.
69 Knapp, *The Concept and Practice of Jihād in Islam*. 82.
70 Al-Bayt, *Jihād and the Islamic Law of War*.
71 Al-Qaradawi, *Fiqh al-Jihād (2 vols.)* [Jurisprudential Reasoning and Jihād].
72 ibid, 56.
73 ibid, 68.
74 Heck, *Jihād Revisited*. 96.
75 Firestone, *Jihād: The Origins of Holy War in Islam*. 25.
76 Heck, *Jihād Revisited*. 97.
77 Knapp, *The Concept and Practice of Jihād in Islam*. 83.
78 Qur'ān 2:256.
79 Heck, *Jihād Revisited*. 98.
80 Nawawi, *Riyadh as-Salihin [Gardens of the Righteous]*. 222.
81 ibid.
82 ibid, 223.
83 ibid, 227.
84 ibid.
85 ibid, 228.
86 ibid, 224.
87 ibid, 228.
88 Knapp, *The Concept and Practice of Jihād in Islam*. 83.
89 Heck, *Jihād Revisited*. 106.
90 ibid, 114.
91 Al-Qaradawi, *Fiqh al-Jihād*. 70.

92 Hegghammer, *Jihādi-Salafis or Revolutionaries? On Religion and Politics in the Study of Militant Islamism*. 74.
93 Al-Qaradawi, *Fiqh al-Jihād*. 88.
94 ibid 77-82.
95 K'Umar, *Islamic Political Thought: A Study of the Diverse Interpretation of Medieval Muslim Political Leaders*. 1055.
96 Heck, *Jihād Revisited*. 118.
97 Lahoud, *The Jihadis' Path to Self-Destruction*. 202.
98 Heck, *Jihād Revisited*. 117.
99 This *Ḥadīth* was recorded by Ahmad ibn Abd al-Halim from Anas b. Mālik. See Farrukh, U. (1966), *Ibn Taymiyya on Public and Private Law in Islam*, p.141. Beirut: Khayats.
100 Sharif, *The Concept of Jihād and Baghy in Islamic Law: With Special Reference to Ibn Taymiyya*. 109-111.
101 ibid, 112.
102 See Schleifer, S.A. (1983), 'Understanding Jihād: Definition and Methodology', *Islamic Quarterly*, London, 26:121-129; Morabia, A. (1978), 'Ibn Taymiyya, Dernier Grand Thoéricien Du Gihâd Médiéval', *Bulletin D'Etudes Orientales*, Paris, 30:85-100.
103 Qur'ān 3:110.
104 Sharif, *The Concept of Jihād and Baghy in Islamic Law: With Special Reference to Ibn Taymiyya*. 120-121.
105 Knapp, *The Concept and Practice of Jihād in Islam*. 84.
106 Yakubovych, *A Neglected Ottoman Sufi Treatise from 16th Century*. 155.
107 Saritopark *et al.*, *Spiritual Jihād among U.S. Muslims: Preliminary Measurement and Associations with Well-Being and Growth*. 3.
108 Knapp, *The Concept and Practice of Jihād in Islam*. 85.
109 Holtmann, *A Primer to the Sunni-Shia Conflict*. 142.
110 Moghadam, *The Shi'i Perception of Jihād*. 2.
111 ibid.
112 Dabashi, *Shi'ism: A Religion of Protest*.
113 Mottahedeh, *Keeping the Shi'ites Straight*.
114 Moghadam, *The Shi'i Perception of Jihād*. 3.
115 ibid.
116 Knapp, *The Concept and Practice of Jihād in Islam*. 86.
117 Al-Qaradawi, *Fiqh al-Jihād*. 128.
118 ibid, 76.
119 ibid.

120 Haykel, *On the nature of salafi thought and action*. 33.
121 Permanent Committee for Scholarly Research and Ifta', "What is 'al-Salafiyah?' What do you think of it?" *Vol.2: Al-Aqida (2)*, Fatwā no. 1361.
122 *Sahih Muslim*, Book 31, no. 6159.
123 Maher, *Salafi-Jihadim: The History of an Idea*. 7.
124 ibid, 8.
125 *Sahih al-Bukhari*, Book 96, no. 42.
126 Sheikh Salih al-Fawzaan on Differentiating between ʿaqīda and Manhaj, *Qawa'id al-Manhaj al-Salafī*, July 2010. Retrieved from: http://www.manhaj.com/manhaj/articles/vnbnh-shaykh-saalih-al-fawzaan-on-differentiating-between-aqidah-and-manhaj.cfm.
127 Sheikh Naasir ud-Deen al-Albani on Differentiating between ʿaqīda and Manhaj, *Qawa'id al-Manhaj al-Salafī*, July 2010. Retrieved from: http://www.manhaj.com/manhaj/articles/lvzvm-shaykh-al-albaanee-on-differentiating-between-aqidah-and-manhaj.cfm.
128 Atwan, *Islamic State: The Digital Caliphate*. 197.
129 ibid, 187.
130 Alsulaiman, *Het Jihadi Salafisme: Politieke and religieuze wortels*. 180.
131 The *First Fitna* broke out following the Battle of the Camel, led by ʿAisha, the Prophet's younger wife, against ʿAli, which ended with a heavy defeat for ʿAisha's army. ʿAli was later involved in a second, larger, civil war that put him in confrontation with the Umayyads. The tension developed into a major battle known as the Battle of Ṣiffīn, where ʿAli's supporters fought against the supporters of Moʿawiya ibn Abi Sufian, the founder of the Umayyad dynasty.
132 Fadl, *Reasoning with God: Reclaiming Shari'a in the Modern Age*. 421.
133 Toth, *Sayyid Qutb: The Life and Legacy of a Radical Islamic Intellectual*. 71.
134 Wiktorowicz, *Anatomy of the Salafi Movement*. 207.
135 Hegghammer, *Jihādi-Salafis or Revolutionaries? On Religion and Politics in the Study of Militant Islamism*. 27.
136 Hafez, *Suicide Bombers in Iraq: The Strategy and Ideology of Martyrdom*. 65.
137 Abu Muhammad al-Maqdisi, "Hiwar al-Sheikh Abu Muhammad al-Maqdisi ma'a Majallat al-'Asr", *Minbar al-Tawhid wa'l-Jihād*, March 2002. Retrieved from: http://www.ilmway.com /site/maqdis/MS_121.html.
138 Sadiq al-Karkhi, "Limādha 'al-Salafīya al-Jihādīya?!'", *Minbar al-Tawhid wa'l-Jihād*, February 2002. Retrieved from: http://www.ilmway.com/site/maqdis/MS_36508.html.
139 Hafez, *Suicide Bombers in Iraq: The Strategy and Ideology of Martyrdom*. 66.

140 Brachman, *Global Jihadism: Theory and Practice*. 41.
141 Alsulaiman, *Het Jihadi Salafisme: Politieke and religieuze wortels*. 185.
142 Maher, *Salafi-Jihadim: The History of an Idea*. 13-14.
143 ibid, 15.
144 Alsulaiman, *Het Jihadi Salafisme: Politieke and religieuze wortels*. 188.
145 Al-Hammadi, *Al-Wahhābiyya wa 'l-salafiyyah al-jihādiyyah. Qirā'ah fī 'iltibasāt al 'alaqāh*. 38.
146 Atwan, *Islamic State: The Digital Caliphate*. 197-198.
147 Hegghammer, *Jihadi-Salafis or Revolutionaries? On Religion and Politics in the Study of Militant Islamism*. 61.
148 Pargeter, *The New Frontiers of Jihād: Radical Islam in Europe*. 119.
149 Maher, *Salafi-Jihadim: The History of an Idea*. 16.
150 Knapp, *The Concept and Practice of Jihād in Islam*. 87.
151 Wright *et al.*, *The Jihadi Threat: ISIS, al-Qaeda, and Beyond*. 8.
152 Streusand, *What Does Jihād Mean?* 5.
153 Knapp, *The Concept and Practice of Jihād in Islam*. 89.
154 Tibi, *Islamism and Islam*. 3.
155 Ayoob, *The Many Faces of Political Islam: Religion and Politics in the Muslim World*. 2.
156 Chamkhi, *Neo-Islamism Post Arab Spring*. 5.
157 Euben, *The Oxford Handbook of Political Theory*. 298.
158 Hourani, *The Emergence of the Modern Middle East*. 183.
159 Abdo, *No God but God: Egypt and the Triumph of Islam*. 6.
160 Chamkhi, *Neo-Islamism Post Arab Spring*. 6.
161 Toth, *Sayyid Qutb: The Life and Legacy of a Radical Islamic Intellectual*. 256.
162 ibid, 257.
163 ibid, 251.
164 Kedouri, *Afghani and ʿAbduh*. 5-38.
165 Soage, *Rashid Rida's Legacy*. 2-10.
166 Nasr, *Sayyid Abu al-Aʿla Mawdudi*. 72-75.
167 Ushama, *Hasan al-Banna*. 76-79.
168 Toth, *Sayyid Qutb: The Life and Legacy of a Radical Islamic Intellectual*. 64.
169 ibid, 70.
170 Tibi, *Islamism and Islam*. 15.
171 ibid, 46.
172 Sayyid Qutb, *Ma'ālim fi al-Tarīq*. 6-7.
173 Abu al-Ala Mawdudi, *al-Islam wal-Madaniyya al-Ḥadītha*, in Dharif, M., *al-Islam al-Siyasi fi al-Watan al-Arabi*, 98-99.

174 De Koning *et al. Salafisme: Utopische idealen in een weerbarstige praktijk*. 45-47.
175 ibid, 59-60.
176 ibid, 62.
177 Toth, *Sayyid Qutb: The Life and Legacy of a Radical Islamic Intellectual*. 95
178 ibid, 121.
179 ibid, 147-154.
180 ibid, 163.
181 ibid, 164-178.
182 Hourani, *The Emergence of the Modern Middle East*. 7.
183 ibid, 9.
184 Balakian, *Raphael Lemkin, Cultural Destruction, and the Armenian Genocide*. 57.
185 Finkel, *Osman's Dream: The History of the Ottoman Empire*. 104.
186 Marx, *Faith in Nation: Exclusionary Origins of Nationalism*. 6.
187 Antonius, *The Arab Awakening: The Story of the Arab National Movement*. 79.
188 Hourani, *The Emergence of the Modern Middle East*. 190.
189 Ibid, 191.
190 Barr, *A Line in the Sand: Britain, France and the Struggle that Shaped the Middle East*. 31.
191 Ibid, 2.
192 Antonius, *The Arab Awakening: The Story of the Arab National Movement*. 304.
193 Kedouri, *In the Anglo-Arab Labyrinth: The McMahon-Husayn Correspondence and its Interpretations 1914-1939*. 159.
194 Friedman, *The Question of Palestine, British-Jewish-Arab Relation: 1914-1918*. 187.
195 Hourani, *The Emergence of the Modern Middle East*. 219.
196 Salibi, *A House of Many Mansions: The History of Lebanon Reconsidered*. 20.
197 Payind and McClimans, *Keys to Understanding the Middle East*. 24.
198 The term *minorization* is used in the social sciences to critically describe the processes which create inequity between groups in a given country. It emphasizes the historical nature of inequity and it refers to the culmination of laws and popular culture which favor the perspectives and interests of the more powerful group, which identifies with national identity and is more supported by the country's

political, social and economic systems, in contrast with less powerful communities (Payind & McClimans, 2016).

199 See Hourani *et al.*, *The Modern Middle East: A Reader.*

200 Campo, *Encyclopedia of Islam*. 81.

201 Hourani, *The Emergence of the Modern Middle East*. 118.

202 See Collelo, T. (1987). *Syria: A Country Study.*

203 Wright, *Dreams and Shadows: The Future of the Middle East*. 201.

204 Jung, *The Middle East and Palestine: Global Politics and Regional Conflict*. 138-139.

205 Vanly, *The Kurds: A Contemporary Overview*. 156.

206 Collelo, *Syria: A Country Study*. 21.

207 The popular protests and demonstrations that commenced in 2010 across the Middle East and North Africa became known as '*Arab Spring*', '*Arab Uprisings*', '*Arab Awakening*' and sometimes '*Arab Spring and Winter*'. Although the popular movements were identified as 'Arab', not all the participants were Arabs. It took the form of a revolutionary wave of both violent and non-violent protests, coups and civil wars in the region.

208 Bouazizi set himself ablaze opposite the governor's office in Sidi Bouzid, on 17 December 2010, in response to the confiscation of his wares and the humiliation and harassment that was reportedly inflicted on his by a policewoman and her aides. Bouazizi was named as 'Person of 2011'. *"Bouazizi was no revolutionary, but his lonely protest served as the catalyst for a wave of revolts that have transformed the Middle East."* (The Times, 2011).

209 Online media activism led to the internationalization of local popular issues and related developments in the Middle East during the Arab Spring, which led to the emergence of dozens of new 'revolutionary' media outlets with the declared objective of founding free media in post-tyranny states, although this objective was rarely attained as a revolutionary tone remained predominant over the discourse of such outlets and basic principles of journalism such as objectivity and impartiality remained invisible. In addition, the already existing media organizations insisted to take sides during these developments in accordance with the tendencies of their owners and sponsoring parties.

210 Chamkhi, *Neo-Islamism Post Arab Spring*. 5.

211 Euben, *The Oxford Handbook of Political Theory*. 298.

212 Hourani, *The Emergence of the Modern Middle East*. 183.

213 Abdo, *No God but God: Egypt and the Triumph of Islam*. 6.
214 Chamkhi, *Neo-Islamism Post Arab Spring*. 6.
215 Bradley, *After the Arab Spring: How Islamists Hijacked the Middle East Revolts*.
216 Ayoob, *The Many Faces of Political Islam: Religion and Politics in the Muslim World*. 2.
217 The narrative of reformism as being a purely secular historical force is deemed untrue. While many secularists played a role in the Tunisian reformist tradition, Islam and Ṣūfism were at the heart of founding the reformist movement (Wolf, 2017).
218 Louden, *Political Islamism in Tunisia: A History of Repression and a Complex Forum for Potential Change*. 2.
219 Rached Ghannouchi: "Il n'y a plus de justification à l'islam politique en Tunisie". Le Monde, 19 May 2016: http://www.lemonde.fr/international/article/2016/05/19/rached-ghannouchi-il-n-y-a-plus-de-justification-a-l-islam-politique-en-tunisie_4921904_3210.html.
220 President Assad said in an interview with the Wall Street Journal in January 2011: "Syria is stable...because we are very closely linked to the beliefs of the people...we have to keep up...as a state and as institutions...political, administrative, economic: These are the changes we need...reform in politics is important, even if slowly and at the tail-end of other priorities." (*Interview with the Syria President Bashar al-Assad*, The Wall Street Journal, Jan. 31, 2011)
221 The story started when a doctor in the southern Syrian city of Daraa received a phone call from a friend about the fall of the Egyptian dictator. The female doctor's reaction was: "We hope that our dictator will be next." One day later, she was arrested. While the elders failed to find a way to release her, young members of her family reacted directly by drawing fearless graffiti on the walls of their schools, such as: "People want to overthrow the regime," and "You are next."
222 Leverett, F. (2005). *Inheriting Syria: Bashar's Trial by Fire*.
223 Hulme, M. (2017). *Weathered: Cultures of Climate*.
224 Allan, S. (2017). *Photojournalism and Citizen Journalism: Co-operation, Collaboration and Connectivity*.
225 According to a study by the World Bank Group, as of early 2017, the Syrian conflict had already inflicted significant damage to the country's physical capital stock (7 percent housing stock destroyed and 20 percent partially damaged), led to the death of nearly 470,000 people

and the forced displacement of half of Syria's 2010 population, amid depressing economic activity. (*The Toll of War: The Economic and Social Consequences of the Conflict in Syria*, World Bank Group, 2017.)

226 In an interview with Denmark's TV-2 in October 2016, President Assad said: "The moderate opposition is a myth...we won't accept that terrorists take control of any part of Syria...if there is opposition, what is the definition of opposition? Could you accept an opposition in your country that belongs to other countries? ...this is an intervention in internal matters. This is against the sovereignty, against the international law."

227 Moore, E. (2014). *Russia-Iran Relations Since the End of the Cold War.*

228 Karam, Z. (2016). *Life and Death in ISIS: How the Islamic State Builds Its Caliphate.*

229 Chemical weapons were repeatedly used during the Syrian civil war, causing hundreds of casualties. Hereby several attacks that were documented by the Arms Association Control: 23 December 2012, first alleged gas attack on Homs; 20 March 2013, chemical weapons attack reported in Aleppo and Damascus suburb; 24 March 2013, regime-led chemical attack reported in Adra town; 13 April 2013, another chemical attack on rebel-held area in Aleppo; 29 April 2013, the town of Saraqeb exposed to chemical attack; 21 August 2013, the largest chemical weapons attack launched by the regime hit the Ghouta region causing over 1000 casualties; 11 April 2014, chlorine-gas attack hit Kafr Zita town; 10 August 2016, Chlorine gas used in attack on opposition-held neighborhood in Aleppo; 7 September 2016, renewed chlorine attack on Aleppo; 13 December 2016, Hama targeted by chemical weapons; 4 April 2017, regime attacks rebel-held Idlib governorate with chemical missiles. (*Timeline of Syrian Chemical Weapons Activity, 2012-2017*, by Kawashima, Y. and Sanders-Zakre, A., Arms Control Association.).

230 Dawoody, A. (2016). *Eradicating Terrorism from the Middle East: Policy and Administration Approaches.*

231 Gleditsch, K. (2016). *Civil War from a Transnational Perspective.*

232 Moore, E. (2014). *Russia-Iran Relations Since the End of the Cold War.*

233 Bernauer, E. (2016). *Identities in Civil Conflict: How Ethnicity, Religion and Ideology Jointly Affect Rebellion.*

234 See *Timeline: Spillover of the Syrian Civil War into Lebanon*, The Daily Star, 21 July 2017.

235 Israeli Air Force hit Syrian military targets several times during the Syrian civil war: On 31 January, an Israeli raid hit a weapons convoy near Damascus. On 3 May, an Israeli aircraft struck a shipment of surface-to-surface missiles in Syria. On 5 May 2013, Israel bombed multiple Syrian military sites (*Timeline: Israeli Attacks on Syrian Targets*, Aljazeera, 5 May 2013). On 7 September 2017, Israeli officials reported an airstrike on Syrian military sites believed to have been producing chemical weapons and advances missiles (*Airstrikes on Syrian Military Sites Renew Focus on Chemical Missiles*, The New York Times, 7 Sept. 2017). The al-Mezzeh Airport of the Syrian army was struck by Israeli aircraft in December 2016 and January 2017. The Syrian Fourth Division's weapons arsenal was also exposed to an Israeli strike in November 2016 (*Israeli Airstrikes in Syria: The International Law Analysis*, Just Security, 3 May 2017).

236 See *Turkey's occupation of northern Syria*. Available at: https://www.al-monitor.com/pulse/ originals/2020/ 05/turkey-syria-population-transfers-tell-abyad-irk-kurds-arabs.html.

237 Weitsman, P. (2014). *Waging War: Alliances, Coalitions, and Institutions of Interstate Violence*.

238 Mabon, S. and Royle, S. (2017). *The Origins of ISIS: The Collapse of Nations and Revolution in the Middle East*.

239 Zuhur, S. (2007). *A Hundred Osamas: Islamist Threats and the Future of Counterinsurgency*.

240 Thaler *et al.* (2008). *Future U.S. Security Relationships with Iraq and Afghanistan*.

241 Paya, A. and Esposito, J. (2011). *Iraq, Democracy and the Future of the Muslim World*.

242 Bensahel *et al.* (2008). *After Saddam: Prewar Planning and the Occupation of Iraq*.

243 Göl, A. (2006). *Iraq and World Order: A Turkish Perspective*.

244 The term is used to refer to the four parts of Kurdistan or the Kurdish inhabited areas in Syria, Turkey, Iraq and Iran (Irwani, 2015: 40).

245 Voller, Y. (2014). *The Kurdish Liberation Movement in Iraq: From Insurgency to Statehood*.

246 The United States repeatedly emphasized the crucial role of the Kurdish Peshmerga forces in the fight against ISIS or ISIS. The U.S. State Department said in one of its statements in this regard: "With effective training, equipping, command and control, and Coalition

firepower, Iraqi forces, including the Kurdish Peshmerga, have seized the initiative and removed ISIS from nearly all of Iraq's major population centers while preventing ISIS from retaking any territory in the process." *U.S. Security Cooperation with Iraq*, U.S. Department of State, 22 March 2017. Retrieved on 15 Nov. 2019 from: https://www.state.gov/r/pa/prs/ps/2017/03/ 269040.htm.

247 Steele, J. (2008). *Defeat: Why the Lost Iraq.*

248 The so-called *disputed areas* mainly include territories in the governorates of Nineveh, Kirkuk, Erbil and Diyala.

249 The Iraqi Central Government in Baghdad has cut the annual financial allocations to the Kurdistan Regional Government since 2014, although these were approved under and protected by the constitution. Ever since, the Kurdistan Region started to suffer deteriorating economic conditions. (Iraqi Kurdistan Economy Suffers Amid Budget Dispute with Baghdad, Al-Monitor, 16 May 2014. Retrieved on 16 No. 2019 from: https://www.al-monitor.com/pulse/tr/ business /2014/05/iraq-kurdistan-region-budget-dispute-economic-effects.html).

250 Schmid, A. (2014). *Violent and Non-Violent Extremism: Two Sides of the Same Coin?*

251 Lipset, S. and Raab, E. (1978). *The Politics of Unreason: Right-Wing Extremism in America 1790-1977.*

252 Coleman, P. and Bartoli, A. (2014). *Addressing Extremism.*

253 Martin, G. (2017). *Essentials of Terrorism: Concepts and Controversies.*

254 Backes, U. (2010). *Political Extremes: A Conceptual History from Antiquity.*

255 Schmid, A. (2014). *Violent and Non-Violent Extremism: Two Sides of the Same Coin?*

256 Ayman al-Zawahiri, leader of al-Qaeda organization which is considered as one of the main extremist Islamic groups, in February 2014 denied any links between his organization and ISIS or ISIS, emphasizing that the leaders of ISIS "disavow sedition among the mujahideen factions in the Levant [and were involved in] shedding protected blood... al-Qaeda is not responsible for ISIS's actions." (*Al Qaeda disavows ISIS militants in Syria,* BBC News - Middle East, 3 February 2014. Retrieved on 9 Nov. 2019 from: http://www.bbc.com/news/world-middle-east-26016318).

257 Sivan, E. and Friedman, M. (1990). *Religious Radicalism and Politics in the Middle East.*

258 Wiktorowicz, Q. and Kaltenthaler, K. (2006). *The Rationality of Radical Islam.*
259 Richards, A. (2003). *Socio-economic Roots of Radicalism? Towards Explaining the Appeal of Islamic Radicals.*
260 Lahaye, T. and Hindson, E. (2015). *Target Israel: Caught in the Crosshairs of the End Times.*
261 Mabon, S. and Royle, S. (2017). *The Origins of ISIS: The Collapse of Nations and Revolution in the Middle East.*
262 Gerges, *A History of ISIS.* 223.
263 *Mujahideen* (*mujāhidīn*), singular *Mujahid* (*Mujahid*), is a term describing those involved in *Jihād* (*jihād*) or the struggle for a praiseworthy goal. The term was broadly used with reference to Islamist Afghan fighters combatting Soviet troops subsequent to the 1979 invasion. Ever since, the term continued to be used and extended to other jihadist groups in different parts of the world.
264 Michael, *The Legend and Legacy of Abu Musab al-Zarqawi.* 339.
265 Moubayed, *Under the Black Flag: At the Frontier of the New Jihād.* 91.
266 See *Timeline: Rise and Spread of the Islamic State*, Wilson Center; https://www.wilsoncenter.org/article/timeline-rise-and-spread-the-islamic-state.
267 Cordesman and Davies, *Iraq's Insurgency and the Road to Civil Conflict.* 576.
268 Glenn, C. (2016). *Timeline: Rise and Spread of the Islamic State.* Wilson Center. Retrieved from: https://www.wilsoncenter.org/article/timeline-rise-and-spread-the-islamic-state.
269 See *Maliki's Authoritarian Regime*, Middle East Security Report 10, by Marisa Sullivan, April 2013; http://www.understandingwar.org/sites/default/files/Malikis-Authoritarian-Regime-Web.pdf.
270 Sullivan, *Maliki's Authoritarian Regime.* 6.
271 "In what may have been the most publicized incident of al-Maliki-Sunni strife, the Prime Minister accused the Vice President Tareq al-Hashemi, a Sunni, of plotting bombings and organizing assassination missions. Vice President al-Hashemi was tried in absentia and found guilty after fleeing to Kurdistan. The charges against Hashemi, the highest-ranking Sunni in Iraq, followed a decision by the Sunni bloc, in Iraq's parliament, to boycott future legislative proceedings...as a result of al-Maliki's refusal to...expand government positions open to Sunnis." (Covarrubias, J., Lansford, T. and Pauly, R., 2016: 40).

272 Sekulow, J., Ash, R. and French, D. (2014). *Rise of ISIS: A Threat We Cannot Ignore.*

273 Atwan, *Islamic State: The Digital Caliphate.* 117.

274 The so-called "Breaking the Walls" campaign began on 21 July 2012 and ended on 23 July 2013. See *Al-Qaeda in Iraq Resurgen: The Breaking the Walls Campaign*, Part I; Middle East Security Report 14; Lewis, J., 2013, pp.12.

275 See *Timeline: Rise and Spread of the Islamic State*, Wilson Center.

276 Lister, *Profiling Jabhat al-Nusra.* 5.

277 The Syrian opposition factions operating in Raqqa at that time included some moderate revolutionary forces, driven by a struggle against the Assad regime, whereas al-Nusra Front and ISI had an Islamist agenda.

278 Mendelsohn, *The al-Qaeda Franchise: The Expansion of al-Qaeda and its Consequences.* 189.

279 Assisted by local Sunni tribal groups, ISIS was able to take over Fallujah and parts of Ramadi on 30 December 2013. See *Ambtsbericht Veiligheidssituatie in Iraq*, Ministerie van Buitenlandse Zaken, Den Haag, pp.9, September 2014.

280 Gerges, *A History of ISIS.* 11.

281 More detailed information on the weaponry seized by ISIS in 2014 could be found in: *Dispatch from the Field, Islamic State Weapons in Iraq and Syria, Analysis of Weapons and Ammunition Captured from Islamic State forces*; London: Conflict Armament Research Ltd, September 2014: http://conflictarm.com/wp-content/uploads/2014/09/Dispatch_IS_Iraq_Syria_Weapons. pdf. ISIS also used chemical agents, such as the mustard gas, on several occasions, which indicates that the group once possessed a certain quantity of chemical weapons. See *Non-State Actors & WMD: Does ISIS have a Pathway to a Nuclear Weapon?*, BASIC, Eweiss, N, March 2016: http://www.basicint. org/sites/default/files/NonStateActors_WMD_Mar2016.pdf.

282 Williams, *Counter Jihād: America's Military Experience in Afghanistan, Iraq, and Syria.* 289.

283 Hyde, *Jihād: The Ottomans and the Allies 1914-1922.* 6.

284 Caris, and Reynolds, *ISIS Governance in Syria.* 4.

285 Neumann *et al.*, *Caliphate in Decline: An Estimate of Islamic State's Financial Fortunes.* 7.

286 Karam, *Life and Death in ISIS: How the Islamic State Builds Its Caliphate.* 168.

287 Details on abuses by parties to conflict are illustrated in *Iraq Report 2016-2017*, Amnesty International: https://www.amnesty.org/en/countries/middle-east-and-north-africa/iraq/report-iraq/. Also see *Syria Report 2016/2017*, Amnesty International: https://www.amnesty.org/en/countries/middle-east-and-north-africa/syria/report-syria/. Further details provided by Human Rights Watch: -https://www.hrw.org/world-report/2015/country-chapters/iraq; https://www. hrw.org/news/2015/07/03/syria-deliberate-killing-civilians-isis; https://www.hrw.org/world-report/2016/country-chapters/syria; https://www.hrw.org/news/2016/01/31/iraq-possible-war-crimes-shia-militia.

288 Tucker, *Modern Conflict in the Greater Middle East*. 122.

289 *Iraqi Shi'ite Cleric Issues Call to Arms*, The New York Times, 13 June 2014: https://www. nytimes.com/2014/06/14/world/middleeast/iraq.html.

290 Abbas, *The Myth and Reality of Iraq's al-Hashd al-Shaabi (Popular Mobilization Forces): A Way Forward*. 4-5.

291 Sullivan, *Maliki's Authoritarian Regime*. 6.

292 Abbas, *The Myth and Reality of Iraq's al-Hashd al-Shaabi (Popular Mobilization Forces): A Way Forward*. 6.

293 See *al-Hashd al-Shaabi: Origin and Future*, Rawabet Center for Research and Strategic Studies, 29 August 2016: http://rawabetcenter.com/en/?p=1037.

294 O'Driscoll and Zoonen, *The Hashd al-Shaabi and Iraq: Subnationalism and the State*. 9.

295 Details on the al-Hashd atrocities in Tikrit after ISIS expulsion to be found in *Special Report: After Iraqi Forces Take Tikrit, A Wave of Looting and Lynching*, Reuters, 3 April 2015: https://www.reuters.com/article/us-mideast-crisis-iraq-tikrit-special-re/special-report-after-iraqi-forces-take-tikrit-a-wave-of-looting-and-lynching-idUSKBN0MU1DP20150403.

296 The Human Rights Watch documented 140 cases of starvation in Fallujah under siege, many of them elderly and young children. See *Iraq: Fallujah Siege Starving Population*, HRW, 7 April 2016: https://www.hrw.org/news /2016/04/07/iraq-fallujah-siege-starving-population.

297 Residents of the city of Fallujah were exposed to mounting attacks during the anti-ISIS campaign. See *Iraq: Fallujah is Liberated, Now What?*, Aljazeera, 30 June 2016: http://www. aljazeera.com/news/2016/06/iraq-fallujah-liberated-160629074425645.html.

298 Obeidi, M. (2016, June 29). *Al-Hashd al-Shaabi Burns Down Homes in Fallujah*. Al-Sharq al-Awsat: English Archive: https://eng-archive.

aawsat.com/munaf-al-ubaidi-and-hamza-mustafa /news-middle-east/ al-hashd-al-shaabi-burns-homes-fallujah.

299 According to the Mayor of Fallujah, Isa Sayer Al-Issawi, Fallujah's infrastructure was exposed to heavy destruction and members of al-Hashd al-Shaabi "have committed acts of arson, crimes and violations and destroyed houses and shops." Quoted by Al-Sharq Al-Awsat, 29 June 2016; available at: https://eng-archive.aawsat.com/munaf-al-ubaidi-and-hamza-mustafa/news-middl e-east/al-hashd-al-shaabi-burns-homes-fallujah.

300 The city of Mosul in Iraq's northwestern Nineveh province used to be a de-facto capital for ISIS in Iraq.

301 A report by Amnesty International voiced concerns about the use of arms by Shia militants in atrocities against Sunni civilians in Iraq. See *Iraq: End Irresponsible Arms Transfers Fuelling Militia War Crimes*, Amnesty International, 5 January 2017: https://www.amnesty.org/en/latest / news/2017/01/iraq-end-irresponsible-arms-transfers-fuelling-militia-war-crimes/.

302 Mabon and Royle, *The Origins of ISIS: The Collapse of Nations and Revolution in the Middle East*. 120.

303 Haidar al-Abadi remained in office as the Prime Minister of Iraq from September 2014 to October 2018.

304 See *From Militia to State Force: the Transformation of al-Hashd al-Shaabi*, Carnegie Middle East Center, 16 November 2015: http://carnegie-mec.org/diwan/61986.

305 Yesiltas and Kardas, *Non-State Armed Actors in the Middle East: Geopolitics, Ideology, and Strategy*. 179-180.

306 Sekulow *et al.*, *Rise of ISIS: A Threat We Cannot Ignore*. 8.

307 Atwan, *Islamic State: The Digital Caliphate*. 12.

308 Bolanos, *Hi-Jacked Islam: Wahhabism and Terrorism*. 106.

309 Hashemi and Postel, *Sectarianization: Mapping the New Politics of the Middle East*. 72.

310 Atwan, *Islamic State: The Digital Caliphate*. 10.

311 Bakker and Singleton, *Foreign Fighters in the Syria and Iraq Conflict: Statistics and Characteristics of a Rapidly Growing Phenomenon*. 15.

312 Badie, *After Saddam: American Foreign Policy and the Destruction of Secularism in the Middle East*. 143.

313 ISIS's recruitment efforts made a remarkable success in the years 2014-2015, and the group succeded to double the number of its

foreign recruits in 2015 in comparison to 2014, raising the number from 15,000 foreign recruits to 30,000 by end of 2015. See *Thousands Enter Syria to Join ISIS Despite Global Efforts*, The New York Times, 26 September 2015: https://www. nytimes.com/2015/09/27/world/ middleeast/thousands-enter-syria-to-join-isis-des pite-global-efforts. html?partner=rss&emc=rss.

314 Karam, Z. (2016). *Life and Death in ISIS: How the Islamic State Builds Its Caliphate*. 150.

315 Howie and Campbell, *Crisis and Terror in the Age of Anxiety: 9/11, the Global Financial Crisis and ISIS*. 37.

316 Al-Baghdadi's audio statement was first broadcasted by the ISIS-affiliated al-Furqan Foundation for Media Production on 1 July 2014. Available at http://ia600300.us.archive.org /6/items/mm_259336/ risala.mp3.

317 Western countries targeted by ISIS terror attacks were mainly members of the Global Anti-Terror Coalition, led by the United States, whose air forces carried out hundreds of strikes against the group's key facilities in Syria and Iraq, which eventually led to a remarkable decline in the group's power on the ground. Such states were considered by ISIS as 'Crusaders' trying to invade its self-proclaimed Caliphate, and with its decline on the ground the group's cells of supporters and recruits in the West were called upon to hit these states at home and make them suffer.

318 Since declaring its Caliphate, ISIS launched over 140 attacks abroad. The main attacks in Europe included the Paris attacks on 13 November 2015; Brussels attacks on 22 March 2016; Nice attack on 14 July 2016; Berlin attack on 19 December 2016; Stockholm attack on 7 April 2017; Manchester attack on 22 May 2017; London attack on 3 July 2017; Barcelona attack on 17 August 2017.

319 More details available on *ISIS Goes Global: 143 Attacks in 29 Countries have Killed 2,043*, CNN, 13 February 2017: http://edition.cnn. com/2015/12/17/world/mapping-isis-attacks-arou nd-the-world/ index.html.

320 This issue was raised and widely debated by European officials. See *Europe's Dilemma – how to deal with returning jihadists*, Al-Monitor, 16 June 2017: https://www.al-monitor.com/pulse/ afp/2017/06/eu-attacks-jihadists.html

321 El-Tobgui, *Ibn Taymiyya: Life, Times, and Intellectual Profile*. 78-102.

322 "Ibn Abd al-Wahhab, Muhammad," in *The Oxford Dictionary of Islam.*
323 Keddi, *Sayyid Jamal ad-Din "al-Afghani"*, 153-226.
324 Kedouri, *Afghani and ʿAbduh*, 5-38.
325 Soage, *Rashid Rida's Legacy*, 2-10.
326 Nasr, *Sayyid Abu al-Aʿla Mawdudi*, 72-75.
327 Ushama, *Hasan al-Banna*, 76-79.
328 This was the title of Paul Berman's famous article "The Philosopher of Islamic Terror," *New York Times Magazine*, March 23, 2003.

Bibliography

Abbas, H. (2017). *The Myth and Reality of Iraq's al-Hashd al-Shaabi (Popular Mobilization Forces): A Way Forward*. Amman: Friedrich Ebert Stiftung (FES), Policy Paper.

Abdo, G. (2000). *No God but God: Egypt and the Triumph of Islam*. Oxford: Oxford University Press.

Abdulmajid, A. (2018). Religious Diversity and Conflict in the Middle East. *International Journal of Social Science and Humanities Research*, 6(3): 1-7.

Abdul-Raof, H. (2012). *Theological Approaches to Qur'anic Exegesis: A Practical Comparative-Contrastive Analysis.* London and New York: Routledge, Taylor & Francis Group.

Al-Bayt, A. (2009). *Jihād and the Islamic Law of War*. Amman: The Royal Aal al-Bayt Institute for Islamic Thought.

Allan, S. (2017). *Photojournalism and Citizen Journalism: Co-operation, Collaboration and Connectivity*. London and New York: Routledge, Taylor & Francis Group.

Al-Hammadi, S. (2014). *Al-Wahhābiyya wa 'l-salafiyyah al-jihādiyyah. Qirā'ah fī 'iltibasāt al''alaqāh* [Wahhabism and Salafi-Jihadism. An insight into the confusions of the relation]. Casablanca: Matba'at al-Najāh al-Jadīda. (pp.37-45).

Al-Qaradawi, Y. (2009). *Fiqh al-Jihād (2 vols.)* [Jurisprudential Reasoning and Jihād]. Cairo: Maktabat Wahbah.

Alsulaiman, A. (2016). Het Jihadi Salafisme: Politieke and religieuze wortels. *Ethnische Perspectieven*, 26(3): 177-197.

Antonius, G. (1938). *The Arab Awakening: The Story of the Arab National Movement*. London: Hamish Hamilton. (pp.79-100).

Arjomand, S. and Brown, N. (2013). *The Rule of Law, Islam, and Constitutional Politics in Egypt and Iran*. New York: State University of New York Press, Albany.

Asatrian, G. and Arakelova, V. (2014). *The Religion of the Peacock Angel: The Yezidis and their Spirit World*. New York: Routledge.

Atwan, A. (2015). *Islamic State: The Digital Caliphate*. California: University of California Press.

Ayoob, M. (2008). *The Many Faces of Political Islam: Religion and Politics in the Muslim World.* United States of America: The University of Michigan Press.

Backes, U. (2010). *Political Extremes: A Conceptual History from Antiquity.* London: Routledge.

Badamchi, M. (2017). *Post-Islamist Political Theory: Iranian Intellectuals and Political Liberalism in Dialogue.* Istanbul: Springer International Publishing.

Badie, D. (2017). *After Saddam: American Foreign Policy and the Destruction of Secularism in the Middle East.* Londond: Lexington Books. (pp.137-145).

Bakker, E. and Singleton, M. (2016). *Foreign Fighters in the Syria and Iraq Conflict: Statistics and Characteristics of a Rapidly Growing Phenomenon.* The Hague: Asser Press.

Balakian, P. (3013). *Raphael Lemkin, Cultural Destruction, and the Armenian Genocide. Holocaust and Genocide Studies,* 27(1): 57-89.

Barr, J. (2011). *A Line in the Sand: Britain, France and the Struggle that Shaped the Middle East.* London: Simon & Schuster UK Ltd.

Bensahel, N., Oliker, O., Crane, K., Brennan, R., Sullivan, T. and Rathmell, A. (2008). *After Saddam: Prewar Planning and the Occupation of Iraq.* Santa Monica, Arlington and Pittsburgh: Rand Corporation.

Bernauer, E. (2016). *Identities in Civil Conflict: How Ethnicity, Religion and Ideology Jointly Affect Rebellion.* Mannheim: Springer VS.

Blanchard, C. (2009). *Islam: Sunnis and Shiʿites.* Washington: Congressional Research Service.

Bolanos, H. (2016). *Hi-Jacked Islam: Wahhabism and Terrorism.* Norwalk: ICS Inc. (pp.99-107).

Bonine, M., Amanat, A. and Gasper, M. (2012). *Is There a Middle East? The Evolution of a Geopolitical Concept.* Stanford: Stanford University Press.

Brachman, J. (2009). *Global Jihadism: Theory and Practice.* Abingdon: Routledge.

Bradley, J. (2012). *After the Arab Spring: How Islamists Hijacked the Middle East Revolts.* Basingstoke: Palgrave Macmillan.

Brewer, J. (1992). *'Sectarianism and racism, and their parallels and differences'.* Ethnic and Racial Studies.

Brunner, R. (2013). *Sunnis and Shiʿites in Modern Islam: Politics, Rapprochement and the Role of Al-Azhar.* In *The Dynamics of Sunni-Shia Relationships,* ed. Marechal, B. and Zemni, S. United Kingdom: C. Hurst & Co. Publishers Ltd.

Campo, J. (2009). *Encyclopedia of Islam*. New York: Facts on File Library for Religion and Mythology, an imprint of Infobase Publishing. (pp.81).

Caris, C. and Reynolds, S. (2014). *ISIS Governance in Syria*. Middle East Security Report 22. Washington: Institute for the Study of War.

Chamkhi, T. (2013). *Neo-Islamism Post Arab Spring*. Australian Political Studies Association, Murdoch University.

Champion, D. (2003). *The Paradoxical Kingdom: Saudi Arabia and the Momentum of Reform*. London: C. Hurst & Co.

Coleman, P. and Bartoli, A. (2014). *Addressing Extremism*. New York: The International Center for Cooperation and Conflict Resolution, Columbia University.

Collelo, T. (1987). *Syria: A Country Study*. Washington: GPO - the Library of Congress.

Cornell, V. (2007). *Voices of Islam*. London: Preacher Publishers.

Croucher, S. (2017). *Global Perspectives on Intercultural Communication*. New York and London: Routledge.

Dabashi, H. (2011). *Shi'ism: A Religion of Protest*. Cambridge: The Belknap Press of Harvard University.

Dabashi, H. (1989). *Auhority in Islam: From the Rise of Muhammad to the Establishment of the Umayyads*. New York: Routledge, Taylor & Francis Group.

Dawoody, A. (2016). *Eradicating Terrorism from the Middle East: Policy and Administration Approaches*. Scranton: Springer.

Dharif, M. (1992). *Al-Islam al-Siyasi fi al-Watan al-Arabi* [Political Islam in the Arab World]. Casablanca: Maktabat al-Umma.

Dixon, P. (2017). '*Beyond Sectarianism in the Middle East: Comparative Perspectives on Group Conflict*'. In Wehrey, F. (ed.), *Beyond Sunni and Shia: The Roots of Sectarianism in a Changing Middle East*. London: C. Hurst & Co. Ltd. (pp.11-36).

El-Hirbi, T. (2010). *Parable and Politics in Early Islamic History: The Rashidun Caliphs*. New York: Columbia University Press.

El-Tobgui, C. S. (2020). *Ibn Taymiyya: Life, Times, and Intellectual Profile*. The Hague: Brill.

Enayat, H. (1982). *Modern Islamic Political Thought: The Response of the Shi'i and Sunni Muslims to the Twentieth Century*. Macmillan Education UK.

Euben, R. (2006). *The Oxford Handbook of Political Theory*. London and Oxford: Oxford University Press.

Fadl, K. (2014). *Reasoning with God: Reclaiming Shari'a in the Modern Age.* London: Rowman & Littlefield.

Fattah, H. and Caso, F. (2009). *A Brief History of Iraq*. New York: Infobase Publishing, Facts On File Inc.

Finkel, C. (2007). *Osman's Dream: The History of the Ottoman Empire*. New York: Basic Books. (pp.104).

Firestone, R. (1999). Jihād: *The Origins of Holy War in Islam*. Oxford: Oxford University Press.

Friedman, I. (1973). *The Question of Palestine, British-Jewish-Arab Relation: 1914-1918*. New York: Schocken Books.

Gerges, F. (2016). *A History of ISIS*. Princeton and Oxford: Princeton University Press.

Glassé, C. (2008). *The New Encyclopeia of Islam*. Lanham, New York, Toronto and Boulder: Rowman & Littlefield Publishers Inc.

Gleditsch, K. (2016). *Civil War from a Transnational Perspective*. Oslo: Peace Research Institute of Oslo & University of Essex.

Glenn, C. (2016). *Timeline: Rise and Spread of the Islamic State*. Wilson Center. Retrieved from: https://www.wilsoncenter.org/article/timeline-rise-and-spread-the-islamic-state.

Göl, A. (2006). *Iraq and World Order: A Turkish Perspective*. In *The Iraqi Crisis and World Order: Structural, Institutional and Normative Challenges*, ed. Thakur, R and Sidhu, W. Tokyo, New York and Paris: United Nations University Press, Pearson Longman.

Gunderson, C. (2004). *Religions of the Middle East*. Minnesota: ABDO & Daughters.

Hafez, M. (2007). *Suicide Bombers in Iraq: The Strategy and Ideology of Martyrdom*. Washington: United States Institute of Peace.

Hashemi, N. and Postel, D. (2017). *Sectarianization: Mapping the New Politics of the Middle East*. Oxford and New York: Oxford University Press.

Hassan, H. (2017). '*The Sectarianism of the Islamic State: Ideological Roots and Political Conflict*'. In Wehrey, F. (ed.), *Beyond Sunni and Shia: The Roots of Sectarianism in a Changing Middle East*. London: C. Hurst & Co. Ltd. (pp.39-59).

Haykel, B. (2009). 'On the nature of salafi thought and action', in Meijer, R. (ed.), *Global Salafism: Islam's New Religious Movement*. London: Hurst.

Heck, P.L. (2004). Jihād Revisited. *Journal of Religious Ethics Inc*, 32(1): 95-128.

Hegghammer, T. (2009). "Jihādi-Salafis or Revolutionaries? On Religion and Politics in the Study of Militant Islamism," in Meijer, R. (ed.), *Global Salafism: Islami's New Religious Movement*. London: Hurst.
Hegghammer, T. (2010). The Rise of Muslim Foreign Fighters: Islam and the Globalization of Jihād. *International Security*, 35(3): 53-94.
Higgins, I. and Brewer, J. (2003). *The Roots of Sectarianism in Northern Ireland*. Queen's University of Belfast.
Hitti, P. (1996). *The Arabs: A Short History*. Washington: Regnery Publishing, Inc.
Holtmann, P. (2014). A Primer to the Sunni-Shia Conflict. *Perspectives on Terrorism*, 8(1): 142-145.
Hourani, A. (1981). *The Emergence of the Modern Middle East*. Hampshire: Macmillan Academic and Professional Ltd. (pp.7-219).
Hourani, A., Khoury, P. and Wilson, M. (2004). *The Modern Middle East: A Reader*. London: I.B. Tauris & Co Ltd.
Howie, L. and Campbell, P. (2017). *Crisis and Terror in the Age of Anxiety: 9/11, the Global Financial Crisis and ISIS*. London: Macmillan Publishers Ltd. (pp.37-45).
Hulme, M. (2017). *Weathered: Cultures of Climate*. London, Los Angeles, New Delhi, Singapore, Washington and Melbourne: Sage Publications.
Hyde, A. (2017). *Jihād: The Ottomans and the Allies 1914-1922*. Gloucestershire: Amberley Publishing.
Jarman, N. (2012). *Defining Sectarianism and Sectarian Hate Crime*. Belfast: Institute for Conflict Research.
Joseph, J. (2004). *Language and Identity: National, Ethnic, Religious*. New York: Palgrave Macmillan.
Jung, D. (2004). *The Middle East and Palestine: Global Politics and Regional Conflict*. New York: Palgrave Macmillan. (pp.138-139).
Karam, Z. (2016). *Life and Death in ISIS: How the Islamic State Builds Its Caliphate*. New York and Miami: Associated Press and Mango Media Inc.
Keddi, N. (1972). *Sayyid Jamal ad-Din "al-Afghani": A Political Biography*. Berkeley: University of California Press.
Kedouri, E. (1966). *Afghani and 'Abduh: An Essay on Religious Unbelief and Political Activism in Modern Islam*. London: Frank Cass.
Kedouri, E. (1976). *In the Anglo-Arab Labyrinth: The McMahon-Husayn Correspondence and its Interpretations 1914-1939*. Cambridge: The Press Syndicate of the University of Cambridge. (pp.159-184).

Kia, M. (2016). *The Persian Empire: A Historical Encyclopedia*. Caliornia and Colorado: ABC-Clio, Llc.

Knapp, M.G. (2003). The Concept and Practice of Jihād in Islam. *Parameters*, 33(1): 82-94.

De Koning, M., Wagemakers, J. and Becker, C. (2014). *Salafisme: Utopische idealen in een weerbarstige praktijk*. Almere: Parthenon.

Kreyenbroek, P. and Sperl, S. (2005). *The Kurds: A Contemporary Overview*. London and New York: Routledge.

K'Umar, M. Y. (2017). Islamic Political Thought: A Study of the Diverse Interpretation of Medieval Muslim Political Leaders. *Saudi Journal of Humanities and Social Sciences*, 2(11): 1050-1057.

Lahaye, T. and Hindson, E. (2015). *Target Israel: Caught in the Crosshairs of the End Times*. Oregon: Harvest House Publishers.

Lahoud, N. (2010). *The Jihadis' Path to Self-Destruction*. London: Hurst & Co. Ltd.

Lambton, A. (1993). *Social Change in Persia in the Nineteenth Century*. In *The Modern Middle East*, ed. Hourani, A., Khoury, P. and Wilson, M. Berkeley and Los Angeles: University of California Press, I.B. Tauris & Co Ltd.

Leverett, F. (2005). *Inheriting Syria: Bashar's Trial by Fire*. Washington: Brookings Institution Press.

Lewis, J. (2013). *Al-Qaeda in Iraq Resurgent: The Breaking the Walls Campaign, Part I*. Washington: Institute for the Study of War.

Liechty, J. and Clegg, C (2001). *Moving Beyond Sectarianism: Religion, Conflict and Reconciliation in Northern Ireland*. Blackrock, Co. Dublin: The Columba Press.

Lipset, S. and Raab, E. (1978). *The Politics of Unreason: Right-Wing Extremism in America 1790-1977*. Chicago: University of Chicago Press.

Lister, C. (2016). *Profiling Jabhat al-Nusra*. Washington: Brookings Institution.

Longva, A. and Roald, A. (2011). *Religious Minorities in the Middle East: Domination, Self-Empowerment, Accommodation*. Leiden: Koninklijke Brill NV.

Louden, S. (2015). *Political Islamism in Tunisia: A History of Repression and a Complex Forum for Potential Change*. Chicago: University of Illinois.

Mabon, S. and Royle, S. (2017). *The Origins of ISIS: The Collapse of Nations and Revolution in the Middle East*. London and New York: I.B.Tauris & Co. Ltd.

Maher, S. (2017). *Salafi-Jihadism: The History of an Idea*. London: Penguin Random House.

Makdisi, U. (2000). *The Culture of Sectarianism: Community, History, and Violence in Ninteenth-Century Ottoman Lebanon*. Berkeley and Los Angeles: University of California Press.

Malbouisson, C. (2007). *Focus on Islamic Issues*. New York: Nova Science Publishers, Inc.

Martin, G. (2017). *Essentials of Terrorism: Concepts and Controversies*. London: Sage Publications, Inc.

Marx, A. (2003). *Faith in Nation: Exclusionary Origins of Nationalism*. Oxford: Oxford University Press Inc.

Mendelsohn, B. (2016). *The al-Qaeda Franchise: The Expansion of al-Qaeda and its Consequences*. Oxford and New York: Oxford University Press.

Michael, G. (2007). *The Legend and Legacy of Abu Musab al-Zarqawi*. London: Routledge.

Moaddel, M. and Karabenick, S. (2013). *Religious Fundamentalism in the Middle East*. Leiden: Koninklijke Brill NV.

Moezzi, M. (2011). *The Spirituality of Shi'i Islam*. New York: I.B.Tauris & Co. Ltd.

Moghadam, A. (2003). *The Shi'i Perception of Jihād*. Medford: Al Nakhlah/Tufts University. (pp.1-8).

Moore, E. (2014). *Russia-Iran Relations Since the End of the Cold War*. New York: Routledge.

Mottahedeh, R. (2003). *Keeping the Shi'ites Straight*. Religion in the News, Vol. 6, No. 2.

Moubayed, S. (2015). *Under the Black Flag: At the Frontier of the New Jihād*. London and New York: I.B.Tauris & Co. Ltd.

Nasr, S. (1995). "Sayyid Abu al-A'la Mawdudi." In *The Oxford Encyclopedia of the Modern Islamic World*. Ed. Espesito, J. L. New York: Oxford University Press.

Nawawi, I. (2006). *Riyadh as-Salihin [Gardens of the Righteous]*. Translated by: Muhammad Zafrulla Khan. London: Curzon Press Ltd.

Neumann, P., Heibner, S., Holland-McCowan, J. and Basra, R. (2017). *Caliphate in Decline: An Estimate of Islamic State's Financial Fortunes*. London: ICSR-The International Centre for the Study of Radicalisation and Political Violence. Retrieved from: http://icsr.info/wp-content/uploads/2017/02/ICSR-Report-Caliphate-in-Decline-An-Estimate-of-Islamic-States-Financial-Fortunes.pdf.

O'Driscoll, D. and Zoonen, D. (2017). *The Hashd al-Shaabi and Iraq: Subnationalism and the State*. Erbil: Middle East Research Institute, MERI.

Pargeter, A. (2008). *The New Frontiers of Jihād: Radical Islam in Europe*. London: I.B. Tauris.

Paya, A. (2006). *Recent Developments in Shi'i Thought*. In *Islamic Democratic Discourse: Theory, Debates and Philosophical Perspectives*, ed. Khan, M. Oxford: Lexington Books, Rowman & Littlefield Publications Inc.

Paya, A. and Esposito, J. (2011). *Iraq, Democracy and the Future of the Muslim World*. London and New York: Routledge, Taylor & Francis Group.

Payind, A. and McClimans, M. (2016) *Keys to Understanding the Middle East*. The Ohio State University: The Middle East Studies Centre.

Qutb, S. (1989). *Ma'ālim fi al-Tarīq* [Signposts on the Road]. 13th legal ed. Cairo: Dar al-Shuruq.

Redha, M. (1999). *Al-Hasan and Al-Hussein: The Two Grandsons of the Messenger of Allah*. Beirut: Dar al-Kotob al-Ilmiyah.

Richards, A. (2003). *Socio-economic Roots of Radicalism? Towards Explaining the Appeal of Islamic Radicals*. Carlisle: Strategic Studies Institute SSI.

Sachedina, A. (1981). *Islamic Messianism: The Idea of the Mahdi in Twelver Shi'ism*. New York: State University of New York Press.

Salibi, K. (1988). *A House of Many Mansions: The History of Lebanon Reconsidered*. London: I.B.Tauris & Co Ltd. (pp.20-24).

Sanders, P. (1994). *Ritual, Politics, and the City in Fatimid Cairo*. New York: State University of New York Press.

Sardar, Z. and Davies, M. (2004). *The No-nonsense Guide to Islam*. Oxford: New Internationalist Publications Ltd.

Saritopark, S.N., Exline, J.J., and Stauner, N. (2018). 'Spiritual Jihād among U.S. Muslims: Preliminary Measurement and Associations with Well-Being and Growth'. *Religions*, 9(158): 1-22.

Schneider, F. (2013). *A Toolbox for Analysing Political Texts: How to Do Discourse Analysis*. East Asia Politics. Retrieved from: http://www.politicseastasia.com/studying/how-to-do-a-discourse-analysis/.

Sekulow, J., Ash, R. and French, D. (2014). *Rise of ISIS: A Threat We Cannot Ignore*. New York: Howard Books, Simon & Schuster Inc.

Schmid, A. (2014). *Violent and Non-Violent Extremism: Two Sides of the Same Coin?* The Hague: International Centre for Counter-Terrorism. Retrieved from: https://www.icct.nl/download/file/ICCT-Schmid-Violent-Non-Violent-Extremism-May-2014.pdf.

Sharif, M.F.M. (2006). *The Concept of Jihād and Baghy in Islamic Law: With Special Reference to Ibn Taymiyya*. Edinburgh: University of Edinburgh.

Shoup, J. (2011). *Ethnic Groups of Africa and the Middle East: An Encyclopedia*. California: ABC-Clio, Llc. (pp.131-140).
Sivan, E. and Friedman, M. (1990). *Religious Radicalism and Politics in the Middle East*. New York: State University of New York Press, Albany.
Soage, A. (2008). "Rashid Rida's Legacy." *The Muslim World 98*. 1-23.
Sourdel, D. and Thomine, J.S. *A Glossary of Islam*. Edinburgh: Edinburgh University Press.
Steele, J. (2008). *Defeat: Why the Lost Iraq*. London and New York: I. B. Tauris. (pp.203-206).
Stefon, M. (2010). *Islamic Beliefs and Practices*. New York: Britannica Educational Publishing.
Stokes, J., Gorman, A. and Newman, A. (2009). *Encyclopedia of the Peoples of Africa and the Middle East*. New York: Infobase Publishing, Inc.
Streusand, D.E. (1997). "What Does Jihād Mean?" *Middle East Quarterly*, 4(3).
Sullivan, M. (2013). *Maliki's Authoritarian Regime*. Middle East Security Report, 10. Washington: Institute for the Study of War, ISW.
Thaler, D., Karasik, T., Kaye, D., Moroney, J., Wehrey, F., Younossi, O., Ali, F. and Guffey, R. (2008). *Future U.S. Security Relationships with Iraq and Afghanistan*. Santa Monica, Arlington and Pittsburgh: Rand Corporation.
Tibi, B. (2012). *Islamism and Islam*. New Haven: Yale University Press.
Toth, J. (2013). *Sayyid Qutb: The Life and Legacy of a Radical Islamic Intellectual*. Oxford and New York: Oxford University Press.
Tucker, S. (2017). *Modern Conflict in the Greater Middle East*. California: ABC-CLIO, LLC.
Ushama, T. (1995). *Hasan al-Banna: Vision and Mission*. Kuala Lumpur: A.S. Noordeen.
Vanly, I.C. (1992). *The Kurds: A Contemporary Overview*. London: Routledge.
Versteegh, K. (2014). *The Arabic Language, Second Edition*. Edinburgh: Edinburgh University Press.
Voller, Y. (2014). *The Kurdish Liberation Movement in Iraq: From Insurgency to Statehood*. New York: Routledge.
Weitsman, P. (2014). *Waging War: Alliances, Coalitions, and Institutions of Interstate Violence*. Stanford: Stanford Security Studies, Stanford University Press.
Wiktorowicz, Q. (2006). Anatomy of the Salafi Movement. *Studies in Conflict & Terrorism*, 29: 207.

Wiktorowicz, Q. and Kaltenthaler, K. (2006). *The Rationality of Radical Islam*. The Academy of Political Science, Political Science Quarterly, Vol. 121, No. 2, pp.295-319.

Williams, B. (2017). *Counter Jihād: America's Military Experience in Afghanistan, Iraq, and Syria*. Pennsylvania: University of Pennsylvania Press.

Wright, R. (2008). *Dreams and Shadows: The Future of the Middle East*. New York: The Penguin Press. (pp.201-241).

Wright, R., Berger, J.M., Braniff, W., Bunzel, C., Byman, D., Cafarella, J., Gambhir, H., Ross, D., Hassan, H. and Lister, C. (2017). *The Jihadi Threat: ISIS, al-Qaeda, and Beyond*. Washington, DC: U.S. Institute of Peace, Wilson Center.

Yakubovych, M.M. (2015). A Neglected Ottoman Sufi Treatise from 16th Century: *Mawāhib al-Rahman fī bayān Marātib al-Akwān* by Ibrāhīm al-Qirīmī. *The Journal of Ottoman Studies*, XLV: 137-160.

Yesiltas, M. and Kardas, T. (2017). *Non-State Armed Actors in the Middle East: Geopolitics, Ideology, and Strategy*. Cham: Springer International Publishing AG. (pp.179-182).

Zuhur, S. (2007). *A Hundred Osamas: Islamist Threats and the Future of Counterinsurgency*. In *Focus on Terrorism, Volume 7*, ed. Linden E. New York: Nova Science Publishers, Inc.

INDEX

A
ʿAdl, 30, 194, 211
'Ahl al-Bayt, 20, 31, 194
'Ahl al-ḥall wal-ʿaqd, 29, 30, 194
'Ahl al-Sunna, 19, 30, 194, 217
Alawite, 17, 18, 29, 32, 36, 123, 127, 133, 161, 164, 195,
Al-firqa al-nājiya, 67, 199
Al-Hashd al-Shaabi, 8, 9, 82, 153,154, 163, 166, 177, 178, 179, 180, 181, 182, 183, 243, 257, 258
'Al-Khulafā' 'al-Rāshidūn, 21, 26, 208, 212
Al-Mahdi, 24, 28, 61, 155, 179, 199, 205
Al-Nusra Front, 148, 161, 173, 174, 175, 256
Al-Qaeda, 8, 9, 56, 74, 75, 76, 77, 82, 147, 153, 154, 155, 161, 166, 168, 169, 170, 173, 174, 175, 183, 184, 248, 254, 256
Al-Salafiyya al-Jihādiyya, 168
Al-salaf al-ṣāliḥ, 66, 67, 77, 98, 213, 214, 217, 218
Al-ṭā'ifa al-manṣūra, 67, 218
Al-walā' wa-l-barā', 71, 73, 76, 101, 102, 221
ʿAmalu l-badan bil-qitāl, 47, 196
'Amānah, 56
Apostasy, 72, 167, 177, 208, 213
ʿAqīda, 67, 71, 72, 99, 196, 224, 226, 247
Arab Spring, 137, 138, 140, 141, 143, 144, 145, 146, 248, 250, 251
Arkān al-Islām, 55, 64, 196
ʿAṣabiyya, 16, 196
ʿAshurā', 28, 61, 197
Awaited Imām, 24, 25, 28, 29, 61, 199, 205, 222,
Ayatollah, 24, 28, 81, 178

B
Baath Party, 129, 130, 132, 133, 154, 158, 172
Bayʿa, 30, 197
Bidʿa, 71, 72, 77, 197, 217, 219, 224, 228

C
Caliphate, 22, 23, 24, 25, 26, 30, 57, 60, 81, 168, 172, 175, 176, 177, 178, 183, 184, 185, 186, 187, 188, 199, 203, 207, 211, 217, 232, 233, 242, 247, 248, 252, 256, 258, 259
Crusaders, 156, 224, 259
Cultural diversity, 7,10, 26, 33, 40, 41, 148, 189

D
Dār al-Islām, 49, 54, 58, 96, 197
Dār al-Ḥarb, 49, 54, 197
Daʿwa, 47, 57, 58, 70, 98, 179, 196, 198, 206
Defensive Jihād, 54, 62,
Democracy, 97, 98, 107, 109, 110, 130, 138, 139, 143, 145, 167, 253

E
Ethnic cleansing, 155, 181, 243
Extremism, 8, 11, 33, 77, 131, 148, 151, 153, 188, 191, 210, 219, 254

F

Farḍ ʿayn, 55, 198
Farḍ kifāya, 55, 63, 198
Fasād, 56, 198
Fatwā, 101, 102, 117, 178, 179, 199, 223, 232, 247

G

Ghayba, 61, 199
Globalization, 9, 82, 189, 191

H

Ḥadīth, 21, 27, 48, 52, 53, 55, 57, 64, 66, 67, 98, 199, 200, 209, 213, 214, 217, 218, 223, 228, 246, 248
Ḥākimiyya, 71, 72, 73, 76, 77, 95, 96, 97, 99, 100, 104, 105, 106, 110, 200, 219, 239
Ḥanafī, 26, 90, 91, 200, 201, 209, 214, 217, 226, 233
Ḥanbalī, 26, 27, 64, 68, 89, 90, 91, 94, 201, 209, 217, 220, 223, 228,
Heretical, 30, 31, 38, 71, 72, 197, 217, 228
Heterodox, 30
Hidden Imām, 28, 61, 62, 65, 199, 205,
Hijra, 20, 201, 221, 242
Ḥisba, 72, 195, 202
Hezbollah, 32, 136, 147, 148, 163, 174, 179

I

Ibn Abd al-Wahhab, 68, 90, 220, 227, 229, 260
Ibn Nusayr an-Namiri, 29, 195
Ibn Taymiyya, 56, 58, 68, 77, 79, 90, 94, 95, 206, 220, 223, 228, 246, 259
Ijmāʿ, 29, 202, 226
'Īmān, 67, 72, 76, 99, 104, 195, 196, 203, 205, 212, 225, 244
'Imāmah, 24, 30, 203
Imām ʿAli, 148
Imām al-Mahdi, 24, 199
Iran, 17, 24, 25, 27, 32, 34, 40, 74, 115, 125, 126, 130, 136, 155, 156, 161, 163, 169, 174, 179, 182, 227, 229, 242, 252, 253
Iraq, 8, 10, 15, 17, 18, 22, 24, 26, 28, 31, 32, 35, 40, 61, 75, 80, 101, 115, 118, 120, 122, 123, 125, 127, 130, 151, 153, 158, 166, 175, 178, 183, 185, 186, 188, 190, 197, 200, 227, 229, 241, 243, 244, 247, 253, 259
IRGC, 180
Islamism, 9, 11, 46, 66, 68, 74, 79, 83, 85, 86, 88, 92, 94, 98, 100, 102, 104, 106, 108, 111, 132, 143, 148, 149, 189, 220, 231, 238, 246, 248, 250, 251
Islamic State, 54, 75, 98, 115, 131, 148, 161, 168, 170, 173, 175, 184, 233, 242, 247, 248, 252, 255, 256, 258, 259

J

Jahl, 56, 99, 205, 208
Jamāʿa, 30, 74, 75, 76, 155, 168, 194, 217
Jihād al-Dafʿ, 47, 63, 205
Jihād al-Ṭalab, 47, 205
Jihād fī sabīl allāh, 45, 206
Jihād Madanī, 57, 58, 206
Jihād Makkī, 57, 58, 206
Jihadism, 7, 11, 43, 46, 48, 50, 52, 54, 56, 58, 60, 62, 64, 66, 82, 113, 177, 189, 248
Jihād of the sword, 62, 65, 105, 106, 206
Jihādī-yul manhaj, 71

K

Kāfir, 68, 69, 99, 101, 207, 208, 218
Khawārij, 23, 69, 207
Khilāfah, 30, 175, 186, 187

Khalīfah, 30, 175
Kuffār, 70, 96, 100, 102, 207, 218, 220
Kufr, 57, 96, 99, 101, 208
Kurds, 18, 35, 40, 116, 119, 121, 123, 125, 126, 130, 131, 133, 134, 155, 158, 161, 164, 244, 245, 250, 253
Kurdistan, 18, 40, 121, 125, 126, 157, 158, 245, 253, 255

L

M
Maʿād, 30, 209, 226
Mālikī, 26, 90, 91, 209, 217
Manhaj, 67, 68, 71, 73, 77, 96, 209, 220, 232, 239, 247
Martyrdom, 28, 53, 56, 61, 63, 96, 185, 197, 215, 247
Monotheism, 30, 67, 71, 72, 75, 173, 128, 219
Mujāhid, 47, 63, 81, 96, 210
Mujāhidīn, 49, 74, 185, 187, 255
Mujtahids, 24, 28, 61, 62, 65
Munāfiq, 57, 210
Mushrik, 210
Muslim Brotherhood, 74, 79, 92, 93, 132, 133, 139, 144, 146, 147, 160, 234, 235, 237, 239

N
Nationalism, 40, 90, 95, 107, 110, 115, 117, 119, 121, 129, 132, 134, 158, 231, 232, 239, 249
Nifāq, 211
Nubuwwa, 30, 212
Nuṣayriyya, 29, 195

O
Offensive Jihād, 62, 65
Ottoman Empire, 25, 36, 91, 115, 119, 121, 124, 200, 232, 249

P
Polytheism, 229
Propaganda, 9, 82, 134, 184, 187, 189
Prophet Muhammad, 19, 22, 27, 48, 53, 67, 85, 104, 142, 194, 200, 201, 208, 213, 217, 218, 221, 228, 242

Q
Qitāl, 46, 47, 196, 212
Qur'ān, 20, 31, 34, 46, 48, 49, 50, 51, 52, 54, 57, 64, 69, 94, 95, 103, 109, 168, 188, 194, 197, 200, 204, 206, 207, 214, 215, 216, 217, 228, 232, 233, 236, 239, 242, 245, 246, 261

R
Rāfiḍa, 26, 212, 216
Ridda, 72, 213
Rojava, 126

S
Salafism, 10, 11, 66, 68, 70, 71, 79, 83, 86, 88, 90, 92, 94, 96, 98, 100, 102, 104, 106, 108, 110, 219, 220
Salafī-yul ʿaqīda, 71
SDF, 161, 164
Sectarianism, 7, 10, 13, 15, 34, 36, 38, 40, 113, 147, 160, 177, 218, 241, 243
Secularism, 92, 93, 95, 97, 107, 110, 145, 167, 238, 239, 258
Shāfʿī, 26, 90, 91, 209, 214
Shahāda, 53, 55, 64, 96, 195, 196, 214
Sharīʿa, 52, 56, 57, 58, 79, 81, 85, 86, 89, 90, 91, 94, 95, 96, 98, 99, 108, 109, 117, 145, 177, 197, 199, 202, 204, 206, 212, 215, 216, 220
Shia Imamate, 60, 64, 217
Shiʿism, 27, 28, 29, 31, 61, 177, 199, 204, 216, 225
Shirk, 215, 224, 229

Ṣūfī, 58, 59, 72, 90, 196, 205, 216, 217, 224, 228, 231, 234, 246, 247, 251
Sunnism, 177, 217
Sunni Caliphate, 60, 217
Sykes-Picot, 122, 125, 127, 176
Syria, 8, 10, 15, 17, 18, 23, 26, 31, 32, 35, 38, 40, 75, 115, 118, 120, 122, 125, 127, 130, 136, 138, 140, 146, 148, 151, 153, 156, 158, 164, 166, 167, 172, 176, 183, 185, 188, 190, 223, 224, 244, 250, 254, 256, 259
Syrian Civil War, 148, 163, 164, 252, 253

T

Tābiʿīn, 66, 213, 217, 218
Ṭāghūt, 72, 75, 77, 218
Takfīr, 68, 70, 71, 73, 75, 77, 99, 100, 218, 220
Takfīri, 72, 95
Tawḥīd, 30, 67, 68, 71, 72, 73, 75, 76, 77, 89, 92, 99, 100, 102, 104, 107, 108, 155, 168, 173, 174, 208, 211, 218, 219, 226, 228, 247
Terrorism, 102, 126, 158, 182, 183, 252, 254, 258
Twelver Shiʿism, 28, 61, 199, 204

U

ʿUlamā', 29, 60, 61, 90, 134, 219
'Umma, 19, 21, 31, 46, 62, 65, 69, 73, 81, 85, 87, 88, 89, 90, 91, 92, 94, 95, 98, 100, 103, 104, 105, 109, 110, 143, 144, 194, 198, 215, 219, 228, 229, 235
ʿUnf, 46, 220

V

W

Wahhabism, 68, 72, 74, 77, 201, 220, 227, 229, 258
Wilāya, 30, 222
Wilāyat al-Faqīh, 74, 222

X

Y

Yezidis, 18, 38, 39, 176, 244
YPG, 126, 161

Z

Zakāt, 55, 64, 108, 195, 196, 222, 235
Ẓann, 56, 222

Made in United States
North Haven, CT
19 September 2023

41732669R00164